CONCISE DICTIONARY OF MANAGEMENT

Abhishek Sharma

HIMACHAL BOOKS
NEW DELHI & HIMACHAL PRADESH

Published by

Himachal Books

New Delhi-110090 (INDIA)

email : himachalbooks@gmail.com

Second Edition 2021

Price : Rs. 895.00

ISBN 13 : 978-93-82526-76-6

Printed by Deepak Offset, Delhi
Type Setting & Designed by Aradhya Art Work, Delhi

Contents

A

360 survey
An employee feedback programme whereby an employee is rated by surveys distributed to his or her co-workers, customers, and managers. HR departments may use this feedback to help develop an individual's skill or they may integrate it into performance management programmes.

401(k) Plan
An employer-sponsored retirement plan that has become an expected benefit and is therefore important in attracting and retaining employees. A 401(k) plan allows employees to defer taxes as they save for retirement by placing before-tax dollars directly into an investment account. Employers also contribute to the plan tax-free, for instance by matching contributions. Some plans enable employees to direct their own investments. These plans can be expensive and complex to manage. It is common for companies to outsource all or part of their plan.

Abandonment rate
Number of incomplete transactions (or abandoned shopping carts). Can be caused by misleading ads, such as promoting low prices, but requiring customers to purchase a different or more of a product to get that price.

Above the line
Marketing and advertising through mass-media, such as television, radio, newspapers, magazines, Internet, etc., which is less personal than Below The Line Marketing. Companies usually use advertising agencies for ATL marketing.

Abram's law
Construction industry theory relating to concrete strength as determined by the ratio of water to cement.

Absenteeism policy
A policy about attendance requirements, scheduled and unscheduled time off, and measures for dealing with workplace absenteeism. Repeated absenteeism can lead to termination.

1. **Scheduled time off:** Excused absences from regular work hours scheduled in advance by an employee for such things as vacation, medical appointments, military service, jury duty, etc.
2. **Unscheduled time off:** Absence from work during regular work hours that was not scheduled in advance by the employee (e.g. sickness). Absences are generally accepted and sometimes compensated if their frequency and rationale fall within an organization's attendance policy.

Absolute advantage
One country enjoying total lower costs of production than another country (ies).

Abstract
A brief summary covering the main points of a written article or research project.

Accelerator
A company which supplies office space, marketing services, etc., in exchange for payment, to help get new companies started.

Acceptance bonus
The amount paid to an employee who agrees to perform a difficult task.

Accessibility
The extent to which a contractor's or employer's facility is readily approachable and does not inhibit the mobility of individuals with disabilities, particularly such areas as the personnel office, worksite and public areas.

Accounts
An individual's or company's financial records. Also an arrangement to keep money with a financial institution, e.g., a bank, building society, etc.

Accretion
Growth or increase in the value or amount of something.

Accrual
The accumulation of payments or benefits over time.

Acid test
A stern measure of a company's ability to pay its short term debts, in that stock is excluded from asset value. (liquid assets/current liabilities) Also referred to as the Quick Ratio.

Across the board
The involvement of, or affect on, everyone or everything in an industry or company.

Acting out
Activities engaged in by consumers during purchase decision-making, such as feeling the weight of the product, inspecting ingredients, and reading instructions. Savvy marketers must anticipate these expectations as part of the product utility.

Actuals
Real costs, sales, etc., that have occurred, rather than estimations or expectations.

Ad hoc
Created or done for a particular purpose as necessary and not planned in advance.

Ad rotation
Describes the rotation of advertisements on a web page-each time a user clicks on a different page or returns to a page they've viewed previously in the same session, a different advert appears on the screen.

Adaptation
Goods or service adapted in either product, distribution or advertising form to take account of unique conditions in any one country(ies).

Added value
Enables and justifies a profit in business.

Addendum
An added section of information in a letter or report.

Adjunct
A thing which is added or attached as a supplementary, rather than an

essential part of something larger or more important.

Administrative services only (ASO)

The hiring of a firm (usually a health care vendor) to handle certain administrative tasks. The firm does not assume any risk but merely carries out the specialized functions that the employer cannot or does not want to do. For example, an employer funds its own dental insurance claim payments but pays the ASO firm to process the claims.

Adoption curve

A graph showing the rate at which a new piece of technology is bought by people for the first time. It is based on the idea that certain people are more open for adaptation than others.

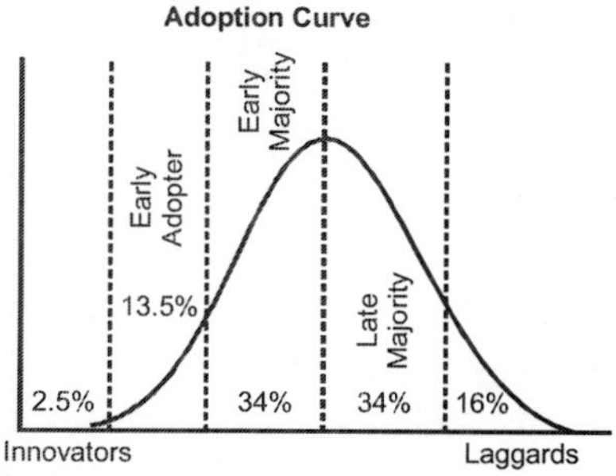

Adverse event

Term used when a volunteer in a clinical trial has a negative or unfavourable reaction to a drug, etc.

Advertising

Paid form of a non-personal communication by industry, business firms, nonprofit organizations, or individuals delivered through the various media. Advertising is persuasive and informational and is designed to influence the purchasing behavior and thought patterns of the audience. Advertising may be used in combination with sales promotions, personal selling tactics, or publicity.

Advertising elasticity

Change in sales that result from each monetary unit spent on advertising. Formula: (“Q)/(Q)÷(“A)//(A) Q is quantity sold A is ad expenditure “Q is change in quantity sold “A is change in ad expenditure Ex: Rockwell Tools leveraged ad elasticity and increased sales by 25%.

Advertising metrics

Ways and means to evaluate, compare, and contrast the effectiveness and efficiency of Internet promotions: Click-through, click-through rate (CTR), conversion rate, cost-per-click (CPC), cost-per-action (CPA), customer acquisition costs, hits, hybrid models, impressions, page view, pay per click (PPC), pay per lead (PPL), pay per sale (PPS), site stickiness, surround session, unique visitors, and website traffic.

Advertising network

Intermediary between advertisers and publishers that sells web properties (space) to advertisers. Often an efficient way to reach social media audiences.

Advertising slogan

Catchy words or phrases that help consumers remember a particular product or service. They tend to reflect the product’s sustainable competitive advantage or unique selling proposition in simple 2-3 word phrases or jingles. Through repetition over time, a marketer can establish top of mind awareness and recall.

Advertising standards authority (ASA)

The UK self-regulatory body funded by the advertising industry for ensuring that all advertising adheres to ASA standards, notably not to offend or mislead people. Equivalents named the same exist in other countries.

Advertorial
An advert in a magazine or newspaper that is written like an article giving facts rather than appearing as an advertisement for a product.

Advocacy advertising
Communication aimed at espousing a point of view, usually about controversial issues. Ads can be directed at specific targets, such as political activists, media, consumer groups, government agencies, or competitors.

Affidavit
A sworn signed statement of fact used as evidence in court whose signature has been witnessed by a commissioner of oaths or other authorised officer, for example a notary. Medieval Latin for 'he has stated on oath', from affidare, meaning to trust.

Affiliate
A company or person controlled by or connected to a larger organisation. In web marketing an affiliate normally receives a commission for promoting another company's products or services.

Affiliate marketing
Using a network of partners to market a company—usually internet-based in which a company rewards or compensates an affiliate for each customer directed to it. Affiliates can include blogs, shopping sites, and comparison sites.

Affinity diagram
A tool used to organize ideas, usually generated through brainstorming, into groups of related thoughts. The emphasis is on a pre-rational, gut-fell sort of grouping, often done by the members of the group with little or no talking. Also known as the KJ method after its creator, Kawakita Jiro.

Affinity marketing
Any number of marketing activities targeted to individuals sharing common interests.

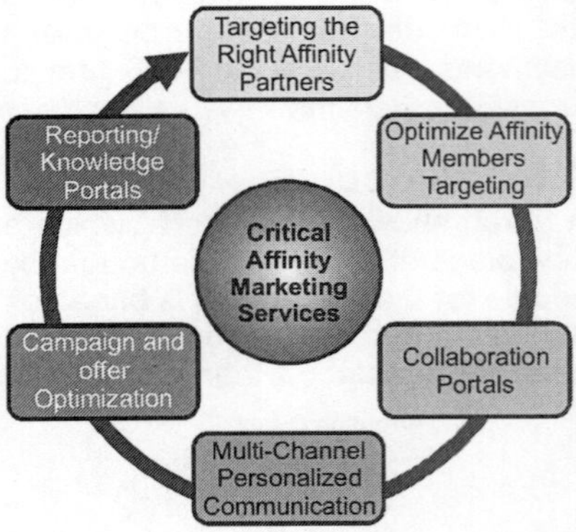

Ex: an auto accessories manufacturer targeting readers of motoring magazines.

Affirmative action
Proactive policies aimed at increasing the employment opportunities of certain groups (typically, minority men and/or women of all racial groups). Title 5, Section 503 of the Rehabilitation Act requires that affirmative action be taken in employment of persons with disabilities by Federal contractors. Affirmative action was designed to rectify past discrimination but has been controversial since its inception.

Affirmative action plan (AAP)
A written set of specific, results-oriented procedures to be followed. Intended to remedy the effects of past

discrimination against or underutilization of women and minorities. The effectiveness of the plan is measured by the results it actually achieves rather than by the results intended and by the good faith efforts undertaken.

Ageism
Unfair prejudice or discrimination on the grounds of a person's age.

Agent
A channel institution which represents one or more suppliers for a fee.

Agent (insurance)
An employee who sells the products owned by the company, in contrast to a broker, who sells the insurance products of several companies.

Aggregate
A whole consisting of the combination of smaller separate elements.

Aggregate planning
The process of planning and developing the best way of producing the right amount of goods, at the right time and at the minimum cost, based on the total number of items which need to be produced, and the amount of materials, equipment and workers necessary for production.

Aggregation
Form of segmentation that assumes most consumers are alike.

Aggressive exporter
An organisation which develops clear marketing strategies for what it intends to do in a foreign markets.

Aggressive growth fund
A high risk investment fund in which shares are expected to increase in value very quickly in the hope of making large profits.

Agile development method
A type of business development which gets things moving quickly and adapts during the development, as distinct from conventional planning and project management implementation.

Agile marketing
Term used for marketers that handle/adjust to the dynamic (ever-changing) shift or change in attitudes and behavior among various target markets due to changes in the environment, technology, economy, and competition. Ex: Facebook acknowledges the value of instant messaging and videos that can be uploaded within minutes.

Agile organization
Also known as agile manufacturing, this is a term applied to an organization that has created the processes, tools, and training to enable it to respond quickly to customer needs and market changes while still controlling costs and quality.

Agio
The percentage charged by a bank for exchanging one form of currency or money, into another that is more valuable.

Agitprop
Political propaganda (published ideas designed to motivate people into certain political views or actions) typically in art, music, literature, etc., a portmanteau word combining the original Russian words agitsiya (agitation) and propoganda, where the term grew from the state department responsible for disseminating communist ideas and information to its people in the 1930s. In the west the term is more associated with publication of left-wing or socialist ideas, often targeted

against a governing right-wing authority.

Agribusinesss

Farming industry on a large corporate scale.

AIDA

Attention, Interest, Desire, Action - an early and fundamentally useful model/ process for effective communications. Also called the 'hierarchy of effects' - we all buy things, and decide to change something, after passing through these four key stages.

A-list

A list of the most celebrated or sought-after companies or individuals, especially in show business and entertainment.

Alpha test

The first stage of testing a new product, especially computer software or hardware, carried out by a developer under controlled conditions.

Alternate dispute resolution (ADR)

An informal process to resolve disputes. Involved parties meet with a trained third party who assists in resolving the problem by arbitration, mediation, judicial settlement conferences, conciliation or other methods. Though usually voluntary, ADR is sometimes mandated by a judge as a first step before going to court.

Amalgamate

When two or more companies combine or unite to form one large organisation.

Ambush marketing

A covert promotional strategy used by a non-sponsoring organizations to capitalize on the popularity and prestige of its product or service by giving the false impression that it is a sponsor. Nike and Pepsi piggybacked on the atmosphere during the World Cup during which their ads gave the illusion that they were sponsors of the event, even using some of the players in their ads.

Americanization

Conformation to American standards and practices by foreigners or immigrants to the United States. This shift towards the American culture has an impact on mainstream entertainment, consumer trends, and consumer needs. With targeted marketing practices, Americanization can also take place in other countries outside of the United States.

Americans with disabilities act (ADA)

Title I of the Americans with Disabilities Act of 1990 is part of a federal law that prohibits discrimination against someone with a disability, defined as "a physical or mental impairment that substantially limits a major life activity." Disability is decided on a case-by-case basis and does not include conditions such as substance abuse. This law applies to the whole employment cycle, from application through advancement and termination.

Amortize

To gradually reduce and write off the cost of an asset in a company's accounts over a period of time.

Anchor tenant

The first and most prestigious tenant, typically a store in a shopping centre, that will attract other tenants or shoppers.

Ancillary staff

People who provide necessary support to the primary activities and work of an organization, e.g: schools, hospitals.

Annual report

The write-ups and financial statements given every year to investors and inquiring members of the public concerning a corporation's business.

Annuity

Often used to provide a pension. An annuity is a fixed regular payment payed over a number of years to a person during their lifetime.

Antediluvian

An interesting and humorous metaphorical description of something (for example a product or service or concept) that is obsolete, old-fashioned or primitive, or devised a long time ago. 'Ante' is Latin for 'before', and 'diluvian' is from Latin 'diluvium' meaning 'deluge', so the overall literal meaning is 'before the flood', being the biblical flood and Noah's Ark, etc. Antediluvian is therefore a clever way to say that something is (so old as to be) 'out of the Ark'.

Anthropology

The discovery of beliefs, motives and values through the study of a society's overt and covert behaviour.

Anthropomorphic/ anthropomorphism/ anthropomorphous

Also called personification - this refers to giving human characteristics to an non-human thing, such as an animal, or a tree, or the Sun, Moon, a god, cartoon character, etc., for dramatic, visual, metaphorical, and amusing effect, etc. It's a very very old concept. Anthropomorphic characterizations have been found on ancient scuptures dating back more than 30,000 years. The word is Greek, originally from athropos, human, and morphe, form.

Appellant

A person appealing to a higher court against a decision of a lower court or other decision-making body.

Apple box

Used in films, TV, etc. Wooden boxes of various sizes which are used to elevate actors and celebrities.

Applicant tracking system (ATS)

A software application that began as a way to electronically handle recruitment needs but has since expanded to the entire employment life cycle. Onboarding, training and succession planning capabilities now exist, for example. An ATS can be implemented on an enterprise level or small business level, depending on the size and needs of the company. Applicant Tracking Systems may also be referred to as Talent Management Systems. An ATS saves time and increases efficiency and compliance for those tasked with managing human capital.

Application service provider (ASP)

Other common terms are SaaS (software as a service), on-demand or Web-based services. A business that provides computer-based services to customers over a network, as opposed to installing the software on a company server (hosted). This is a cost-effective solution for small and medium-sized businesses, who may find it hard to keep up with the increasing costs of specialized software, distribution and upgrades. Smaller, periodic payments replace one-time lump sum pricing. The ASP can be accessed from any location via the Internet. HRmarketer.com is an example.

Appraisal
A review of performance, capability, needs, etc., typically of an employee, in which case the full term is normally 'performance appraisal'.

Arbiter
A person who settles a dispute or has the ultimate authority to decide the outcome of a matter.

Arbitrator
An independent person or body officially appointed to settle a dispute.

Archive/archives
A collection of records no longer active. Also pluralized-archives-meaning the same, and referring to the place of storage.

Area organisation
A form of international organisational structure used by highly marketing oriented organisations with stable products.

Articles of association
The document which lists the regulations which govern the running of a company, setting out the rights and duties of directors and stockholders, individually and in meetings.

Aspirational brand
A brand or product which people admire and believe is high quality, and wish to own because they think it will give them a higher social position.

Asset
A resource of money value, including cash, accounts receivable, inventory, real estate, machinery, collectibles, and securities.

Asset stripping
Buying a stricken company and selling off its assets with no thought for the future of the company or its people, customers, etc.

Assets
Anything owned by the company having a monetary value; eg, 'fixed' assets like buildings, plant and machinery, vehicles (these are not assets if rentedand not owned) and potentially including intangibles like trade marks and brand names, and 'current' assets, such as stock, debtors and cash.

Assorting
Putting together a variety of products to give a target market what it wants, as in selecting various or different item for a gift basket or first aid kit.

Attention
A momentary attractions to a stimulus, something someone senses via sight, sound, touch, smell, or taste. Attention is the starting point of the perceptual process in that attention of a stimulus will either cause someone to decide to make sense of it—or reject it.

Attitude
A person's point of view toward something (feelings, values, mores).

Attitudes and values
A predisposition towards a person or object based on cultural mores and values which is a precursor of behaviour.

Attributes data
Data that is counted in discrete units such as dollars, hours, items, and yes/no options. The alternative to attributes data is variables data, which is data that is measured on a continuous and infinite scale such as temperature or distance. Charts that use attribute data include bar charts, pie charts, Pareto charts and some control charts.

Attrition
A gradual voluntary reduction of employees (through resignation and retirement) who are not then replaced, decreasing the size of the workforce.

Attrition
The process of reducing the number of employees in an organisation by not replacing people who leave their jobs.

Auditor
A qualified person who officially examines the financial records of a company to check their accuracy.

Auteur
An artist or creative, for example a film director, whose personal style is recognizable because he/she keeps tight control over all aspects of the work.

Autocratic
Offensively self-assured or given to exercising unwarranted power. Expecting to be obeyed and not caring about the opinions and feeling of others.

AV
Anti-Virus, a common abbreviation referring to virus protection software/services for computer and internet use.

Availability
A product or service's ability to perform its intended function at a given time and under appropriate conditions. It can be expressed by the ratio operative time/total time where operative time is the time that it is functioning or ready to function.

Avant garde
New or original and often unconventional techniques, concepts, products, etc, usually associated with the arts and creative areas.

Avatar
An identity, often in cartoon form, which can be chosen from a selection or created by the person using it to represent themselves in a website chatroom, etc.

Average chart (X-bar chart)
A control chart in which the average of the subgroup, represented by the X-bar, is to determine the stability or lack thereof in the process. Average charts are usually paired with range charts or sample standard deviation charts for complete analysis.

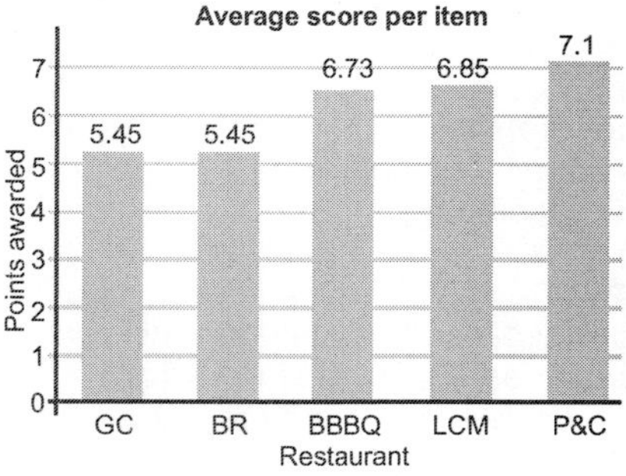

Average daily rate
In the hotel industry a calculation of the average price at which a hotel room is booked each night based on total daily revenue divided by the number of rooms sold.

B

B2b
Business to business. This refers to a commercial trading model by which a business supplies other businesses, and by implication does not generally supply consumers, i.e., domestic private customers. A B2B provider is therefore a provider of business services or products, for example: company auditors, manufacturers of industrial machinery, conference organizers, corporate hospitality, advertising agencies, trade journals, wholesalers, warehousing and logistics, management consultancies, mining, farming, industrial chemicals, papermills, etc.

B2c
Business To Consumer – Business conducted between companies and individual consumers rather than between two companies. A retailer such as Walmart is an example of a B2C company.

B2g
Businesses that sell products and services (or information) to government or government agencies. U.S. Federal Government spends approximately $530bn annually for a wide range of products and services.

Back shift
A group of workers or the period worked from late afternoon until late at night in an industry or occupation where there is also a day shift and a night shift.

Back with music
In the entertainment business, films, TV, etc., dialogue which is spoken over music.

Back-end load
A fee or commission paid by an individual when they sell their shares in an investment fund.

Background Screening / Pre-employment Screening
Testing to ensure that employers are hiring qualified and honest employees and that a prospective employee is capable of performing the functions required by the job. The screening can involve criminal background checks, verification of Social Security numbers, past addresses, age or year of birth, corporate affiliations, bankruptcies, liens, drug screening, skills assessment and behavioral assessments. If an employer outsources pre-employment screening, the federal Fair Credit Reporting Act requires that there must be a consent and disclosure form separate from an employment application.

Backscratching
Informal term for reciprocity or returning favours, as in the term 'you scratch my back and I'll scratch yours'.

Back-to-back loan

A loan in which two companies in separate countries borrow each other's money at the same time for a specific period at an agreed upon interest rate.

Backward integration

Actions taken to acquire greater control over suppliers. Ex: Starbucks formerly purchased coffee beans from a supplier in Colombia; it now operates its own farm in China to control the quality and cost of its beans.

Bait and switch

Dishonest and illegal tactic to attract potential buyers based on attractive special promotional offers (bait); then attempt to sell a more expensive product (switch).

Balance of payments

A measure of all economic transactions between one country and all other countries.

Balance sheet

The Balance Sheet is one of the three essential measurement reports for the performance and health of a company along with the Profit and Loss Account and the Cashflow Statement. The Balance Sheet is a 'snapshot' in time of who owns what in the company, and what assets and debts represent the value of the company. (It can only ever be a snapshot because the picture is always changing.) The Balance Sheet is where to look for information about short-term and long-term debts, gearing (the ratio of debt to equity), reserves, stock values (materials and finsished goods), capital assets, cash on hand, along with the value of shareholders' funds. The term 'balance sheet' is derived from the simple purpose of detailing where the money came from, and where it is now. The balance sheet equation is fundamentally: (where the money came from) Capital + Liabilities = Assets (where the money is now). Hence the term 'double entry' - for every change on one side of the balance sheet, so there must be a corresponding change on the other side - it must always balance. The Balance Sheet does not show how much profit the company is making (the P&L does this), although pervious years' retained profits will add to the company's reserves, which are shown in the balance sheet.

Balanced scorecard

A strategic planning and management system that is used to tie business activities to the vision and strategy of the organization, improve internal and external communications, and monitor performance against goals. Developed in the early 1990's by Drs. Robert Kaplan and David Norton, the balanced scorecard measure four areas of business: internal business processes, financial performance, customer knowledge, and learning and growth.

Balloon

Describes a long term loan in which there is a large final payment when the loan matures.

Bancassurance

The selling of both insurance and banking services, usually by a major bank.

Bandwidth

In computing, the amount of information that can be transmitted through a communication channel over a given period of time, usually measured in 'bits per second' (bps).

Bank loan

A loan made by a bank to an individual, company, etc., for a fixed term, to be repaid with interest.

Bank run

Lots of sudden and heavy cash withdrawals at the same time from a bank or banks, because customers believe the banks may become insolvent.

Bankers hours

A short working day, often with a long lunch break.

Bankruptcy

A term that describes the legal process governed by the U.S. bankruptcy code for companies unable to meet financial obligations.

Bar chart

A chart that compares different groups of data to each other through the use of bars that represent each group. Bar charts can be simple, in which each group of data consists of a single type of data, or grouped or stacked, in which the groups of data are broken down into internal categories.

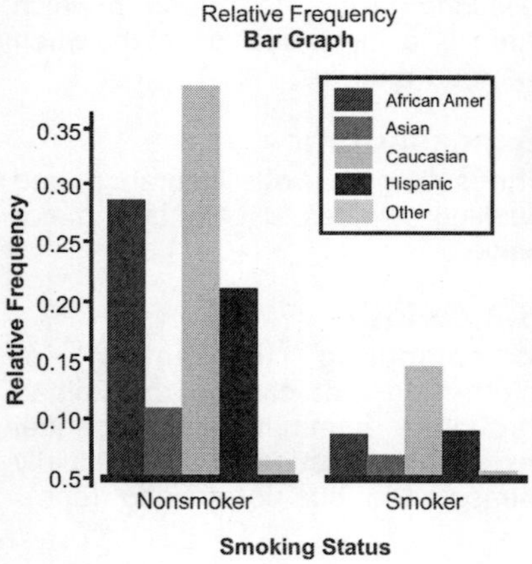

Barista

A person who is a professional speciality coffee maker, for example, cappuccino, latte, espresso, etc.

Barter

Process of exchanging goods or services for other goods or services without the exchange of money. Often used by small business with limited cash flow or limited lines of credit.

Base 2

Also known as the binary system, which is the basis of computer logic. Normal counting is based on 0-9. Binary just has 0-1, which means a new column is started after two, not nine. Binary counting does not go 1, 2, 3, 4, etc. It goes 0, 1, 10, 11, 100, 101, etc. Other than for computing it's not very practical.

Base wage rate (or base rate)

The monthly salary or hourly wage paid for a job, irrespective of benefits, bonuses or overtime.

Basis trading

The difference to new york futures, either on or off.

Bathtub curve

A U-shaped graph, often long horizontally-resembling a bathtub-representing high incidence or measure at the beginning and finish (far left and far right of graph) of a life-cycle or lifetime or period, with much lower incidence over a relatively long middle period (middle of graph), for example when measuring engineering failures in a product over time, in which early development teething problems produce high failure rates, tending to reduce to lower failure rates due to uncommon random faults, with failure rates again peaking at the end of product life, due to natural 'wear and tear'/exhaustion/erosion of components and construction. A Bathtub Curve may also equate to a U-shaped graph, for example in describing a type of recession which contains a prolonged period at the lowest point, i.e., a U-shaped recession.

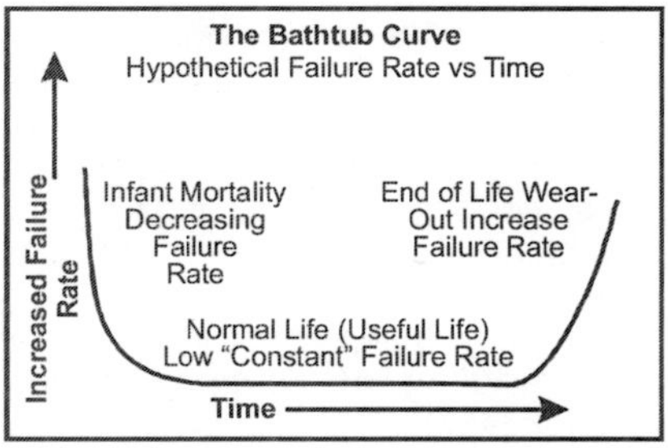

Bean counter
An informal derogatory term for an accountant, especially one who is perceived or suggested to be overly concerned about expenditure detail.

Beanfeast
Also known as a beano-an annual party, dinner, or outing given by an employer for its employees.

Bear market
In the stock market a period of declining prices in which investors continue selling shares, expecting the prices to fall further.

Bear raid
The practice, in the stock market, of attempting to push the price of a stock lower by selling in large numbers and often spreading unfavourable rumours about the company concerned.

Behavioral competency
The behavior qualities and character traits of a person. These act as markers that can predict how successful a person will be at the position he/she is applying for. Employers should determine in advance what behavioral competencies fit the position and create interview questions to find out if the candidate possesses them.

Behavioral risk management
The process of analyzing and identifying workplace behavioral issues and implementing Programmes, policies or services most suitable for correcting or eliminating various employee behavioral problems.

Behavioral targeting
Practice of targeting and ads to groups of people who exhibit similarities not only in their location, gender or age, but also in how they act and react in their online environment: tracking areas they frequently visit or subscribe to; subjects or content or shopping categories for which they have registered. Google uses behavioral targeting to direct ads to people based on the sites they have visited.

Behavioral-based interview
An interview technique used to determine whether a candidate is qualified for a position based on their past behavior. The interviewer asks the candidate for specific examples from past work experience when certain behaviors were exhibited.

Behaviorally anchored rating scale (BARS)
An appraisal that requires raters to list important dimensions of a particular job and collect information regarding the critical behaviors that distinguishes between successful and unsuccessful performance. These critical behaviors are then categorized and appointed a

numerical value used as the basis for rating performance.

Behemoth

A large and powerful organisation. (originally from Hebrew, behemoth-beast)

Bell curve

Survey/sample distribution term. 'Bell curve' is the common informal term for a graph with a large rounded peak in the middle, sloping sharply to the right and left and then tapering more gently at the extreme ends of the graph. It's a bell-shape, hence the name.

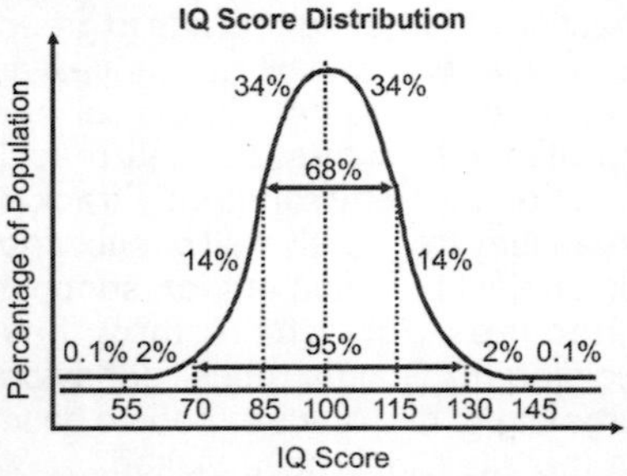

The term 'bell curve' refers also to this sort of statistical distribution, even if it is not actually graphed. Technically in probability theory, mathematics and marketing, etc., the 'bell curve' is 'normal' distribution or Gaussian distribution (after German mathematician ohann Carl Friedrich Gauss). The bell curve is very commonly exhibited in sampling and surveys, where the vast majority of results/subjects/data tend to concentrate towards the average score, with incidence of variation above and below the average (shown graphically right and left) being roughly equal to each other, and much less than the incidence/results towards the average and majority. Business people often refer to a 'bell curve' when anticipating/explaining a situation where the vast majority of members of an audience or market are very similar, and only a very small minority is outside of the 'norm' or average. This terminology is helpful in emphasizing the needs or tendencies of the big majority, and avoiding distraction by or over-estimating the effect of minority interests/needs, which can cause projects to be distorted unnecessarily. There is a broad correlation between the notion of a 'bell curve' and Pareto theory, also known as the '80-20 Rule', i.e., both concepts highlight the significance of concentration and distribution when assessing opportunity, risk, effectiveness, and the targeting of communications, resources, etc.

Bells and whistles

Extra features added often more for show than function, especially on computers, cameras, etc., to make the product more attractive to buyers.

Below the line

BTL. Describes marketing which has a short-term duration, such as non-media advertising, direct-mail, e-mail, exhibitions, incentives, brochures, etc., which is targeted directly at the consumer/customer. Often used by companies on a limited budget.

Bench warrant

An order issued by a judge for an absent defendent to be arrested and brought before a court.

Benchmark job

A job commonly found in the workforce for which pay and other relevant data are readily available. Benchmark jobs are used to make pay comparisons and job evaluations.

Benchmarking

A technique using specific standards to make comparisons between different organizations or different segments of the organizations, with the intent of improving a product or service.

Benefit

A desirable attribute of a good or service, which customers perceives that they will get frompurchasing and consuming/using it. Whereas vendors sell features ("a high speed 1/2" drill bit with tungsten-carbide tip"), buyers seek the benefit (a 1/2" hole).

Benefit principle

A taxation principle which states that those who benefit more from government expenditure, financed by taxes, should pay more tax for the product or service than those who benefit less.

Benefit segmentation

Use of data to define (often narrow) target market segments according to similarities or differences in their unmet needs.

Benefits (benefits package)

Benefits are a form of compensation paid by employers to employees over and above the amount of pay specified as a base salary or hourly rate of pay. Benefits are a portion of a total compensation package for employees.

Benefits administration

Software that helps companies manage and track employee participation in benefits Programmes such as healthcare, flexible spending accounts, pension plans, etc. This software helps automate and streamline the complex and otherwise time-consuming tasks of benefits administration.

Benefits realisation

Also Benefits Realisation Management, or if you prefer the US English it would be Benefits Realization. This refers to the translation of projects into real and perceived positive effects, seemingly a concept devised originally in the field of IT and ICT (Information and Communications Technology) project management, where projects are notoriously difficult to manage successfully and generate clear end-user appreciation.

BEP

Break even point – sales quantity at which the firm's total cost will equal its total revenue.

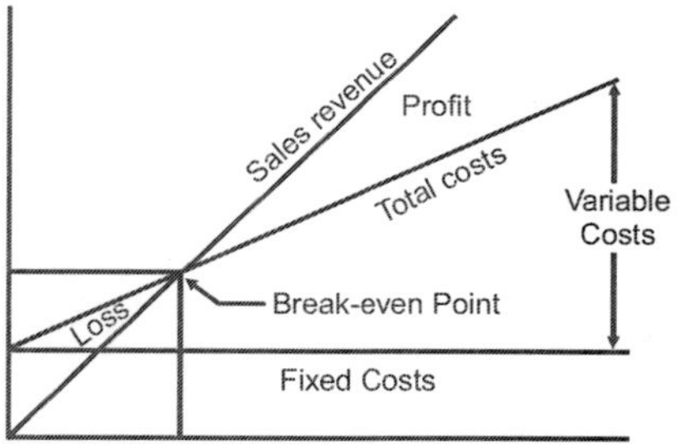

Bereavement leave

Paid or unpaid time off following the death of an employee's relative or friend. This time, generally ranging from one to three days, is given so that the employee can make arrangements, attend the funeral and attend to other matters related to the deceased. Many organizations are flexible in terms of how much time an employee takes off.

Best boy

The person on film sets, TV, etc., who is the assistant to the electrician.

Beta

The indicator used by *Value Line* to measure a stock's risk relative to the market, in this case the NYSE Index. The market's beta is always 1.0 (Based on past statistical records, a beta higher than 1.0 indicates that when the market rises, the stock will rise to a greater extent than that of the market; likewise, when the market falls, the stock will fall to a greater extent. A beta lower than 1.0 indicates that the stock will usually change to a lesser extent than that of the market. The higher the beta, the greater the investment risk.).

Beta test

The second test of a product, such as computer hardware, software, or even a website, under actual usage conditions, before the final version is used by or sold to the public.

Bid bond

A sum agreed to be paid by a company that wins a contract if the work is not carried out.

Bid price

The price one is willing to pay for a security.

Big bang

Occurred (UK) on 27th October 1986, when major technology changes took place on the London Stock Exchange chiefly to replace manual systems with electronic processes.

Bilateral

Agreement or involvement or action by two parties, people, companies, countries, etc.

Bill of lading

The receipt given by the shipping company to the shipper for goods accepted for carriage by sea. (as opposed to an airway bill of lading for goods carried by air).

Bills of exchange

An unconditional order in writing, addressed by one person (drawer) to another (drawee), signed by the person giving it (drawer), requiring the person to whom it is addressed (drawee) to pay on demand, at a fixed or determinable future date, a sum in money to, or to the order of, a specific person (payee) or to bearer.

Biometrics

The biological identification of human features, such as eyes, voices and hands, increasingly used to identify individuals, e.g., in laptop computers, entry systems and passports.

Bit part

In films and TV, a supporting actor who has at least one line of dialogue, and who is usually listed in the credits.

Black economy

Money earned in private cash transactions, which is untraceable, and therefore untaxable.

Black knight

A company which makes a hostile takeover bid for another company that does not want to be bought.

Black market (Underground economy)

Business transactions between sellers and buyers of goods or services that are often not recorded on a financial statement. Thus, an illegal action. Ex: The recent release of Apple's iPhone5 motivated some Chinese to purchase the new products and travel to China where they were resold on the street for hundreds more than the U.S. price.

Black swan/black swan theory

A 'black swan' refers to a random unpredictable and highly influential event (upon economics, society, politics, life, etc) whose potential/ significance is generally only appreciated after it has happened, and even then is commonly rationalized (by commentators and leaders, etc) to have been predictable and part of a predictable pattern of some sort, which actually is not so, or it would have been. The tendency for many people to be in denial as to the true nature of black swan event unpredictability and impact is an important part of the black swan theory itself. Examples of 'black swans' are events such as the September 11 attacks on the US by al-Qaeda; the 1986 Chernobyl disaster; and the 2008 global financial/credit collapse. Black swans can instead be of a more positive nature, for example, the invention of the internet, or the fall of the Berlin Wall. The black swan term/ theory was introduced by Nassim Taleb, a highly regarded Lebanese-American professor, author and theorist, in his best-selling 2001 book Fooled by Randomness: The Hidden Role of Chance in Life and in the Markets, and reinforced by his follow-up 2007 best seller The Black Swan: The Impact of the Highly Improbable. The 'black swan' metaphor alludes to both to the rareness of black swans, and to early beliefs that the creatures did not exist - which relates to general attitudes towards the real nature of 'black swan' events. The word 'black' also suggests negative consequences, which commonly result from black swan events. 'Grey swan' is a related expression, also coined by Nassim Taleb in his books, which refers to a predicted or known event which has uncertain outcomes.

Blamestorming

Portmanteau term contrived from Brainstorming and Blame, referring to meetings or discussions seeking to allocate responsibility for a failure or disaster. Popularised in the late 1990s by viral emails which listed amusing office terminology.

Blatherskite

A person who talks at great length without saying anything useful. Originally a Scottish 16thC expression adopted into American slang from the song Maggie Lauder during the US War of Independence.

Blended workforce

A workforce is comprised of permanent full-time, part-time, temporary employees and independent contractors.

Blind test

Research method in which people are asked to try a number of similar products which are not identified by brand name, to decide which product is the best.

Blind trial

A trial, with two groups of people, to test the effect of a new product, especially in medicine. One group is given the real product while the other group is given a placebo or 'sugar pill', which does not contain any medication.

Bloatware

In computing, software that needs so much computer memory that it takes a long time to load and therefore does not function properly.

Blog

A Web log written for and posted to the Internet using such software as www.blogger.com. Readers access the blog through the Web (e.g., http://hrmarketer.blogspot.com/) or subscribe to the blog's RSS (Really Simple Syndication) feed and receive alerts when there is a new posting. Blogs are becoming increasingly important to HR suppliers in order to increase their company's visibility, communicate with customers, and promote their products or services to establish themselves as thought leaders.

Blue chip
On the stock market, shares of a large company with a good reputation, whose value and dividends are considered to be safe and reliable.

Blue law
In the US, a law which regulates and limits activities for religious reasons, such as Sunday working or shopping.

Blue ocean strategy
Creating new market space that attempts to make a competitor irrelevant.

Blue-sky law
In the US, a law designed to protect the public from buying fraudulent securities.

Blue-sky thinking
Open-minded, original and creative thinking, not restricted by convention.

Bluetooth
Wireless technology which allows data to be transferred over short distances between laptop computers, mobile phones, digital cameras, etc.

Bodhisattva
From Buddhism, a person who seeks enlightenment for the good of, and motivated by a compassion for, other people. In Western thinking we could see this to be similar to Maslow's notion of 'trancendence' in the pursuit of self-actualization, notably helping others to self-actualize. Not an easy concept to explain; in the spectrum of human behaviour it's about as far away that can be imagined from the pursuit of a merchant banker's bonus or the Presidency of Europe, if you'll forgive the clichés.

Boilerplate
A section of standard text, especially a contract clause, inserted into legal documents, or instead increasingly referring to a standard section of code inserted into computer Programmes or other digital applications. The main sense of the 'boilerplate' meaning is that the text/ code is already existing and available to use, is quite fixed, needing little or no alteration, and by implication has a proven and trusted validity or suitability, and is therefore an aid to saving effort and cost compared with originating an equivalent clause or section of code from nothing. Usage and origins of the term boilerplate have become varied and confused, which perhaps helped popularize the term itself because this has made its meanings more flexible and widely applicable. The term 'boiler plate' or 'boiler-plate' seems to have two main original meanings: Firstly, plates of pre-cut/pre-formed metal used in constructing industrial boilers, and scondly, a much smaller plate or metal label attached to a boiler to identify the maker and other important details about the boiler. This latter sense is more iconically meaningful because of the visibility and imagery of steam engines and old industrial machinery. There is also a theory (not especially well-proven) that the term was initially applied metaphorically in traditional printing to the occasional use of hard durable steel printing plates for repeatedly used text/graphic sections, to save time and wear compared with the 'hot metal' and related methods of assembling printing plates from individual print blocks made from much softer metal.

Bold-faced names
Informal term for celebrities, used mostly in the USA.

Bond
The financial meaning of a bond is normally a debt/investment instrument issued by a company or country for a period of more than a year, with fixed interest rates and a firm and full repayment date. Typically a bond will pay a stipulated rate of interest at fixed times, and the debt is repaid at a specified time, i.e., the investor is guaranteed to be repaid the amount loaned/invested in full. More loosely the word bond can refer to a mortgage in some parts of the world, for example South Africa. A bond may also refer to a legal deed or agreement by which one person or party is bound to make payments to another; or to an insurance contract; or (notably in the US) to a sum of money paid as bail. The specific and more general meanings of bond logically derive from the older and original sense of bond, meaning fasten together, or the tie/festening itself.

Bonded warehouse
A warehouse in which imported goods are stored under bond, until the import taxes are paid on them.

Bonus
An extra sum of money given to an employee on top of their salary, often for achieving targets.

Bonus culture
Term used when companies give their executives huge bonuses in addition to their large salaries, even if their performance has been poor, especially leaders of financial institutions.

Book depreciation
A decrease or loss in value of a company's assets, as recorded in the company's finances.

Book value per share
The accounting value of a share of common stock, determined by dividing the company's net worth by the number of shares that are circulating.

Bookkeeping
The recording of a business's transactions, such as sales, purchases, payments, income, etc.

Boomlet
A small period of rapid growth in trade and economic activity.

Bootstrapping
Starting a business from scratch and building it up with minimum outside investment.

Bossnapping
Believed to have started in France, the unlawful imprisonment of a boss, in the offices of a company or on the site of a corporation, by employees who are protesting against redundancy, closure of the company, etc.

Bottom fishing
Buying the cheapest investments available which are unlikely to fall much further in value.

Bounce
In economics a bounce is a small quick partial recovery of the economy after a recession, which may subsequently continue upwards in growth, or plateau neither growing or contracting, or descend back into recession.

Bounce rate
Number of visitors to an e-commerce website. Tells web owners if visitors

are finding what they want and whether they're sufficiently interested to click for more content. A bounce occurs when a web site visitor only views a single page on a website, that is, the visitor leaves a site without visiting any other pages before a specified session-timeout occurs. There is no industry standard minimum or maximum time by which a visitor must leave in order for a bounce to occur. Rather, this is determined by the session timeout of the analytics tracking software.

Bounty hunter
In the US, someone who pursues criminals or fugitives and brings them to the police in exchange for a monetary reward.

Boutique
A small shop or outlet typically selling fashionable and expensive items such as clothing. The term 'boutique' is also now increasingly applied as a descriptive word in various other sectors and products to denote an outlet/supplier of small-scale, highly individual, bohemian, quirky, or hand-made quality, for example Boutique Hotels, below.

Boutique hotel
A small individual hotel, commonly within a historic building, with luxurious stylish themed and furnished rooms, typically independently owned.

Bracket creep
Slowly moving into a higher tax bracket with small pay increases over a period of time.

Brain drain
The loss of highly skilled people to another region, country or industry, where they can work in a better environment and/or earn more money.

Brainstorming
A tool used to encourage creative thinking and new ideas. A group formulates and records as many ideas as possible concerning a certain subject, regardless of the content of the ideas. No discussion, evaluation, or criticism of ideas is allowed until the brainstorming session is complete.

Brand
A unique design, sign, symbol, words, or a combination of these, employed in creating animage that identifies a product and differentiates or positions it from competitors. Over time, this image becomes associated with a level of credibility, quality, and satisfaction in consumers' minds. Thus brands stand for certain benefits and value. Legal name for a brand is trademark and, when it identifies or represents a firm, it is called a brand name.

Brand
A unique identifying symbol, trademark, company name, etc., which enables a buyer to distinguish a product or service from its competitors.

Brand architecture
Method by which a marketer can organize and manage various brands (often terms "sub brands"). Ex: In addition to Coke's various flavored colas, it also owns Sprite and Odwalla.

Brand association
Something or someone which make people think of a particular product.

Brand equity
Value of brand's overall strength in the market as measured in loyalty (those who will not switch).

Brand licensing
Process of creating and managing contracts between brand owners and individuals (often middlemen such as wholesalers and retailers) who wish to use the brand in connection with their product or service for a fixed period of time, or within a defined marketing territory.

Brand loyalty
When a consumer repeatedly buys a particular brand of product and is reluctant to switch to another brand.

Brand positioning
A distinctive position of careful manipulation of the marketing mix so that a brand adopts to ensure that its target market can set the brand apart from competitors. Ex: Loreal's original USP: "Costs more, but you're worth it," using a higher price point to connote quality.

Branded entertainment
Blending or exposure of products into various TV, movie, or web entertainment Programmes/sites. Ex: TV show 30 Rock poked fun at product placement, such as Outback Steakhouse.

Branding
Promoting a product or service by identifying and then marketing its key differentiators from competitors. The differentiator/s often inspire the name, phrase or logo for which the product or service becomes known.

Bread and Butter
The main source of income of a company or an individual.

Break even
To make enough money to cover costs. In business, the point at which sales equals costs. To make neither a profit or loss.

Breakthrough thinking
A management technique which emphasizes the development of new, radical approaches to traditional constraints, as opposed to incremental or minor changes in thought that build on the original approach.

Bridging/Bridging loan/ Bridge
A short term loan, normally at high rates of interest calculated daily, which 'bridges' a period when funds are unavailable, typically when payment has to be made before finance can be released from elsewhere to cover the transaction.

Brinkmanship
The practice of pursuing a tactic or method to the point of danger or damage, typically employed in competitive situations in which it is felt that the tactic will unsettle or cause the withdrawal of the adversary/ies. Dervies from the word brink, meaning the edge of a cliff or other dangerously high point.

British standards institution
BSI. An organisation which sets out formal guidelines to help businesses, etc., produce or perform more efficiently and safely. The BSI operates in more than 25 countries, and represent UK interests in other organisations, such as the ISO - International Organisation For Standardization.

Broadbanding
A pay structure that exchanges a large number of narrow salary ranges for a smaller number of broader salary ranges. This type of pay structure encourages the development of broad employee skills and growth while reducing the opportunity for promotion.

Broker
A channel institution which puts a specific buyer(s) and seller(s) in contact with one another in one or more commodity(ies) or service(s) with a view to achieving a sale or benefit. In general a broker is an independent agent used extensively in some industries. A broker's prime responsibility is to bring sellers and buyers together and thus a broker is the third-person facilitator between a buyer and a seller. An example would be a real estate broker who facilitates the sale of a property.

B-roll
Promotional tactic designed to enhance and increase exposure for a marketer's product or service. Video clips are often provided to media outlets (TV, satellite, Internet news sources) for use when covering stories or events. This can also include photos (screenshots), used as background images as the newscaster is reading the story.

Brown goods
Household electrical entertainment appliances such as televisions, radios and music systems.

Brownfield
Previously developed land, either commercial or industrial, which has been cleared for redevelopment.

Brown-noser
Insulting slang term for a sychophant, originally 1930s US military slang (brown-nose). Brown-nosing describes crawling or creeping to please a boss; an amusingly disturbing interpretation of various expressions which juxtapose the head of the follower with the backside of the boss, as in the rude slang metaphors: kissing arse/ass, arse-licking, bum-licker, etc.

Brussels nomenclature
An international convention aimed at grouping articles, mainly according to their material composition, into a simplified classification system for tariff administration.

Bubble economy
An unstable boom when the economy experiences an unusually rapid growth, with rising share prices and increased employment.

Budget
In a financial planning context the word 'budget' (as a noun) strictly speaking means an amount of money that is planned to spend on a particularly activity or resource, usually over a trading year, although budgets apply to shorter and longer periods. An overall organizational plan therefore contains the budgets within it for all the different departments and costs held by them. The verb 'to budget' means to calculate and set a budget, although in a looser context it also means to be careful with money and find reductions (effectively by setting a lower budgeted level of expenditure). The word budget is also more loosely used by many people to mean the whole plan. In which context a budget means the same as a plan. For example in the UK the Government's annual plan is called 'The Budget'. A 'forecast' in certain contexts means the same as a budget - either a planned individual activity/ resource cost, or a whole business/ corporate/organizational plan. A 'forecast' more commonly (and precisely in my view) means a prediction of performance - costs and/ or revenues, or other data such as

headcount, percentage performance, etc., especially when the 'forecast' is made during the trading period, and normally after the plan or 'budget' has been approved. In simple terms: budget = plan or a cost element within a plan; forecast = updated budget or plan. The verb forms are also used, meaning the act of calculating the budget or forecast.

Built to flip

Companies which have been sold soon after they have been created, so that money can be made quickly.

Bull market

On the Stock Market, a prolonged period in which share prices are rising and investors are buying.

Bullet point

A symbol, e.g. a dot or a square, printed at the beginning of each item on a list.

Bullying (workplace bullying)

Workplace bullying is "repeated, health-harming mistreatment, verbal abuse, or conduct which is threatening, humiliating, intimidating, or sabotage that interferes with work, or some combination of the three."

Bumping

Giving long-standing employees whose positions are to be eliminated the option of taking other positions within the company that they are qualified for and that are currently held by employees with less seniority.

Bundling

Combining products as a package, often to introduce other products or services to the customer. Ex: AT&T offers discounts for customers by combining 2 or more of the following services; cable television, home phone service, wireless phone service, and internet service.

Business angel

Also known as Private Investor. A, usually wealthy, individual who invests money in developing (often high risk) companies, and who provides their advice, skills, knowledge and contacts in return for an equity share of the business.

Business continuity planning

Broadly defined as a management process that seeks to identify potential threats and impacts to the organization, and provide a strategic and operational framework for ensuring the organization is able to withstand any disruption, interruption, or loss to normal business functions or operation.

Business name

These are a very vague terms indeed. Precise interpretation may depend on the actual legal definitions of these terms in the territory/state/country concerned. And also the way a business perceives and interprets the terms, and whether they fill in the forms/checkboxes correctly. Generally business names and trade/trading names may be registered and licensed. A lot depends on the interpretation of the term 'Business name'. Business name can refer to a trade/trading name, or also could refer to the the over-arching or parent or holding company, which is ultimately responsible for a trade/trading name within or of the business. A trade name is normally a division or branded operation/service, or product brand, within/of a (legally titled) business, but the terms are very broad and it's difficult to be specific because circumstances and legal interpretations vary. Be careful to avoid applying a strict definition to such loose terms and certainly if serious implications stem from interpretation then seek expert local clarification.

Business plan

A written document which sets out a business's plans and objectives, and how it will achieve them, e.g. by marketing, development, production, etc.

Business process outsourcing (BPO)

The managing of an organizations business applications by a technology vendor.

Business process redesign or Reengineering

A management method which stresses the fundamental rethinking of processes, questioning all assumptions, in an effort to streamline organizations, and to focus on adding value in core processes.

Button ad

A small advertisement on a website, typically measuring 120 x 90 pixels.

Buy and sell orders

An intent to buy or sell a security.

Buy-and-hold

A strategy in which the stock portion of one's portfolio is fully invested, including dividends reinvestments, at all times.

Buy-in

Purchase of a company where outside investors buy more than 50% of the shares, so they can take over the company.

Buzz marketing

A viral marketing technique that attempts to make each encounter with a "prospect" appear to be a personal, spontaneous interaction instead of an obvious marketing pitch. For example, the advertiser reveals information about their new product to a few opinion leaders within their target audience. In theory, these opinion leaders then talk about your product with their peers, thus beginning a word-of-mouth campaign where other buyers are flattered to be included in the group of those "in the know". A typical buzz marketing campaigns is initiated in chat rooms, where marketing representatives assume an identity appropriate to their target audience and pitch their product.

Buzzword

A word or phrase which has become fashionable or popular, or sounds technical or important and is used to impress people.

C

CE mark
Conformite Europeenne (European Conformity). A symbol on many products sold in the European Union indicating that they have met health, safety and/or environmental requirements, ensuring consumer and workplace safety.

CIF
A contract of sale "cost, insurance freight" of the documents of title, not the goods, whereby the buyer is under an obligation to pay against the shipping documents irrespective of the arrival of the goods.

Cafeteria plan
A plan in which an employer offers employees a variety of different benefits. The employee is able to choose which benefits would fit their individual needs. Examples of benefits offered in the cafeteria include group-term life insurance, dental insurance, disability and accident insurance, and reimbursement of healthcare expenses.

Calculated risk
A risk which has been undertaken after careful consideration has been given to the likely outcome.

Call account
A bank account, which usually pays a higher rate of interest, from which investors can make instant withdrawals.

Call option
The right given a buyer to buy stock at a specified price within a certain time period.

Callable
Usually applies to bonds or convertible securities which can be bought back, at an agreed price, before maturity, by the company or government which sold them.

Callable bond
A bond that can be officially repaid by the issuer prior to its maturity date (Out of courtesy, a premium is usually paid when the bond is repaid.)

Cannibalization
Occasions when a new product will take market share away from an older brand, as in the addition of a diet soda product to a previously existing brand line of sodas. The new diet soda will compete with and perhaps eat away at the profits of the previously existing products. Cannibalization may also be said to occur when product sales fall at a particular sales outlet or set of retail outlets as the result of the opening of a new store, because sales at the new outlet are eating away at sales at the older ones.

CAN-SPAM Act (Controlling the Assault of Non-Solicited Pornography and Marketing Act)

Congressional legislation that regulates commercial emails (i.e. commercial advertisement or promotion) and sets clearly defined opt-out standards. Any billing, warranties, product updates or customer service information is not included in this act. E-mail newsletters that are not considered advertisements are also exempt.

Cap and collar

The upper and lower limits of interest rates on a loan, usually fixed for a specific period of time.

Capital

The net worth of a business, including assets, cash, property, etc., which exceeds its liabilities (debts). The amount of money invested in a business to generate income.

Capital allowance

Money spent by a company on fixed assets, such as buildings, vehicles, machinery, which is deducted from its profits before tax is calculated.

Capital employed

The value of all resources available to the company, typically comprising share capital, retained profits and reserves, long-term loans and deferred taxation. Viewed from the other side of the balance sheet, capital employed comprises fixed assets, investments and the net investment in working capital (current assets less current liabilities). In other words: the total long-term funds invested in or lent to the business and used by it in carrying out its operations.

Capital flight

The sudden movement of money from one country or investment to another in order to reduce risk, such as high inflation, or to increase profit.

Capital gain

An increase from the purchase price to the selling price of common stock or any other capital asset; profit from the sale of investments or property (A capital gain that persists for one year or less is called a short-term capital gain. Likewise, one that persists for more than one year is called a long-term capital gain.)

Capital gains tax

Tax payable on profit made on the sale of certain types of assets by a company or individual.

Capital loss

A decrease from the purchase price to the selling price of common stock or any other capital asset; a loss from the sale of investments or property.

Capital outlay

Money which is spent for the acquisition of assets, such as land, buildings, vehicles, machinery.

Capitalization issue

When a company converts its spare profits into shares, which are then distributed to existing shareholders in proportion to the amount of shares they already hold.

Capitated pricing

Vendors deliver contracted services for a set amount of money per employee per month. This can be a risky strategy for vendors whose profitability is directly tied to how much the services are or are not used (e.g., EAPs).

Capitialism
When an economic system of a country is controlled and profited by private individuals and corporations, rather than the government.

Capped-rate
Interest rate, usually on a loan, which cannot rise above the upper set level but can vary beneath this level.

Caption
Usually appears in the form of text added to help explain the features or benefits that accompany an illustration or photograph in an advertisement.

Carbon credit
Allows the right to emit a measured amount of harmful gases, such as carbon dioxide, into the air, and can be traded between businesses and countries.

Care mapping
Medical procedure for a particular diagnosis in a diagrammatic form that includes key decision points used to coordinate care and instruct patient.

Carey street
To be heavily in debt or bankrupt. Originates from Carey Street in London where the bankruptcy court was situated.

Carload
A shipment of goods which, typically by weight, qualifies for a lower shipping rate. The term 'Less than carload' refers to a shipment which is below the given size/weight necessary to qualify for such a rate. The term originated from USA railway freight car transportation and also applies to other methods of freight transport, notably shipping containers, hence similar terms containerload and 'less than containerload'.

Carnet
An international official permit which allows you to take certain goods, e.g. for display or demonstration, into another country, duty free, for a specific period-usually 12 months.

Carpet bomb
To send an advertisement to a large number of people by e-mail or onto their computer screens.

Carrier
A vendor in the employee benefits space. More commonly used in reference to health care. Carriers (e.g., Met Life, Blue Cross, Aetna, etc.) sell their products through Brokers & Consultants, but may also sell to an employer directly.

Cartel
A group of separate companies or nations which together agree to control prices and not compete against each other. Also known as a Price Ring.

Carve-out
The elimination of coverage of a specific category of benefit services (e.g. vision care, mental health/ psychological services, or prescription drugs). The employer opts out of certain services with one vendor and contracts another to deliver them.

Cash call
A request by a company to its shareholders to invest more money.

Cash cow
A steady dependable source of income which provides money for the rest of a business.

Cash flow forecast
Also called Cash Flow Projection. An estimate of the amounts of cash outgoings and incomings of a company over a specific time period, usually one year.

Cash flow per share
Earnings after taxes and depreciation, divided by the number of a firm's shares.

Cashflow
The movement of cash in and out of a business from day-to-day direct trading and other non-trading or indirect effects, such as capital expenditure, tax and dividend payments.

Cashflow statement
One of the three essential reporting and measurement systems for any company. The cashflow statement provides a third perspective alongside the Profit and Loss account and Balance Sheet. The Cashflow statement shows the movement and availability of cash through and to the business over a given period, certainly for a trading year, and often also monthly and cumulatively. The availability of cash in a company that is necessary to meet payments to suppliers, staff and other creditors is essential for any business to survive, and so the reliable forecasting and reporting of cash movement and availability is crucial.

Casting vote
The deciding vote cast by the presiding officer to resolve a deadlock when there are an equal number of votes on both sides.

Casual employment
The practice of hiring employees on an as-needed basis, either as a replacement for permanent full-time employees who are out on short and long-term absences or to meet employer's additional staffing needs during peak business periods.

Catch-22
Much misused expression, it refers properly only to a problem whose solution is inherently self-defeating. Wrongly it is used to describe any insurmountable or difficult problem.

Category killer
Large companies that put smaller and less efficient competing companies out of business.

Cattle call
Term used in the entertainment industry for a large number of actors, etc., who are all auditioning for the same job.

Cause & effect diagram
A tool used to analyze all factors (causes) that contribute to a given situation or occurrence (effect) by breaking down main causes into smaller and smaller sub-causes. It is also known as the Ishikawa or the fishbone diagram.

Cause-related marketing
Joint funding and promotional strategy in which a percentage of a firm'ssales are linked to a charity or other public cause. Unlike philanthropy, money spent in cause-related marketing is considered an expense and is often expected to show a return.

Caveat emptor
When the buyer takes the risks and is responsible for checking the condition or quality of the item purchased.

Central counterparty
Acts on behalf of both parties in a transaction, so that the buyer and

seller do not have to deal with each other directly.

Central reservation system (CRS)

A computer database system used by a chain of hotels (and other services providers) enabling availability and rates to be monitored and bookings to be made.

Certificate of deposit (CD)

An interest-bearing bank receipt for a specified amount of money (CD's usually mature between three months and three years. The interest rate depends on the amount of money and length of time of the deposit.).

Chain of command

A system in a business, or in the military, in which authority is wielded and delegated from top management down through every level of employee. In a chain of command instructions flow downwards and accountability flows upwards.

Chamber of commerce

A group of business owners in a town or city who form a network to promote local business.

Change management

A deliberate approach for transitioning individuals or organizations from one state to another in order to manage and monitor the change. Change management can be conducted on a continuous basis, on a regular schedule (such as an annual review), or when deemed necessary on a Programme-by-Programme basis.

Channel of distribution

Also known as Distribution Channel. A means of distributing a product from the manufacturer to the customer/end user via warehouses, wholesalers, retailers, etc.

Channels

Any series of firms or individuals that participate in the movement/flow of goods and services from producer to final user.

Characteristic

Distinguishing feature or attribute of an item, person, or phenomenon that usually falls into either a physical, functional, or operational category.

Check sheet

A customized form used to record data. Usually, it is used to record how often some activity occurs.

Check the gate

A term used in the film industry after a shot is taken on a film set. The gate, or opening in front of the camera, is checked to make sure that there is no dirt, hair, etc., present.

Checklist

A list of important steps that must take place in a process or any other activity. A list of things to do.

Churn rate

Rate of customers lost (stopped using the service) over a specific period of time, often over the course of a year. Used to compare against new customers gained.

Clapper boy

On a film or TV set, the person who holds the clapperboard (which has information on it, for example film title, shot number, etc) in front of the camera for about one second at the start of each shot after the camera starts rolling.

Class a spot

In the media, commercials which are run on a prime time network.

Class action
A lawsuit in which one person makes a claim and sues on behalf of a large group of people who have similar legal claims, usually against a company or organisation.

Clicklexia
Ironic computing slang for a user's tendency to double-click on items when a single click is required, often causing the window or utility to open twice.

Clicks and mortar
Also known as Clicks and Bricks. Refers to businesses which trade on the Internet as well as having traditional retail outlets, such as shops.

Clickstream
A record of an internet user, including every web site and web page which have been visited, and e-mails sent and received.

Click-through
When a person clicks on an advertisement on a web page which takes them to the advertisers website.

Clinical practice guidelines
A general term for statements of accepted medical procedure for a particular diagnosis.

Clip-art
Ready made pictures of computerised graphic art which can be copied by computer users to add to their own documents.

Close company
In the UK, a company which is controlled by five or less directors.

Cluster analysis
A technique for grouping similarities or differences between a set of objects or persons.

Clusters
Customer profiles based on lifestyle, demographic, shopping behavior, or appetite for fashion. Example: Ready-to-eat meals may be heavily influenced by the ethnic make-up of a store's shoppers, while beer, wine, and spirits categories in the same store may be influenced predominantly by the shopper's income level and education.

CMSA
Consolidated Metropolitan Statistical Area - (adjacent to MSA/PMSA with 1 million population).

Coaching
A method of training an individual or group in order to develop skills or overcome a performance problem. Coaching can be between a manager and a subordinate or an outside professional coach and one or more individuals. There are many coaching methods and models, but close observation, accountability and feedback on progress and performance are usually included.

Co-branding
An agreement between two brands to work together in marketing a new product, such as Dreyer's Ice Cream flavored with Baby Ruth candy pieces (promoting both brands on the label).

Code-sharing
An arrangement between different airlines in which they all agree to carry passengers on the same flight using their own flight numbers.

Co-employment
The relationship between a Professional Employer Organization (PEO), or employee leasing firm and an employer, based on a contractual sharing of liability and responsibility for employees.

Coercion

Forcing someone, by some method or other, to do something or abstain from doing something against their will.

Cognitive ability testing

A testing instrument used during the selection process in order to measure the candidate's learning and reasoning abilities.

Collective bargaining

One or more unions meeting with representatives from an organization to negotiate labour contracts.

Combined ratio

In insurance, a way of measuring how much profit has been made by comparing the amount of money received from customers to the amount paid out in claims and expenses.

Commercial monopoly

The control of a commodity or service by one provider in a particular market, virtually eliminating competition.

Commercial paper

An unsecured and unregistered short-term agreement in which organizations can borrow money from investors who cannot take the assets from the organization if the loan is not repaid.

Commercialization

Stage in product development process where the decision to order full-scaleproduction and launch is made. The act of exchange, buying, selling of a commodity on a large scale for profit. This also describes the flow of goods and services from producer to consumer.

Commission

A broker's fee is given for assisting in buying or selling securities.

Commission

In finance, a payment based on percentage of transaction value, according to the local interpretation of value (e.g., based on total revenue, or gross profit, etc).

Commission broker

A person who buys and sells shares, bonds, etc., on a commission basis on behalf of their clients.

Commoditization

When mature industries, slowing innovation, excessive supply, or fickle price-conscious consumers push margins to the floor. Often occurring when products lack differentiation or strong brand identities.

Common causes

Inherent causes of variation in a process. They are typical of the process, not unexpected. That is not to say that they must be tolerated; on the contrary, once special causes of variation are largely removed, a focus on removing common causes of variation can pay big dividends.

Common stock

Shares in a company that represent part ownership of that company.

Companies house

A government agency in the UK which is responsible for collecting and storing information about limited companies. The companies must file annual accounts or face penalties.

Comparative advantage

One country enjoying a lower production ratio (input to outputs) than another country under total specialisation.

Comparative advertising

Promotional messaging in which there is specific mention or presentation of competing brands, and a comparison is made or implied. Cellular companies often compare their features or advantages, as in this example of Verizon Wireless using a U.S. map to show 5 times more coverage than AT&T for its 3G network.

Comparative analysis

Comparing the same set of statistics within a category of one country with another for the purpose of estimating potential demand.

Compensation

Pay structures within an organization. It can be linked to employee appraisal. Compensation is effectively managed if performance is measured adequately.

Compensation fund

A fund set up by a company or organisation from which to pay people who have suffered loss or hardship which has been caused employees or members of the company or organisation.

Compensatory time-off plan

The practice of giving employees paid time off that can be used in the future in lieu of paying them overtime for hours worked in excess of 40 per week. While an acceptable practice in the public sector, the FLSA places very strict limitations on the use of compensatory time off for private sector employers.

Competency modeling

A set of descriptions that identify the skills, knowledge, and behaviors needed to effectively perform in an organization. Competency models assist in clarifying job and work expectations, maximizing productivity, and aligning behavior with organizational strategy.

Competency-based pay

Competency-based pay, alternately known as skill-based and knowledge-based pay, determines compensation by the type, breadth and depth of skills that employees gain and use in their positions.

Competition

A product, organisation or individual, in either the same or another category which can be directly substituted one for the other in fulfilling the same needs or wants.

Competition law

Known as Antitrust law in the US, regulates fair competition between companies, including the control of monopolies and cartels.

Competitive advantage

In the context of Human Resources, competitive advantage refers to the quality of the employees, as a competing organization's systems and processes can be copied but not its people. All other things being equal among competing companies, it is the company with better employees that has the competitive advantage.

Competitive cost advantage

An advantage that a firm has over competitors, allowing it to generate greater sales margins and/or retain more customers. It supports the firm's cost structure, product offerings, distribution network and customer support.

Competitive intelligence

Process of gathering actionable information on your business' competitive environment. Ex: In 2006, after extensive research to diversify and move into the organic fish market (available at Whole Foods), Walmart bought all the organic fisheries so it would have no competition, and could keep prices low in sync with its USP.

Competitive strategy
The adoption of a specific target market and marketing mix stance in the market place.

Competitor
A business rival, usually one who manufactures or sells similar goods and/or services.

Competitor analysis
Also called Competitive Analysis. A company's marketing strategy which involves assessing the performance of competitors in order to determine their strengths and weaknesses.

Compliance officer
A corporate official whose job is to ensure that a company is complying with regulations, and that its employees are complying with internal policies and procedures.

Compound interest
Interest which is calculated on not only the the initial loan, but also on the accumulated interest.

Compounding
The paying of interest on the accrued interest as well as on the principal.

Compulsory purchase
When an organisation has the legal right to force the sale of land, property, etc., usually to build motorways or railways.

Concentrated marketing
A growth strategy in which a firm's resources are focused on a well-defined market niche or population segment.

Concept
A thought or notion. An idea for a new product, advertising campaign, etc.

Concierge
An employee of e.g. an hotel who provides a service to guests, such as handling luggage, delivering mail and messages, making tour reservations, etc.

Conciliation
To bring two disputing sides together to discuss the problem with the aim of reaching an agreement.

Concordance
In publishing, a concordance is an alphabetical list of the key words from a text showing their meanings. Concordances are rare in old large books because of the time and effort required to compile them, but more commonly arise in modern computer-generated applications.
A concordance is a sort of cross-referenced index, but in (sometimes very much) more detail than the standard index of chapters and subjects typically shown before the main content. There are other more complex and different meanings of the word concordance relating to various technical applications (mathematics, genetics, etc) where often the meanings concern duality or cross-referencing of some sort.

Condition of employment
An organization's policies and work rules that employees are expected to abide by in order to remain continuously employed.

Conditional sale
A purchasing arrangement, usually where the buyer pays in instalments but does not become the legal owner

of the goods until the full purchase price has been paid.

Conference call
A telephone call which allows three or more people to take part at the same time.

Confidentiality agreement
An agreement between an employer and employee in which the employee may not disclose proprietary or confidential information.

Conflict of interest
A much overlooked, under-estimated, yet highly prevalent factor in the execution of any responsibility or activity, where an organization/group/individual is subject to incompatible demands, opportunities, incentives, or responsibilities, etc., and especially where there is potential for one demand to distort the proper honest diligent execution of responsibility in achieving the second demand, i.e.., the incompatibility is competing and mutually unhelpful. A conflict of interest produces divided loyalties, for example where a person represents two different competing businesses, or an employee is responsible for managing family members or personal friends.

Conformance
Meeting requirements or specifications.

Conglomerate
A corporation which consists of several smaller companies with different business activities.

Conservator
In law, a guardian or protector appointed by a court to manage the affairs, finances, etc., of someone who is too ill or incapable of doing so themselves.

Consortium
A group of businesses, investors or financial institutions working together on a joint venture.

Constructive dismissal
An employer's behaviour (either one serious incident or a pattern of incidents) creates a negative work environment, leading to an employee's resigning. Such behaviour is considered a breach of contract and gives the employee the right to seek compensation in court.

Constructive spending
Helping the local economy by buying home produced goods, holidaying in your own country, etc., rather than buying imported goods and holidaying abroad.

Consultants
An outside individual who supplies professional advice or services to companies for a fee. Large HR consulting firms include Aon, Mercer, Hewitt and Watson Wyatt. Large HR consulting firms typically work with companies who have more than 1,500 employees.

Consumer
A purchaser of a good or service at retail, or an end user not necessarily a purchaser, in the distribution chain of a good or service (gift recipient).

Consumer credit
Also called Personal Credit or Retail Credit. Loans given to consumers by financial institutions for household or personal use.

Consumer debt
Money owed by people in the form of loans from banks or purchase agreements from retailers, such as 'buy now pay later'.

Consumer panel
A group of selected people, usually a cross-section of a population, whose purchasing habits are monitored by an organization, in order to provide feedback on products, services, etc., which are used.

Consumer price
The price which the general public pays for goods and services.

Consumer price index
A measure of inflation which involves regularly monitoring the change in price for everyday goods and services purchased by households.

Consumer protection
Laws which protect consumers against unsafe or defective products, deceptive marketing techniques, dishonest businesses, etc.

Consumer watchdog
An independent organization that protects the rights of individual customers and monitors companies to check for illegal practices.

Consumer-to-business (C2B)
A system in which consumers use online agents (middlemen) to look for a product or service that suits their needs.
Examples include Priceline.com and shopbot.com.

Consumption tax
Tax paid which is based on the price of services or goods, e.g. value added tax.

Contango
A situation in which the price of a commodity to be delivered in the future exceeds the immediate delivery price, often due to storage and insurance costs.

Contextual advertising
Method of deciding and posting specific advertising offers on websites. A contextual ad system scans the text of a website for keywords and returns ads to that webpage based on what the user is viewing (as in sports-related products on a physical fitness site).

Contingency fee
In law, a fee that is payable to the lawyer out of any damages which have been awarded to the client by a court. There is no payment if the case is unsuccessful.

Contingency recruiting (search)
Contingency recruiters conduct frontline talent searches and represent either employers or individuals seeking placement. Contingency firms are not paid unless a candidate is successfully placed.

Contingent liability
This is recorded as a debt on a company's accounts which may or may not be incurred, depending on the outcome of a future event, such as a court case.

Contingent staff
Temporary staff that supplements a companys workforce. Contingent staff may be hired through a staffing firm. Businesses that have fluctuating seasonal staff demands or are in need of temporary call center representatives often use contingent workers.

Continuous improvement
On-going improvement of any and all aspects of an organization including products, services, communications, environment, functions, individual processes, etc.

Contra entry
In accounting, an amount entered which is offset by another entry of the same value, i.e., a debit is offset by a credit.

Contraband
Goods prohibited by law from being exported or imported. Smuggling.

Contract for services
An agreement with a self-employed person for a specific job.

Contract of employment
A contract between an employee and an employer which specifies terms and conditions of employment, such as hours to be worked, duties to perform, etc., in return for a salary, paid benefits, paid holiday, etc., from the employer.

Contract of purchase
Also called Purchase Agreement. A legal document which states the terms and conditions, including price, of the sale of an item.

Contract of service
Another term for employment agreement.

Contract worker
A person who is hired by a company (but not as an employee), often through an employment agency, for a specific period of time to work on a particular project.

Contractor
An individual, company, etc., who agrees to provide goods and/or services to another individual or company under the terms specified in the contract.

Control account
An account which a company keeps in addition to its official accounts, in order to cross-check balances, etc., to ensure that the official accounts are accurate.

Control chart
A chart that indicates upper and lower statistical control limits, and an average line, for samples or subgroups of a given process. If all points on the control chart are within the limits, variation may be ascribed to common causes and the process is deemed to be "in control." If points fall outside the limits, it is an indication that special causes of variation are occurring, and the process is said to be "out of control."

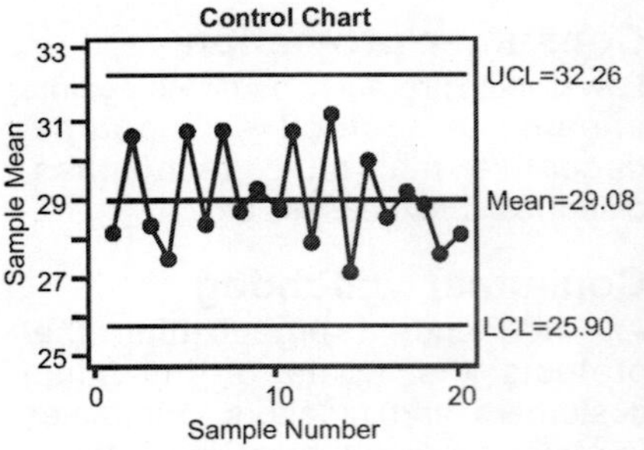

Control limit
A statistically-determined line on a control chart used to analyze variation within a process. If variation exceeds the control limits, then the process is being affected by special causes and is said to be "out of control." A control limit is not the same as a specification limit.

Controlling interest
The ownership of more than 50% of the voting shares in a company, which enables the owner of these shares to make decisions, direct operations, etc.

Convene
To gather together for an official or formal meeting.

Convention
A large formal meeting of politicians, members, delegates, sales people, etc.

Conversion rate
A conversion rate is defined as the relationship between visitors to a web site and actions considered to be a 'conversion', such as a sale or request to receive more information. Search optimization (SEO) is far less expensive than an aggressive paid search campaign and gets you the same amount of traffic. Plus, the effects are longer lasting, and conversions are frequently in the same range (or even higher) than paid ads on engines.

Conversion rate
Percentage of customers to purchase a product or service. Also includes percentage of website visitors to sign up for a newsletter, register for membership, or apply for a credit card.

Convertible
Refers to a security (bonds or shares) which can be exchanged for another type of security in the same company.

Convertible currency
Currency which can be quickly and easily converted into other countries currencies.

Conveyancer
A specialist lawyer who is an expert in conveyancing, i.e., legal work carried out connected to the selling and buying of property.

Cookie
On a computer, coded information that an Internet website you have visited sends to your computer which contains personal information, such as identification code, pages visited, etc., so that the website can remember you at a later time.

Cooling-off period
A period of time after the exchange of contracts, purchasing agreements, etc., during which the purchaser can change their mind and cancel the contract, and usually get any deposit paid reimbursed.

Cooperative
A collection of organisations or individuals, pooling their resources in order to gain commercial or non-commercial advantage in buying, selling or processing goods and/or services.

Cooperative marketing
Also known as Cooperative Advertising. When two companies work together to promote and sell each others products. A manufacturer or distributor who supports, and often pays for, a retailers advertising.

Copyright
An exclusive legal right to make copies, publish, broadcast or sell a piece of work, such as a book, film, music, picture, etc.

Core competencies
The particular set of strengths, experience, knowledge and abilities that differentiate a company from its competitors and provide competitive advantage. Employees should possess these qualities in order to advance business goals.

Core earnings
A company's revenue which is earned from its main operations or activities minus expenses, such as financing costs, asset sales, etc.

Corporate advertising
Also called Institutional Advertising. Advertising that promotes a company's image, rather than marketing its products or services.

Corporate hospitality
Entertainment provided by companies in order to develop good relationships with its employees, customers, other businesses, etc.

Corporate image
The mental image held by others at the mention of a firm's name. It's a compositepsychological impression that's dynamic based on circumstances, media coverage, performance, pronouncements, etc. Similar to a firm's reputation or goodwill, it is the public perception of the firm rather than a reflection of its actual state or position. Large firms use various corporate advertisin techniques to enhance their image to improve their desirability as a supplier, employer, customer, borrower, etc

Corporate ladder
The order of rank, position, etc., in a company from junior to senior, which can be progressed or 'climbed' by employees.

Corporate raider
A term used for an individual or company who purchases large numbers of shares in other companies, against their wishes, in order to gain a controlling interest in the other companies, or to resell the shares for a large profit.

Corporate social responsibility
CSR. An obligation of a company to adhere to legal guidelines in order to meet the needs of its employees, shareholders and customers, and also to be concerned about social and environmental issues.

Corporate veil
A term which refers to the fact that a company's shareholders are not liable for the company's debts, and are immune from lawsuits concerning contracts, etc.

Corporation
A large company or a group of companies which is legally authorised to act as a single entity, separate from its owners, with its liabilities for damages, debts, etc., limited to its assets so that its shareholders and owners are protected from personal claims.

Corporation tax
A tax which limited companies and other organisations, such as societies, clubs, associations, etc., pay on their profits after adjustments for certain allowances.

Correspondence course
A study course using written correspondence, books, etc., which are sent to you by post from learning institutes.

Corruption
Lack of honesty or integrity. Illegal behaviour, such as bribery, by people in positions of authority, e.g. politicians.

Cost accounting
Managerial accounting which calculates, records and controls the operating costs of producing goods or services.

Cost control
A management process which ensures that departments within a company or organisation do not exceed their budget.

Cost cutting
Reducing an individual's, company's, etc, expenditure.

Cost effective
Producing a product, offering a service, etc., in the most economical way to the benefit of the company and the customer.

Cost leader
A company which has a competitive advantage by producing goods or offering services at a lower cost than its competitors.

Cost of debt ratio
Despite the different variations used for this term (cost of debt, cost of debt ratio, average cost of debt ratio, etc) the term normally and simply refers to the interest expense over a given period as a percentage of the average outstanding debt over the same period, ie., cost of interest divided by average outstanding debt.

Cost of goods sold (COGS)
The directly attributable costs of products or services sold, (usually materials, labour, and direct production costs). Sales less COGS = gross profit.

Cost of living
The standard cost of basic necessities which people need to live, such as food, housing and clothes.

Cost of living allowance
COLA. A salary supplement which a company pays to employees because of an increase in the cost of living.

Cost of poor quality
The costs incurred by producing products or services of poor quality. These costs usually include the cost of inspection, rework, duplicate work, scrapping rejects, replacements and refunds, complaints, and loss of customers and reputation.

Cost of quality
Philip Crosby's term for the cost of poor quality.

Cost of sales (COS)
Commonly arrived at via the formula:

opening stock + stock purchased - closing stock.

Cost of sales is the value, at cost, of the goods or services sold during the period in question, usually the financial year, as shown in a Profit and Loss Account (P&L). In all accounts, particularly the P&L (trading account) it's important that costs are attributed reliably to the relevant revenues, or the report is distorted and potentially meaningless. To use simply the total value of stock purchases during the period in question would not produce the correct and relevant figure, as some product sold was already held in stock before the period began, and some product bought during the period remains unsold at the end of it. Some stock held before the period often remains unsold at the end of it too. The formula is the most logical way of calculating the value at cost of all goods sold, irrespective of when the stock was purchased. The value of the stock attributable to the sales in the period (cost of sales) is the total of what we started with in stock (opening stock), and what we purchased (stock purchases), minus what stock we have left over at the end of the period (closing stock).

Cost overrun
The amount by which the actual cost of a project, etc., exceeds the original budget.

Cost per click
CPC. The amount of money an advertiser pays to a website publisher every time a visitor clicks on an advert displayed on the publisher's website which links to the advertisers website.

Cost-benefit analysis
The ability to measure the costs associated with a specific programme, project, or benefit. The cost is then compared to the total benefit or value derived.

Cost-centre
Part of a business or organisation such as a marketing department, or quality assurance department, which is a cost to operations and does not produce external customer revenues or profit through trading.

Cost-per-hire
The costs linked to recruiting talent. These costs can include advertising, agency fees, relocation costs, and training costs.

Cottage industry
A small business in which production of goods or services are based in the home rather than in a factory or on business premises.

Count chart (c chart)
An attributes data control chart that evaluates process stability by charting the counts of occurrences of a given event in successive samples.

Counterbid
To make a higher offer than someone else in a bid to buy something.

Counterclaim
In a court of law, a claim made against you (plaintiff) by the person (defendant) you are making a claim against.

Counterpart
A person or position which has a corresponding function in a different organization, country, etc. The corresponding function naturally is also a counterpart. Also a copy of a legal document.

Countersign
To add a second signature, where required, to a document or cheque, in order to make it valid.

Countertrade
An agreement by the customer to buy goods on condition that the seller buys some of the customer's own products in return.

Countervailing duty
An additional tax imposed on certain imported goods which have been produced very cheaply in their country of origin, in order to bring the price of the goods up to the true market price to protect the importing country's producers.

Count-per-unit chart (u chart)
A control chart that evaluates process stability by charting the number of occurrences of a given event per unit sampled, in a series of samples.

Courier
A person who carries and delivers messages, documents, packages, etc., often between companies. A person employed by a travel company as a tourist guide.

Courseware
Computer software designed to be used in teaching or for self-learning.

Covenant
A written promise, sometimes part of a contract, to perform, or not to perform, a particular action.

Cover charge
A fixed fee charged by a nightclub or a restaurant with live entertainment, which covers, or part covers, the cost of musicians, DJs, etc.

Cowboy
A dishonest, often unqualified, business person, especially one who overcharges for bad quality work. Not to be confused with the cowboy of top-shelf publications.

CP
Commonly used process capability index defined as [USL (upper spec limit) - LSL (lower spec limit)] / [6 x sigma], where sigma is the estimated process standard deviation.

CPK
Commonly used process capability index defined as the lesser of USL - m/3sigma or m - LSL /3sigma, where sigma is the estimated process standard deviation.

CPM
Cost Per Thousand – Used by marketers and advertisers to measure the effectiveness of their media expenditures. Derived by dividing the cost of media purchase divided by the number of consumers reached (in thousands).

Cpm
Critical Path Method – Method to break down complex projects into simpler tasks, thus identifying more efficient, easiest, and fastest path to completion.

Crapola
Items of little importance or poor quality.

Crawling peg
A system of frequently adjusting a country's exchange rate by marginal amounts, because of inflation, etc.

Creative director
A person who usually works in the advertising or entertainment industry and is responsible for planning and managing the creative aspects of an advertising or promotional campaign.

Credit
An arrangement in which an item for sale is received by the purchaser and paid for at a later date. A loan. The positive balance in a bank account. An amount entered in a company's accounts which has been paid by a debtor.

Credit analysis
The process of analysing a company's financial records and assessing its ability to repay a loan, etc.

Credit crunch
Also known as Credit Squeeze. This usually precedes a recession. A situation in which loans for businesses and individuals are difficult to obtain, when a government is trying to control inflation, because of the fear of bankruptcy and unemployment. The term 'Credit Crunch' also became a specific informal name for the 2008 global financial crisis and subsequent prolonged recession, which affected western economies particularly, mainly because of their highly leveraged and indebted nature, and the convoluted inter-dependent chains of credit arrangements between banks, some of which failed completely

resulting in their effective nationalization or absorption into larger competitors.

Credit history

A record of an individual's or company's debt repayment, used by lenders to asses a borrowers ability to repay a loan, mortgage, etc.

Credit rating

Information (based on interpretation by an official credit rating agency or similar financial services data provider) of a person's or company's or other entity's financial history and circumstances, which assesses and indicates their ability to repay debts, loans, etc. Lenders use this information when making a decision regarding a loan approval, and in larger cases will adjust levels of interest and other financial credit terms according to the perceived risk of the loan situation and client, which may be an individual or a whole country or international federation.

Credit rating agency

A credit rating agency is a company which analyses and issues an official recognized assessment of the quality of a debt or debtor, including corporate, institutional or state debt or debt/credit products (specifically the reliability of repayment/recoverability), such as bonds and tradable securities (debts, equities, mortgages, and derivative complex financial credit contracts), and significantly also of organizations, bodies, and entire countries, by virtue of their credit-worthiness (ability to repay their debts). Ratings are visible, published and officially/internationally recognized, especially for countries. Ratings strongly influence interest rates applied to rated organizations, i.e., poor ratings mean that the low-rated organizations/bodies/nations are charged higher rates of interest by lenders, due to the higher perceived level of risk, and the overall market's response to the rating/risk. Conversely, positively-rated organizations/countries enjoy the lowest possible interest rates when borrowing. The same principle applies to debt products, mindful that many debt products are sold from one lender to another, commonly entailing seriously vast sums of money. Ratings are typically expressed on a scale of AAA ('triple A') as the top/best, which equates to the most reliable and secure debt/debtor, down through AA, A, BBB, BB, etc., to CCC with the lowest being C, although there are variations, including lower case letters, numbers, and + and - symbols. This is a highly significant, pivotal, and controversial area of corporate/global finance, economic management, extending to life and society, because:

1. The sums of money involved/affected by these ratings are extremely big (multi-billions) so there is a lot at stake, for corporations, countries, bankers, brokers, and for societies too.
2. While there are hundreds of small credit rating agencies, historically the market is dominated by just three of them, namely Standard and Poor; Moody's, and Fitch ('The Big Three'), which between them control (at 2013) c.95% of the global market (in ratings and related services, significantly at the highest levels of national and corporate debt/credit).
3. The credit rating industry is inherently and worryingly liable to major conflict of interest because agencies provide important and high-value advisory services to the same

organizations whose products the agencies assess, along with rating the client organizations themselves.

There is also huge potential for conflict of interest and corruption on a vast scale because credit ratings affect interest rates and transactions entailing monumental sums of money, and so there is unlimited temptation and opportunity for incestuous deals between the rate-fixers and those who trade in credit and debt, and financial investments and speculation generally. Sadly, as with much else that happens in the financial sector across the globe, combinations of conflict of interest, extreme 'product' complexity, corporate and personal incentive and greed, together with a lack of sufficient regulation and transparency, tend to produce very big outcomes, trends and economical effects that can be arbitrary, distorted, extremely polarized, so that a few powerful people/organizations/entities achieve massive gains and advantages, while others, especially those in weak positions, suffer massive disadvantages. It is an interesting point of note that despite enormous reliance on credit ratings agencies at the level of global corporations and national governments, credit rating agencies can make large misjudgments, as when for example very positive ratings were given to highly toxic derivative mortgages/ debts products whose collapse and virtual irrecoverable value led mainly or substantially to the 2008 global financial disintegration and following recesssion.

Credit rationing

When a bank or money lender limits the amount of funds available to borrowers, or interest rates are very high.

Credit repair

The process of helping to improve a person or company's credit rating, sometimes by disputing or correcting credit history discrepancies.

Credit union

A financial institution, similar to a bank, whose members create the funds from which they can obtain loans at low rates of interest.

Creditor

A person, business, etc., to whom money is owned.

Crib

Plagiarism. To copy someone else's written work and pass it off as your own.

Crisis management

Actions taken by a company to deal with an unexpected event which threatens to harm the organisation, such as a loss of a major customer, bad publicity, etc.

Criterion

A principal or standard by which other things or people may be compared, or a decision may be based.

Critical mass

The minimum amount of customers, resources, etc., needed to maintain or start a business, venture, etc. The point at which change occurs e.g., when a company is able to continue in business and make a profit without any outside help.

CRM

Customer Relationship Management – Broad term that covers concepts used by companiesto manage their relationships with customers, including the capture, storage, and analysis of customer, vendor, partner, and internal process information.

Cronyism
In business and politics, showing favouritism to friends and associates by giving them jobs or appointments with no regard to their qualifications or abilities.

Crosby, philip
One of the quality guru's. Crosby founded several consulting agencies including Career IV, Philip Crosby Associates, and the Quality College. He has authored several books including Quality Is Free and Quality Without Tears. Crosby is well-known for his theory of "zero defects."

Cross guarantee
Also known as Inter Company Guarantee. A guarantee by a group of companies to be responsible for the debts, etc., of another company in the group if it fails to repay them. The group also use the guarantee to raise capital or take out multiple loans.

Cross merchandising
Also known as Add-On Sales. In retailing, the practice of putting related products together on display in order to encourage customers to purchase several items.

Cross-channel marketing
Use of a single marketing channel (such as direct mail or internet) tosupport or promote another channel (such as retailing).

Cross-training
When employees are trained to perform various jobs by other groups or individuals to improve job performance. Often aimed at creating a diverse working group to combat an "narrow-minded" work force. Also known as conditioning.

Crowdfunding
A method of funding and underpinning a project or business venture which became increasingly popular and visible in the 21st century, whereby users or other interested people are involved as investors at project inception, and therefore agree and commit to support a development of one sort or another. A good example of crowdfunding is the raising capital and support from a local community for the construction of nearby wind turbines, which generally otherwise encounter local hostility instead of support.

Crowdsourcing
Term first coined by Jeff Howe in 2006 in Wired magazine. Crowdsourcing refers to an organisation, group or individual delegating a task to a large number of people via the internet, thereby using the general public or a community of followers, users, experts, etc., to do research, make suggestions, solve a problem, etc., usually without being paid. Their reward is mainly a sense of ownership and real involvement, which is proven to be a very powerful and meaningful force for motivation.

Crown jewel
The most valuable and profitable asset of a company or business.

C-suite
The Chief Officers or most senior executives in a business or organisation.

Cube farm
An open office which is divided into cubicles.

Culpability
Blame or liability for harm or damage to others, from Latin culpa meaning fault.

Culture
The sum total of learned behaviourial characteristics or traits which are manifest and shared by members of a particular society.

Cumulative sum chart
Control chart that shows the cumulative sum of deviations from a set value in successive samples. Each plotted point indicates the algebraic sum of the last point and all deviations since. PathMaker does not support cumulative sum charts.

Currency bloc
A group of countries that use the same currency, for example the Euro.

Currency swaps
A method to gain access to foreign capital at favourable rates comprising contracts to exchange cash flow relating to the debt obligations of the two counterparts to the agreement.

Current account
A bank account which can be used to make deposits, withdrawals, cash cheques, pay bill, etc.

Current assets
Cash and anything that is expected to be converted into cash within twelve months of the balance sheet date.

Current liabilities
Money owed by the business that is generally due for payment within 12 months of balance sheet date. Examples: creditors, bank overdraft, taxation.

Current ratio
The current ratio is an indication of a firm's market liquidity and ability to meet creditor's demands. Acceptable current ratios vary from industry to industry and are generally between 1.5 and 3 for healthy businesses. If a company's current ratio is in this range, then it generally indicates good short-term financial strength. If current liabilities exceed current assets (the current ratio is below 1), then the company may have problems meeting its short-term obligations. If the current ratio is too high, then the company may not be efficiently using its current assets or its short-term financing facilities. This may also indicate problems in working capital management.

Current yield
The amount produced by dividing the annual income, both from interest and dividends, by the current price of the security (Stocks do not gain interest; the current yield for stocks is equal to the dividend yield.).

Customer
Any recipient of a product or service; anyone who is affected by what one produces. A customer can be external or outside the organization, or they can be internal to the organization.

Customer advocate
Individual entrusted by management to study the needs of an organization's customers and help it better satisfy them. A role often cited as problem-solver: addressing customer complaints to protect and enhance the organization's image.

Customer loyalty
Describes when a customer prefers to buy a particular brand or type of product, who prefers a particular shop,

or who stays with the same company, such as a bank, insurance company, phone company, etc.

Customer profile

Description of a customer group or type of customer based on various geographic, demographic, and psychographic characteristics; also called shopper profile_(may include income, occupation, level of education, age, gender, hobbies, or area of residence, etc.). Profiles provide knowledge needed to select the best prospect lists and to enable advertisers to select the bestmedia.

Customer relations

The relationship a company has with its customers and the way it deals with them. The department in a company which is responsible for dealing with its customers, for example complaints, etc.

Customer retention

a goal of organizations to keep customers buying their products and services, an essential component to sustaining growth and profitability as it costs more to acquire a new customer than to retain existing customers. Ex: Best Buy has a team that surfs the Internet in search of special offers by competitors on products it offers and make adjustments, as needed.

Customer satisfaction

Customers' state of mind about a company when their expectations have been met or exceeded, most often leading to brand loyalty and product repurchase. Ex: Nordstrom's Department Store emphasizes a 100-year-old customer service philosophy to generate customer satisfaction (best possible service, selection, quality and value).

Customer-centric

An approach to doing business in which a company focuses on creating a positive consumer experiences at the point of sale and post-sale. A customer-centric approach helps organizations to differentiate and position themselves apart from competitors who don't offer the same experiences. Customer-centric organizations are operated from a customers' point of view rather than developing new products and attempting to convince consumers to purchase them.

Customs duty

A tax which must be paid on imported, and sometimes exported, goods, to raise a country's revenue and to protect domestic industries from cheaper foreign competition.

Customs union

A group of nations which have agreed to promote free trade, for example, not to charge tax on goods which they trade with one another, and to set taxes for nations which are not members of the group.

Cutover

Also known as 'Going Live'. The point in time a company or organisation, etc., replaces an old Programme or system with a new one.

Cut-throat

Ruthless and intense competition. An unprincipled, ruthless person.

Cyber monday

In recent times, the busiest online shopping day of the year, in the USA typically the Monday after Thanksgiving Day (the fourth Thursday of November); in the UK typically the first Monday in December.

Cyberspace
Term credited to author William Gibson in 1984 which describes the imaginary place where e-mails, web pages, etc., go to while they are being sent between computers.

Cybersquatting
The illegal activity of buying and registering a domain name which is a well-known brand or someone's name, with the intent of selling it to its rightful owner in order to make a profit.

Cyclical industry
An industry whose success is closely linked to the rise and fall of the general economy (The auto industry is a cyclical industry.).

D

Damage limitation
The process of trying to limit or curtail the amount of damage or loss caused by a particular situation or event.

Dark net
A term for online private websites and networks concealed from and inaccessible to unauthorised users in which materials are shared, normally illegally and anonymously.

Dark store
A retail store adapted or designed for the main or whole purpose of fulfilling online orders. Customers generally do not visit 'dark stores', except where policy/processes allow the collection of pre-ordered goods. The 'dark store' feature of retailing began to emerge seriously in the early 2000s, in which an existing retail store or a purpose-built facility - notably in the supermarkets sector - would be adapted/designed chiefly or entirely for distributing orders placed online, i.e., website sales. Dark stores typically contain similar warehousing/ shelving/aisles arrangements to conventional retail stores, but store staff physically pick the products, rather than customers. Orders are then delivered to customers, or (subject to the policy if the retailer) may be collected.

Data
Facts/figures pertinent to a marketing problem.

Data mining (knowledge discovery)
Process of analyzing data from different perspectives or angles for use in such marketing activities as increasing revenue, cutting costs, etc.

Daughter company
A company that is controlled partly or completely by a holding or parent company.

Dawn raid
A sudden planned purchase of a large number of a company's shares at the beginning of a days trading on the stock exchange.

Day player
In the entertainment industry, actors, etc., who are hired by the day.

Day-after recall test
Research method testing consumers' memories a day after hopefully seeing an advertisement. Designed to assess the ad's effectiveness.

Dead cat bounce
A derogatory term used on the stock exchange to describe a huge decline in the value of a stock, usually a

share, which is immediately followed by a temporary rise in price before continuing to fall. From: "Even a dead cat will bounce if it falls from a great height".

Deadbeat
A person or company who tries to avoid paying their debts.

Dear money
Also known as Tight Money. When money is difficult to borrow, and if a loan is secured then it would be paid back at a very high rate of interest.

Debenture
Unsecured certified loan over a long period of time with a fixed rate, based on the trust that payment will be made in the future.

Debriefing
A meeting or interview in which a person or group of people report about a task or mission just completed or attempted.

Debt
Money owed to another person or organisation, such as a loan, mortgage, etc., which is required to be paid back, usually with interest.

Debt exposure
Money that a lender risks losing if the borrower fails to pay it back.

Debt-equity swap
An arrangement between a lender and a debtor, usually a company, in which the lender agrees to reduce the debt in exchange for newly issued shares from the borrower.

Debt-to-equity ratio
The ratio found by dividing long-term debt by the equity (all assets minus debts) held in stock (This is a measure of financial risk.).

Decentralised plans
A planning system taking into account differences in product/market conditions.

Deceptive advertising (False advertising)
Misleading customers by making claims or promises that are untrue, unproven, or distortions of the truth to promote the sale of goods or services. Often an illegal practice regulated or prosecuted by the secretaries of state.

Decertification
In employment this refers specifically to action taken by workers to disassociate themselves from a trade union which previously represented them. Aside from this the general meaning refers to withdrawal of certification of one sort or another.

Decision consequence analysis
A process for helping decision makers, usually in the pharmaceutical and petroleum exploration industries, decide where resources such as time, money, etc., should be invested.

Decision matrix
A tool used to evaluate problems, solutions, or ideas. The possibilities are listed down the left-hand side of the matrix and relevant criteria are listed across the top. Each possibility is then rated on a numeric scale of importance or effectiveness (e.g. on a scale of 1 to 10) for each criterion, and each rating is recorded in the appropriate box. When all ratings are complete, the scores for each possibility are added to determine which has the highest overall rating

and thus deserves the greatest attention.

Decision tree

A diagram which starts with an initial decision, and possible strategies and actions are represented by branches which lead to the final outcome decided upon.

Decision Tree of Weather

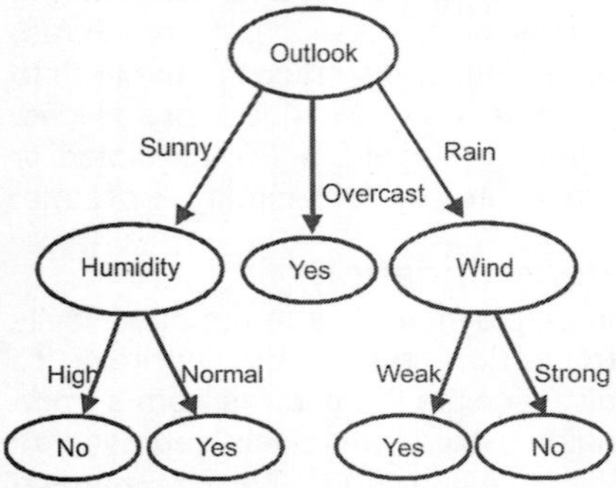

Deed of partnership

A legal document which sets out how a partnership is to be run, and also the rights of the partners. A Deed Of Partnership is not compulsory but it helps to avoid any misunderstandings or disputes in the future.

Deep throat

In business, an anonymous source of top secret information. First used in this sense in the reporting of the US Watergate scandal.

Deep web

Also known as the Invisible Web, said to contain about 500 times more information than the generally accessible world-wide web, the Deep Web comprises data held by secure organizations, for example military and government.

Default

A term that denotes the failure to pay the principal or interest on a financial obligation (such as a bond).

Default risk

The risk that a company will default, or fail to meet its financial obligations, i.e., fail to pay the interest or principal on its bonds.

Defect

An error in construction of a product or service that renders it unusable; an error that causes a product or service to not meet requirements.

Defence document

A document that a company's shareholders receive which explains why an offer to buy the company should be rejected.

Deferred compensation

Payment for services under any employer-sponsored plan or arrangement that allows an employee (for tax-related purposes) to defer income to the future.

Deficit financing

When a government borrows money because of a shortage of funds from taxes. This usually results in pushing up interest rates.

Defined benefit plan

A retirement plan that pays participants a lump-sum amount that has been calculated using formulas that can include age, earnings and length of service.

Defined contribution

A pension plan that clearly defines the amount of contributions, which is usually a percentage of an employees salary. The benefits payable at retirement depend on several factors including future investment return and annuity rate at retirement.

Deflation

Economic decline typified by falling costs of goods and services; falling levels of employment; limited money supply or credit; reduced imports; lower wage increases, often caused by lower personal spending or investment, and/or a reduction in government spending. Deflation is broadly the opposite of inflation.

Delegation
An assignment of responsibility or task, usually by a manager to a subordinate. Separately a delegation refers to a deputation, being a group of people appointed or responsible for representing a nation or corporation or other organization to attend talsk or negotiations, etc.

Deleveraging
An attempt by a company to reduce its debts, for example by selling off assets, laying off staff, etc.

Demand pattern analysis
The analysis of in-country industrial sector growth patterns.

Demerit goods
Products or services such as as alcohol, gambling, drugs, prostitution, etc., which are considered unhealthy or undesirable, and are often subject to extra taxes in order to reduce consumption and potentially to fund remedial actions in response to consumption.

Deming cycle
Alternate name for the Plan-Do-Check-Act cycle, a four-stage approach to problem-solving. It is also sometimes called the Shewhart cycle.

Deming, W. Edwards
Known as the father of quality control. Deming began his work in quality control in the United States during World War II to aid the war effort. After the war, he went to Japan to help in the rebuilding of their country. His methods of quality control became an integral part of Japanese industry. Deming is a celebrated author and is well-known for his "14 Points" for effective management.

Democracy
Majority rule, by which the biggest proportion of members of a group determine decisions for the whole group. Democracy typically refers to a country's political system, in which government is elected through majority vote.

Demographic profile
Used in marketing to describe a particular segment of the population, for example social class, age, gender, income, etc.

Demographic segmentation
The process of identifying and dividing consumers into groups according to their race, age, gender, religion, etc.

Demographics
Consumer statistics regarding socioeconomic factors, including gender, age, race, religion, nationality, education, income, occupation and family size. Each demographic category is broken down according to its characteristics by the various research companies.

Demonetize
To officially decide that a particular coin or banknote can no longer be used as currency.

Deposition
A sworn statement of evidence by a witness taken outside of the court proceedings before a trial.

Depreciation
The decrease in value due to wear and tear, decay, decline in price, e.g., a new car purchased at $20,000

depreciates to $5,000 in five years.

Depression
A prolonged and very deep economic recession, in a country or wider region. Definitions of an economic depression vary greatly, from two to ten years or more, characterized by extremely deep levels of negative indicators such as unemployment, credit and money supply, living standards, and reduced GDP, etc. Historians and economic commentators commonly disagree about the duration of depressions due to the confused methods of defining precisely what a depression is.

Deregulate
The reduction or removal of government regulations from an industry or business.

Deregulation
The removal or revision of laws that regulate the supply of goods and services.

Derived demand
Desire for something produced as a by-product for another product or service, as in the demand for specialty skilled labour for the auto industry, or inherent value in a sports star's endorsement. Ultimate result is customer fulfillment.

Desk jockey
An informal term for someone who spends their working day sitting behind a desk, and who is concerned about administration.

Desktop publishing
Producing printed documents, magazines, books, etc., using a small computer and printer.

Devaluation
The reduction in the value of one currency vis a vis other countries.

Developmental counseling
A form of shared counseling where managers or supervisors work together with subordinates to identify strengths and weaknesses, resolve performance-related problems and determine and create an appropriate action plan.

Diagnostic journey/Remedial journey
A problem-solving approach in which a problem is investigated by looking first at symptoms, and gradually working back towards root causes. Once root causes have been established, experimentation and tracking are used in the remedial journey - the finding of a cure for the roots of the problem.

Didactic
Describes works of literature or art which are intended to be be informative or instructional, especially morally, rather than entertaining. From the ancient Greek word didaskein, which means to teach.

Differentiated marketing
Sales growth strategy in which several market niches or population segments are targeted with different products for each niche or segment.

Differentiation/product
Differentiation seeks to make a product more attractive by contrasting its unique qualities with competing products. This creates a competitive advantage for the seller when customers view these products as unique or superior.

Diffusion theory
A classification for the adoption of innovation(s) through social phenomenon, characterised by a normal distribution.

Digerati
People who consider themselves to be experts of the Internet and computer industry.

Digital marketing
Use of Internet-connected devices to engage customers with online product and service marketing/promotional Programmes. Includes mobile phones, iPads, and other Wi-Fi devices.

Digital wallet
Computer software used to store a persons bank account details, name, address, etc., to enable them to make automatic payments when they are making purchases on the Internet.

Direct marketing
Direct marketing is a sales method by which advertisers approach buyers directly with products or services. The most common forms of direct marketing are telephone sales, emails and print (e.g., catalogs, brochures). Successful direct marketing also involves renting or compiling / maintaining a database of qualified buyers. According to the Direct Marketing Association, average response rates for print direct mail (flat mail) are 2.73%), catalogs are 2.45% and E-mail is 1.12%. HRmarketer.com research shows emails that offer a compelling "offer" in the form of a free downloadable white paper or research report (on a topic that resonates with your buyer) are significantly more likely to generate a response than promotional offers. In all industries, marketers are shifting their spending from brand building tactics like print advertising to direct response-oriented promotional channels such as direct marketing and interactive marketing (online advertising). The HRmarketer.com research report Trends in HR Marketing (http://www.hrmarketer.com/home/whitepaper_main2.htm) verifies this trend in the HR marketplace.

Direct overhead
A portion of the overheads, e.g. lighting, rent, etc., directly associated with the production of goods and services.

Directives
At an official level, directives are instructions, guidelines or orders issued by a governing or regulatory body. They may amount to law. In a less formal way a directive equates to an instruction issued by an executive or manager or organizational department.

Director
A person appointed to oversee and run a company or organisation along with other directors, In the entertainment industry, the person who directs the making of a film, TV Programme, etc.

Dirty money
Money made from illegal activities which needs 'laundering' so that it appears to be legitimate.

Disability
The inability to perform all or part of one's occupational duties because of an accident or illness. This can be due to a sickness, injury or mental condition and does not necessarily have to have been caused by the job itself.

Disability income insurance
Health insurance that is paid to a policyholder who experiences a loss of income due to an injury or an illness. Disability insurance plans pay a portion of the salary of a disabled worker until his/her retirement age.

Disburse
To pay out money from a large fund, e.g. a treasury or public fund.

Disciplinary procedure
A standardized process that an organization commits to when dealing with an employee who has breached the terms of employment in some way. If this procedure is not standardized and fair, the organization may face discrimination or other legal charges.

Discontinuous innovation
Description of how products and services are displaced by other products and services, reducing their intended utility or in some cases rendering them obsolete. Ex: Computers have virtually replaced typewriters. Will cell phones eliminate the need for a land line? Will iPads/ Kindle readers replace college bookstores?

Discount
Reduction off the list price offered by a producer to a buyer; five types of discounts are common: trade, quantity, cash, seasonal and allowances. Marketers issue discounts to increase sales, to move out-of-date items, to reward valuable customers, or use it as a sales promotion.

Discount bond
A bond whose value is less than its face amount.

Discount broker
A stockbroker who charges a smaller commission than other brokers, but provides no counsel in investment.

Discount loan
A loan on which the finance charges and interest is paid before the borrower receives the money.

Discount window
In the US, when banks can borrow money from the Federal Reserve at low interest rates.

Discretionary income
Amount of income after fixed regular expenses (mortgage/rent, car payment, insurance, taxes) have been paid—monies not yet committed and therefore subject to persuasion techniques on the part of marketers. Ex: Take someone living in a $300/ month trailer, who eats Ramen noodles as a staple, and often has his electricity or phone shut off for non-payment. But he drives a brand new Chrysler 300 with $3400 21" custom rims. His esteem need is in direct competition with safety/security and physiological needs for his discretionary income.

Discretionary income
The amount of income a person is left with after taxes and living essentials, such as food, housing, etc., have been deducted.

Discretionary order
Permits a broker to buy or sell shares on behalf of an investor in order to get the best price.

Discriminating duty
A variable tax levied on goods depending from which country they were imported.

Discrimination
The favoring of one group of people, resulting in unfair treatment of other groups.

Disease management
An information-based process involving the continuous improvement of care (prevention, treatment and management) throughout the delivery of health care. Effective disease management can mean decreased health care costs.

Dispatch note
Also called Dispatch Advice. A document giving details of goods which have been dispatched or are ready to be dispatched to a customer.

Distance learning
Educational Programmes using instruction via video or audio tapes, computers etc. instead of attending a class in one centralized location.

Distributable profit
A company's profits which are available for distribution among shareholders at the end of an accounting period.

Distributer
An individual or company who buys products, usually from manufacturers, and resells them to retail outlets or direct to customers. A wholesaler.

Distribution
Movement of goods and services through the distribution channel, to the finalcustomer, consumer, or end user, with the movement of payment (transactions) in the opposite direction back to the original producer or supplier.

Distribution channel
An institution through which goods or services are marketed giving time and place utilities to users.

Distribution channel
Path through which goods and services flow from producer to_consumer. This can be direct from the vendor to the consumer or may include several intermediaries such aswholesalers, distributors, agents, and retailers. Each intermediary receives the item at one pricingpoint and moves it to the next higher pricing point until it reaches the final buyer.

Distributive bargaining
A negotiation between competing parties that involves the distribution of resources. One party prevails, to the detriment of the other.

Diversification
modification of a current product or introduction of a completely new product. that expands the organization's current market. Usually involves creating a new customer base and often acquiring specialized expertise.

Diversion/product diversion
In marketing and business 'diversion' refers to the unofficial distribution/ availability of branded consumer products. In other words this is the supply of branded products through unautorized stockists or retailers or other suppliers, notably via the web. Diversion does not refer to pirated or counterfeit or 'fake' goods. Diversion refers to official goods being sold through unofficial channels. Also called a 'grey market'.

Diversity
The collective mixture of differences and similarities that may include : individual and organizational characteristics, values, beliefs, experiences, backgrounds, preferences and behaviors.

Diversity training

Diversity training is training for the purpose of increasing participants' cultural awareness, knowledge, and skills, which is based on the assumption that the training will benefit an organization by protecting against civil rights violations, increasing the inclusion of different identity groups, and promoting better teamwork.

Dividend

A dividend is a payment made per share, to a company's shareholders by a company, based on the profits of the year, but not necessarily all of the profits, arrived at by the directors and voted at the company's annual general meeting. A company can choose to pay a dividend from reserves following a loss-making year, and conversely a company can choose to pay no dividend after a profit-making year, depending on what is believed to be in the best interests of the company. Keeping shareholders happy and committed to their investment is always an issue in deciding dividend payments. Along with the increase in value of a stock or share, the annual dividend provides the shareholder with a return on the shareholding investment.

Dividend payout ratio

The ratio found by dividing the annual dividends per share by the annual earnings per share.

Dividend yield

The yield found by dividing the annual dividends per share by the price per share (This yield is an indication of the income from a share of stock. Since return on a stock is comprised of capital gain plus dividends, the total return is comprised of dividend yield plus the capital gains percentage for stock.).

Docking station

A device to which a notebook computer or a laptop can be connected so it can serve as a desktop computer.

Document sharing

Used in video-conferencing. A system which allows people in different places to view and edit the same document at the same time on their computers.

DOE (Design of experiments)

DOE is the science of designing sets of experiments which will generate enough useful data to make sound decisions without costing too much or taking too long.

Dollar cost averaging (DCA)

A system of buying securities at regular intervals, using a fixed amount of cash over a considerable period of time regardless of the prevailing prices of the securities (DCA protects against the risk of losing a sum of money invested all at once at an inopportune time, e.g., right before a price drop.).

Dotcom

an internet business, or the internet business sector.

Double

In the film and TV industry, a person who stands in, or is substituted, for a principal actor.

Double indemnity

A clause in a life insurance policy where the insurance company agrees to pay double the face value of the policy in the event of accidental death.

Double-blind

A method of testing a new product, usually medicine, in which neither the people trying the product nor those administering the treatment know who is testing the real product and who has been given a placebo containing none of the product.

Double-dip Recession
A recession during which there is a brief period of economic growth, followed by a slide back into recession, before final recovery. Also called a W-shaped recession.

Double-dipping
The practice, usually regarded as unethical, of receiving two incomes or benefits from the same source, for example receiving a pension and consultancy income from the same employer.

Double-entry bookkeeping
An accounting method which results in balanced ledgers, i.e., for every transaction a credit is recorded in one account and a debit is recorded in another.

Double-loop marketing
Need for marketers to build offer/ share useful information to help consumers make decisions. This is the first loop (and often an enticing free offer), after which a second loop offers other for-profit options. Ex: *Annualcreditreport.com* offers one free credit report with no strings attached; then offers continuing/value-added options such as credit alerts or credit scores for an additional cost.

Doula
A birthing or labour coach, from the greek word doule, meaning female slave.

Dow Jones industrial average
An indicator showing generally how well the market is going, found by averaging the prices of 30 industrial blue-chip stocks trading in the New York Stock Exchange.

Drayage
The fee charged for, or the process of, transporting goods by lorry or truck.

Drip advertising
An advertising campaign in small amounts over a long period of time to ensure that the public is continually aware of a product or service.

Drum-buffer-rope
A method, usually in manufacturing, which ensures an efficient flow of work in a production process by taking into consideration any possible delays or problems which may occur.

Dual labour markets
a situation in an organization where a smaller Core Labour Force and a Peripheral Labour Force co-exist.

Due diligence
In mergers and acquisitions, the process of carefully investigating the details of an investment or purchase to assess risk and potential value and reward.

Dumping
The selling of goods or services in a buying country at less than the production unit price in the selling country, or the difference between normal domestic price and the price at which the product leaves the exporting country.

Duopoly
A market that is dominated by two suppliers to the extent that jointly control pricing of goods or services in a defined market. This way, either seller can exert some control over the output and prices, but must consider

the reaction of its sole competitor (unless both have formed an illegal collusive duo Ex: If AT&T merges with T-Mobil for this would this give AT&T and T-Mobil an advantage to reduce risk.

Dutch auction

A type of auction which opens with a high asking price which is then lowered until someone accepts the auctioneers price, or until the sellers reserve price has been reached.

Duty

The actual custom duty based on an imported good either on an ad valorem, or specification amount per unit or combination of these two.

Dvricide

Phenomena of fast-forwarding through TV commercials that consumers see as an inconvenience (as opposed to the Superbowl, in which ads are sometimes watched more than the football game). According to BBC America, commercials have been skipped by 50- 70 percent of viewers. It will be interesting to see how advertisers begin positioning their products into the content of products (ex: Kia car features in episodes of The Glades).

Dynamic pricing

Sudden or frequent pricing fluctuations based on changes in customer demand. Product bidding is often the result, as witnessed on eBay and other "how much would you offer" websites offering coupons, premiums, or contests. Thanks to the Internet, many businesses are finding it essential to remain competitive.

Dysphemism

The substitution of a neutral or positive word/phrase with a replacement word/phrase that has a more negative/pesimistic effect. The opposite or inverse of a dysphemism is euphemism. Both are widely used in press and public relations communications. Extreme examples are unethical at best, and criminally dishonest at worst.

Dystopia

The opposite of Utopia, a society in which conditions are characterised by human misery, depirvation, squalor, disease, etc. The term is said to have been coined by by John Stuart Mill in 1868 in a UK House of Commons speech criticizing the government's Irish land policy.

E

Eap

An employer-sponsored programme that is designed to assist employees whose job performance is being adversely affected by such personal stresses as substance abuse, addictions, marital problems, family troubles, and domestic violence. For every dollar invested in an EAP, employers save approximately $5 to $16. The average annual cost for an EAP ranges from $12 to $20 per employee. Source: US Department of Labour.

Early return to work programme

Modified work programmes designed to get employees who have been out of work due to injury or illness to return to the workforce sooner by providing them with less strenuous alternative jobs until they are able to resume their full regular duties.

Earnest money

Money paid in good faith as a deposit, usually for a property, to show that the buyer is serious about doing business with the vendor.

Earnings before

There are several 'Earnings Before..' ratios and acronyms: EBT = Earnings Before Taxes; EBIT = Earnings Before Interest and Taxes; EBIAT = Earnings Before Interest after Taxes; EBITD = Earnings Before Interest, Taxes and Depreciation; and EBITDA = Earnings Before Interest, Taxes, Depreciation, and Amortization. (Earnings = operating and non-operating profits (eg interest, dividends received from other investments). Depreciation is the non-cash charge to the balance sheet which is made in writing off an asset over a period. Amortisation is the payment of a loan in instalments.

Earnings per share

Earnings found by dividing the net income of the company by the number of shares of common outstanding stock.

Earnings yield

Yield found by dividing the earnings per share for the last 12 months by the market price per share.

Earn-out

An arrangement in which an extra future conditional payment is made to the seller of a business in addition to the original price, based upon certain criteria being met.

Easterlin paradox

A theory that beyond satisfaction of basic needs, increasing wealth of a country does not produce increasing happiness, suggested by US professor of economics Richard Easterlin based on his research published in 1974.

Easy monetary policy
A policy which enables the public to borrow money easily, at low interest rates, in order to expand the economy by investing the money in business activities.

E-business
Electronic Business. Using the internet to conduct business or enable businesses to link together.

E-commerce
Electronic Commerce. The buying and selling of products and services over the Internet.

Econometrics
Using mathematics and statistics to study the economy.

Economic growth
An increase in a region's or nation's production of goods and services.

Economic life
The period of time during which an asset, e.g. property, vehicle, machinery, etc., is expected to be usable, including repairs and maintenance, before a replacement is required.

Economic union
Also known as a Common Market. An agreement between a group of countries which allows the free flow of goods, services, labour, etc., between the member countries and usually has a common currency.

Economies of scale
Reduction in cost per unit resulting from increased production, realized through operational efficiencies of production or reducing the cost of resources.

Economy
The management of money, currency and trade of a nation. The efficient management of resources.

Ecotourism
Nature based travel to unspoilt places in the world with a view to conservation and to bring economic benefit to the local people. Also known as Ecological Tourism.

E-currency
Electronic currency. Used on the Internet for making and receiving payments. Companies which provide this service include Paypal and E-Gold.

Edutainment
Products or media which both educate and entertain at the same time, such as TV, books, computer software.

E-enabled
Being able to communicate and/or conduct business using the internet.

Egalitarian
Believing that everyone is equal and should all have the same rights and opportunities in life.

E-lance
Freelance working using the Internet to sell services or goods anywhere in the world.

Elasticity of demand
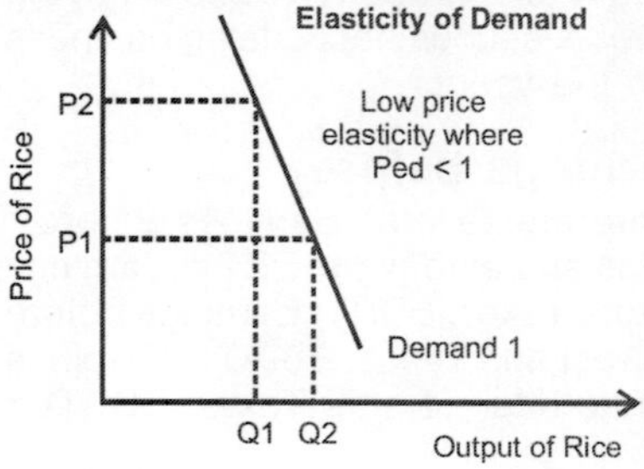

The measure of whether people require more or less of a product or service after a price change.

E-learning
E-learning is a method of education via the Internet or other computer related resources. It presents just-in-time information in a flexible learning plan. E-learning can be combined with face-to-face courses for a blended learning approach.

Electronic cottage
A home which has the necessary electronic equipment, such as telephone, computer, etc., from which to run a business.

Electronic data exchange
A means of exchanging documents between businesses using electronic equipment such as computers.

Electronic media
Includes television, radio, internet, DVD (anything not film- or paper-based).

Electronic purse
A type of microchipped smartcard which stores small amounts of money to enable payment for purchases, especially on the Internet, instead of having to use cash.

E-marketing
Activity of promoting a product in electronic media format, such as internet ads, pop up links, e-commerce cell text, or email messages.

Embezzlement
Dishonestly appropriate goods or money from one's employer for personal gain; steal from one's employer, typically by electronic administrative methods, thus abusing a position of trust or responsibility.

Emolument
Total wages, benefits or compensation paid to someone for the job they do or the office they hold.

Emoticon
Used in e-mails, internet chat rooms and text messages, symbols which represent facial expressions, e.g. :-) = smile.

Emotional capital
Emotional experiences, values and beliefs of a company's employees that make good working relationships and a successful business. Low emotional capital can result in conflict between employees, low morale and poor customer relations.

Emotional intelligence I
Based on the book of the same name by Daniel Goleman, Emotional Intelligence is the ability to recognize, assess and manage their own and others' emotions.

Emotional intelligence II
The ability or skill of a person to understand and control their emotions, and to understand and assess and respond appropriately to the feelings and situations of others. Commonly abbreviated to EQ (Emotional Quotient, alluding to the concept of IQ - Intelligence Quotient), Emotional Intelligence theory seeks to enable a sophisticated practical appreciation and application of the concept of intelligence, especially in work, management, leadership and human relationships.

Empirical
Information derived from experience, observation or experiment rather than from theory or subjective opinion. From Greek- empeiros, meaning skilled - in

turn from peira, meaning trial or experiment.

Employee
An individual who is hired and paid by another person, company, organisation, etc., to perform a job or service.

Employee assessments
Tests used to help employers in pre-hire situations to select candidates best suited for open positions. These tests can sometimes be taken via the Internet and can provide employees with effective training, assist managers in becoming more effective, and promote people into appropriate positions. Types of assessments include those to determine personality, aptitude and skills.

Employee buyout
A transaction in which employees purchase all or most of a company's shares, thereby gaining control of the company.

Employee engagement
Employee engagement, also called worker engagement, is a business management concept. An "engaged employee" is one who is fully involved in, and enthusiastic about their work, and thus will act in a way that furthers their organization's interests.

Employee involvement
Regular participation of employees in decision-making and suggestions. The driving forces behind increasing the involvement of employees are the conviction that more brains are better, that people in the process know it best, and that involved employees will be more motivated to do what is best for the organization.

Employee ownership
A business model and constitutional framework in which staff hold significant or majority shares of a company, thereby ensuring higher levels of loyalty and commitment, and fairness in the way that business performance relates to employee reward. The John Lewis Partnership is one of the prime and most successful examples of the concept.

Employee relations
Developing, maintaining, and improving the relationship between employer and employee by effectively and proactively communicating with employees, processing grievances/ disputes, etc.

Employee retention
Practices and policies designed to create a work environment that makes employees want to stay with the organization, thus reducing turnover.

Employee self service
A programme that allows employees to handle many job-related tasks normally conducted by HR departments including benefits enrollment, and updating personal information. Employees can access the information through the company's intranet, kiosks, or other Web-based applications.

Employee stock option
Allows specified employees the right to purchase shares in the company at a fixed price.

Employer
A person, business, organisation, etc., that pays for the services of workers.

Employment branding
A strategy designed to make an organization appealing as a good

place to work. This targeted marketing effort utilizes both print and Internet tactics and attempts to shape the perceptions of potential employees, current employees and the public / investment community.

Employment equity
Promotes equal employment opportunities for everyone, regardless of gender, race, ability, etc.

Employment law
Also known as Labour Law. The branch of the law that deals with the legal rights of employees, e.g. workplace safety, discrimination, compensation, etc.

Empowerment
Giving employees the resources, skills and authority necessary to share power with management and make decisions. Employees are then held accountable for their decisions and rewarded if appropriate. Empowerment is then the process of obtaining these basic opportunities for marginalized people, either directly by those people, or through the help of non-marginalized others who share their own access to these opportunities. It also includes actively thwarting attempts to deny those opportunities. Empowerment also includes encouraging, and developing the skills for, self-sufficiency, with a focus on eliminating the future need for charity or welfare in the individuals of the group.

Encrypt
Convert data into code which cannot be easily understood by people who have no authorisation to view it.

End consumer
An individual who buys and/or uses a product or service.

End marker
Used at the end of a take in a film, TV Programme or audition to cover a mistake or to remind people who the person auditioning was during auditions.

Enterprise
A company or business. A business project, often one which is sometimes difficult and/or risky.

Enterprise application integration
Software technology that links computer Programmes, data bases, etc., within an organisation, so that information can be shared.

Enterprise compensation management (ECM)
The automation of the compensation process to assist organizations in the acquisition, management and optimization of its workforce.

Entrenpreneur
An ambitious person who starts new business ventures in order to make a lot of money, often taking financial risks.

Environmental impact assessment
The effect that a proposed project, such as a new building or development, will have on the environment.

Environmentalist
An individual who is concerned about the protection, conservation and improvement of the natural environment.

E-procurement
Electronic procurement. Businesses using the internet to purchase from, or

sell goods and services to, other businesses.

Equal employment opportunity (EEO)

A policy statement enforced by the Equal Employment Opportunity Commission that states that equal consideration for a job is applicable to all individuals, and that the employer does not discriminate based on race, color, religion, age, marital status, national origin, disability or sex.

Equilibrium price

The price at which the demand of a particular product or service is equal to the quantity supplied.

Equity

(1) Value determined by subtracting debts from assets.

(2) An alternate term for stock or similar securities which denote a partial ownership.

Equity accounting

When a company records, in its financial records, profits which can be claimed from an affiliated company which they part own.

Equity theory

The idea that people desire to be treated fairly and thus compare their own contributions to the workplace—and resulting rewards—against those of their coworkers, to determine if they are being treated fairly.

E-recruitment

Web-based software that handles the various processes included in recruiting and onboarding job candidates. These may include workforce planning, requisitioning, candidate acquisition, applicant tracking and reporting (regulatory or company analytics).

Erisa (employment retirement income security act)

A federal law that governs pension and welfare employee benefit plans. ERISA requires plans to provide participants with plan information including plan features and funding. It also requires that plans provide fiduciary responsibilities for those who manage and control assets. It gives participants the right to sue for benefits and breaches of fiduciary duty.

ERP

Short for enterprise resource planning, a business management system that integrates all facets of the business, including manufacturing, sales, marketing, finance and human resources. This is slightly different than best-of-breed HRIS applications and the industry continues to debate the merits of one versus the other. With the growing popularity of web-based applications (ease of use, lower costs) ERP seems to be losing out, especially in the mid-market.

Escape clause

A condition in a contract which allows the contract to be broken in particular circumstances.

E-tailer

An retailer who uses the internet to sell goods and/or services to the public.

Ethernet

Technology, invented by The Xerox Corporation, which connects computers in a local area network (LAN).

Ethics committee
In medicine, an independent body which is appointed to examine and consider the rights and safety of people taking part in clinical trials.

Ethnic monitoring
Recording and evaluating the racial origins of employees in a company to ensure that all races are represented fairly.

Ethnocentrism
A home country orientation but with export of surplus production.

Euphemism
The replacement of a strong/offensive word or phrase with an alternative word or phrase considered to be milder/inoffensive. Euphemisms are used widely and very wrongly by politicians and business people attempting to avoid responsibility and personal acknowledgment of mistakes, bad decisions and unjustifiable actions, etc. Euphemisms in such situations are part of 'spin', or spinning a story.

Euroland
Also known as the Eurozone. All the countries in the EU (European Union) that use the Euro as currency.

European union
EU. Previously called the European Community. An international, economical and political organisation which brought the nations of Europe together so that people, goods, money, services, etc., can move freely between member nations.

Ex-gratia
Something given or carried out as a favour or gift, rather than as a legal duty.

Ex-officio
Someone who has a right to be included because of their job or position, e.g. to sit on a committee. (Latin - by virtue of office or position)

Ex-stock
Goods which are available for immediate delivery because the supplier has them in stock.

Ex-works
Goods which are delivered to the purchaser at the plant or place where they are manufactured. The purchaser then pays for transporting and insuring the goods from that point.
Ex: Cirque de Soleil expanded beyond the boundaries of traditional circus acts with its themed Vegas entertainment offerings. It has no competitors.

Exchange rate
Also known as Foreign Exchange Rate. The rate, which can vary from day to day, at which a country's currency can be exchanged for another country's currency.

Exchange rate exposure
When a business risks losing money because of the need to change one currency for another of lower value.

Exclusive distribution
Contracting with single channel members to move the product through the commercialization schedule. (Not to be confused with Exclusive exposure: Selling a product only through a single outlet in a particular region or market. Exclusive retail outlets are expected to perform many, if not most of the marketing functions to promote and support sales.)

Execution risk
The risk that a company's plans, or a project, will fail because of changes

being made, e.g. entering a new market, bad management, etc.

Executive coaching

Executive coaching is a professional relationship between a coach and an executive, or an executive team. The goal is to assist executives with positive leadership development. It can be provided in one-on-one sessions or via the Internet.

Executive compensation

Also called executive pay, compensation packages are specifically designed for executive-level employees that include items such as base salary, bonuses, perquisites and other personal benefits, stock options and other related compensation and benefit provisions.

Executive director

Also called Internal Director. A person who usually works as a full-time senior employee for a company, and is responsible for the day to day running of the business, and is often a member of the company's board of directors.

Executive search

An agency or organization used by employers to assist them with the selection and placement of candidates for senior-level managerial or professional positions.

Exempt versus non-exempt employees

The difference between exempt and nonexempt employees is who gets paid overtime and who doesn't. The U.S. Department of Labour specifically designates certain classes of workers as exempt, including executives, administrative personnel, outside salespeople, highly skilled computer-related employees, doctors, lawyers, engineers, etc. Managers who hire and fire employees and who spend less than half their time performing the same duties as their employees are typically also exempt employees. In general, the more responsibility and independence or discretion an employee has, the more likely the employee is to be considered exempt. Generally, any worker performing repetitive tasks is most likely nonexempt and must be paid overtime.

Exit interview

The final meeting between management, usually someone in the HR department, and an employee leaving the company. Information on why the employee is leaving is gathered to gain insight into work conditions and possible changes or solutions.

Exit strategy

A plan by an investor to dispose of an investment, such as shares in a company, to make a profit, or a business owner to dispose of their company, e.g., by selling the business, floating it on the stock market, ceasing to trade, handing it over to another family member, etc.

Expatriate

An employee who is transferred to work abroad on a long-term job assignment.

Expectancy theory

A theory of motivation developed by Canadian Victor Vroom, Yale professor of management and psychology, established in his 1964 book, Work and Motivation, which essentially states that motivation necessarily comprises and is determined by three elements of belief:

1. Effort will produce success.
2. Success will produce reward.
3. These outcomes will be personally satisfying.

Experience curve
In business, when costs fall and production increases as a result of increase in workers skills and lower material costs.

Expert system
A computer software system which can provide expert knowledge for a specific problem when users ask a series of questions.

Export credit
A loan taken out by an importer with a bank in an exporters country, so that the importer can buy foreign goods and pay for them at a later date.

Export credit guarantee fund
A facility, provided by government treasury, to guarantee the development costs of exports or legal claims arising there from.

Export factoring
A facility offered by banks to exporters. The bank is responsible for collecting payments for exported goods, so that the exporter can borrow money from the bank before the goods have been paid for by the customers.

Export processing zone
A zone, designated within the country, enjoying tax privileges or other status, where goods and services can be brought into, reprocessed and re-exported.

Exporting
The marketing of surplus goods produced in one country into another country.

Exposition
A public event at which businesses, that produce related goods, can showcase their products and/or services.

Exposure
Presentation of a sales promotion piece or advertisement to an individual, such as a person viewing a television commercial or a reader opening a magazine to an advertisement page. The number of exposures achieved is an important measure of the effectiveness of an advertisement as measured in conjunction with the quality of the exposures achieved. For example, if a golf club advertisement is exposed to 1000 golfers; it has greater value than if it is exposed to 1 million non-golfers.

Expropriation
The annexation or seizure of national assets as an extreme form of political action.

Extension strategy
A marketing strategy to stop a product going into decline by making small changes to it, reaching new customers or finding new uses for it, e.g. a drink which was sold as an aid to those recovering from illness is now sold as a sports drink.

External competitiveness
Being able to sell goods and services to customers in foreign countries at a competitive price.

External customer
A person or organization outside your organization who receives the output of a process. Of all external customers, the end-user should be the most important.

External debt
Also known as Foreign Debt. Money that is owed by the government, organisations or individuals to creditors in other countries.

External equity
A situation in which an organisation's employees receive similar pay for the same type of work as employees in other organisations, i.e., pay which is equal to market rates.

Extranet
A private computer network to which a company's customers and suppliers can link and communicate using the Internet.

Eye tracking
Research method used in advertising to determine which parts of an advertisement tend to get consumer attention. Accomplished by tracking eye movements.

Eyeballs
Advertising term. A name given to the number of people who visit a website advertisement, which can be counted by the number of click-throughs.

E-zine
An electronic magazine which is published on the internet, or delivered by e-mail.

F

FAS

A contract of sale "free along side" whereby the seller undertakes to place the goods alongside a ship ready for boarding and carry all charges up to that point.

FOB

A contract of sale "free on board" whereby the seller undertakes to place the goods on board a named ship at a named port and berth and carry all charges up to delivery over the ships rail.

Face value

The value printed on the face of a stock, bond, or other financial instrument or document.

Facilitating agent

Firms or individuals that performs any number of distribution or commercialization tasks other than buying, selling, or transferring title of products or services. They perform these services more effectively and/or efficiently than the producer. Ex: Transportation, warehousing, financing, sorting, etc.

Facilitator

Person who helps a team with issues of teamwork, communication, and problem-solving. A facilitator should not contribute to the actual content of the team's project, focusing instead as an observer of the team's functioning as a group.

Facings

Generally a retail term used to describe the number of products displayed vertically on the same shelf. Marketers often provide incentive or pay to gain this exposure.

Factor comparison

A systematic and scientific comparison, that instead of ranking complete jobs, ranks according to a series of factors. These factors include mental effort, physical effort, skill needed, responsibility, supervisory responsibility, working conditions, etc.

Factory floor

The area of a factory where the goods are made. Also the collective name of the ordinary workers in a factory, rather than management.

Factory price

The price charged for goods direct from the factory, not including transport costs, etc. Factory Price is often quoted by retailers or in advertisements to show that products are for sale at a very low price.

Failure mode effects analysis

A technique that systematically analyzes the types of failures which will be expected as a product is used, and what the effects of each "failure mode" will be.

Fair representation

The duty of fair representation is incumbent upon U.S. labour unions that are the exclusive bargaining representative of workers in a particular group. It is the obligation to represent all employees fairly, in good faith, and without discrimination.

Fairy dust

A term often used in the entertainment business. The final enhancement or touch on a project. The unknown factor which turns something great into something fantastic.

Fallen angel

Term used in finance to describe bonds which once had a good investment value, but have now dropped in value to a much lower rating.

False accounting

A criminal offence. Giving false information in, or destroying, a company's accounts, usually for personal gain. Fraud.

False bottom

On the stock market, selling prices which seem to have already hit their lowest level because of a subsequent price rise then fall through a false bottom because the price falls even lower.

Fast moving consumer goods (FMCG)

Products (and the related industry) which are sold in big volumes by big retailers at low profit margins, at keen prices, to domestic consumers - traditionally foods and groceries, household consumables, etc., and nowadays extending to any products of short life and disposable/ consumable nature.

Fast track

Quick route in a career to success and promotion, associated with high ambition.

Fat cat

A wealthy person living off investments or dividends, or a chief executive of a large company or organisation who is on a very large salary, huge pension, etc.

Fault tolerance

Enables a system, especially in computing, to continue to operate properly even though a component in the system has failed.

Feasibility study

A preliminary assessment of a new project, including costs, risks, etc., to determine whether the project will be successful and practical.

Feather-bedding

A term often used in industry describing the practice of hiring more workers than is necessary to carry out a job, often because of a contract with a union.

Feature/accessory

Characteristics that are offered to the potential consumer that are sought out or desired as an attribute of form, time, place, and possession utility. An accessory is not essential in and of itself, but adds beauty, convenience, or effectiveness to what it is attached.

Federation

An organisation which has been formed by the joining together of a group of companies, clubs, etc.

Fidelity bond
Also known as Fidelity Insurance. Protects an employer against any losses incurred because of dishonesty, or damage caused, by an employee.

Fiduciary
Describes an organisation or individual who manages money or property for a beneficiary.

Figurehead
In business, organizations, politics, etc., a person who holds an important position or office but lacks real power or authority; a 'front man'. Derived from the carved painted figurehead models which traditionally were fixed to the front of sailing ships.

Filibuster
A person who attempts to delay or obstruct legislation by giving long speeches, but does not contravene rules concerning proceedings.

Fill or kill
Also FOK, on the stock exchange, an instruction received by a broker from a client to buy or sell specified shares immediately or not at all.

Finance
To provide or obtain funds for a business, commercial project, an individual, etc. The management of money. To sell or provide goods on credit.

Financial engineering
The practice of solving financial problems or creating financial opportunities in a company, by changing the way money is borrowed, debts paid, etc.

Financial equity
The ownership of interest in a company, usually in the form of shares.

Financial planner
An investment professional who helps with financial plans for specific goals and assists in the coordination of financial concerns.

Financial strength
A company's financial condition as seen by its analysts (*Value Line* rates financial strength on a scale from A++ to C.).

Finite capacity scheduling
A process in which a computer Programme organises tasks, matching the resources available to the most efficient way of production.

Firepower
The amount of power, money and/or influence that is available to a business or organisation.

Firewall
A firewall is a software or hardware-based network security system that controls the incoming and outgoing network traffic by analyzing the data packets and determining whether they should be allowed through or not, based on a rule set. A firewall establishes a barrier between a trusted, secure internal network and another network (e.g., the Internet) that is not assumed to be secure and trusted.

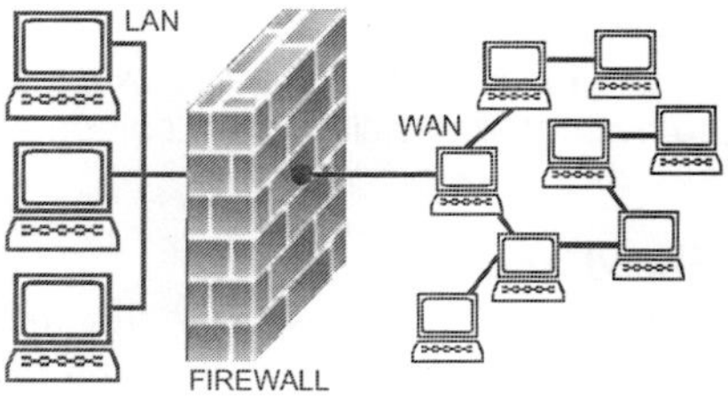

Firmware
Describes the fixed Programmes, which cannot be lost or changed, in

electronic devices such as digital cameras, calculators, remote controls, etc.

First mover
A business that gains an advantage by being the first to establish itself in a specific market by producing a new product or offering a new service, or by being the first to use new technology.

First order of business
The most important task to be dealt with.

Fiscal drag
A situation in which wages rise because of inflation but income tax thresholds are not increased, which can push people into higher tax brackets and therefore makes them pay an increased proportion of their wages in tax.

Fiscal policy
A government policy to regulate a nation's annual economic activity by setting tax levels and determining government expenditure.

Fishbone diagram
Another name for a cause & effect diagram, derived from the original shape of the diagram as used by its creator, Kaoru Ishikawa.

Five nines
Refers to the 99.999% of the time that some companies claim their computer systems work properly.

Fixed assets
Fixed assets, also known as "tangible assets" [Dyckman, Intermediate Accounting,Revised Ed. (Homewood IL: Irwin, Inc. 1992),195.] or property, plant, and equipment (PP&E), is a term used in accounting for assets and property that cannot easily be converted into cash. This can be compared with current assets such as cash or bank accounts, which are described as liquid assets. In most cases, only tangible assets are referred to as fixed. International Accounting Standard (IAS) 16, defines Fixed Assets as assets whose future economic benefit is probable to flow into the entity, whose cost can be measured reliably.

Fixed cost
A cost which does not vary with changing sales or production volumes, eg, building lease costs, permanent staff wages, rates, depreciation of capital items.

Fixed parity
In foreign exchange, when the currency of one country is equal in value to the currency of another country.

Fixed term contract
Also known as Temporary Contract. A contract of employment which ends on a specific date, or on completion of a task or project. Fixed term employees have the rights to the same pay, conditions and benefits as full-time employees.

Fixed term employment
An employee agrees to work for a fixed term—until a certain date, at the completion of a project, etc.

Fixer
A person who makes arrangements for someone else, usually for a fee, by using their influence and often underhand, illegal methods.

Flame
To send a rude or unacceptable message by e-mail, or to post a

message on an Internet forum which is offensive or inciteful.

Flash drive
A small portable device such as a 'pen drive' which connects to a USB port on a computer and is used to store data which can then be transferred to another computer. The term flash drive derives from 'flash' memory, invented by Dr Fujio Masuoka of Toshiba around 1980. The name flash (apparently, according to Wikipedia, 2010) was suggested by Masuoka's colleague, Shoji Ariizumi, who likened the memory erasure function to a camera flash.

Flash mob
A secretly-planned (usually via modern computerised social networking technology), quickly-formed, organized group of people, assembled to engage in a quirky activity, typically for the amusement and entertainment of the participants. Potentially the term may be applied to similar gatherings organized for more conventional promotional, protest or other publicity/pressure purposes, although this strays somewhat from the usual concept, in which the flash mob event is an aim in itself, rather than part of a wider campaign with a specific purpose. The expression is not new.

Flats
In the entertainment industry, these are painted canvas sheets fixed onto wooden frames used on film sets, etc. for scenery.

Flexecutive
A manager who works flexible hours, often from home using the Internet. A multi-skilled executive who can change tasks or jobs with ease.

Flexible spending accounts (FSA)
FSAs allow employees to set aside a portion of their earnings on a pre-tax basis into separate spending accounts to fund allowable health care and/or dependent day care expenses. The funds must be segregated as per IRS regulations.

Flexible work arrangements
Schedules that allow employees to structure their work hours around their personal responsibilities. Examples include flextime, job sharing, telecommuting and a compressed workweek. Home sourcing has become a popular flexible work concept in recent years. In this arrangement, employees work full-time from their homes.

Flexitime
A work system in which employees work a set number of hours each week or month, but they decide when they are going to start and finish each day, usually between a range of given working hours.

Flight capital
The movement of large sums of money from one of investment to another, or from one country to another, to avoid high taxes or financial instability due to political unrest.

Flighting
A cost effective method of advertising. A commercial is scheduled to appear on TV, usually when viewing figures are high (flight). There are periods in between the flights when the commercial does not appear on TV (hiatus). During the TV hiatus the product being advertised will often appear in newspapers or magazines, so the public is continually aware of it.

Floor limit

In retailing, the highest amount of money for a sale for which a debit or credit card can be used by a customer without authorisation from the customer's bank.

Floor trader

Also known as a Local. An investor who is allowed on the trading floor of a stock exchange, to buy and sell shares, etc., for their own account.

Flotation

The process of financing a company by selling shares on the stock exchange for the first time.

Flowchart

A graphical representation of a given process delineating each step. It is used to diagram how the process actually functions and where waste, error, and frustration enter the process.

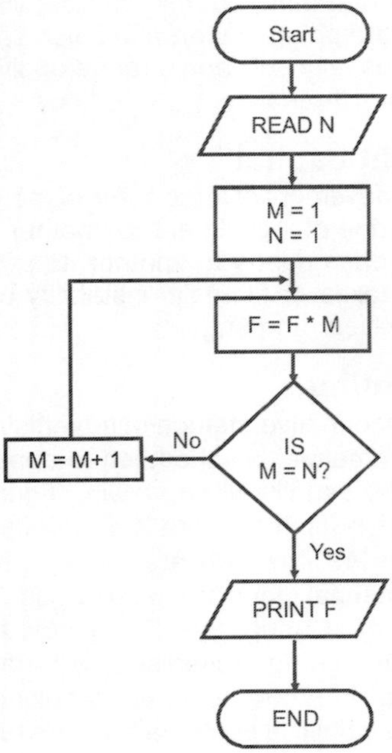

Flyback

Also known as a Callback. A series of screening interviews for a job during which a person, usually a student, is interviewed several times, often on the same same day, by the prospective employer.

Flynn effect

Research showing that the results of IQ (Intelligence Quotient) tests in various countries (i.e. internationally) have risen consistently over several decades, (after political scientist James R Flynn).

FOB - 'Free on board'

The FOB (Free On Board) abbreviation is an import/export term relating to the point at which responsibility for goods passes from seller (exporter) to buyer (importer). It's in this listing because it's commonly misunderstood and also has potentially significant financial implications. FOB meant originally (and depending on the context stills generally means) that the seller is liable for the goods and is responsible for all costs of transport, insurance, etc., until and including the goods being loaded at the (nominated FOB) port. An importing buyer would typically ask for the FOB price, (which is now now often linked to a port name, eg., FOB Hamburg or FOB Vancouver), knowing that this price is 'free' or inclusive of all costs and liabilities of getting the goods from the seller to the port and on board the craft or vessel. Logically FOB also meant and still means that the seller is liable for any loss or damage up to the point that the goods are loaded onto the vessel at the FOB port, and that thereafter the buyer assumes responsibility for the goods and the costs of transport and the liability. From the seller's point of view an FOB price must therefore include/recover his costs of transport from factory or warehouse, insurance and loading, because the seller is unable to charge these costs as extras once the FOB price has been stated. The FOB expression originates particularly from the meaning that the buyer is free of liability and costs of transport up to the point that the goods are loaded on board the ship. In modern times FOB also applies to freight for export by aircraft from airports. In recent years the term has come to be used in slightly different ways, even to the extent that other interpretations are placed on the acronym, most commonly 'Freight On Board', which is technically incorrect. While technically incorrect also, terms such as 'FOB Destination' have entered into common use, meaning that the insurance liability and costs of transportation and responsibility for the goods are the seller's until the goods are delivered to the buyer's stipulated delivery destination. If in doubt ask exactly what the other person means by FOB because the applications have broadened. While liability and responsibility for goods passes from seller to buyer at the point that goods are agreed to be FOB, the FOB principle does not correlate to payment terms, which is a matter for separate negotiation. FOB is a mechanism for agreeing price and transport responsibility, not for agreeing payment terms. In summary: FOB (Free On Board), used alone, originally meant that the transportation cost and liability for exported goods was with the seller until the goods were loaded onto the ship (at the port of exportation); nowadays FOB (Free On Board or the distorted interpretation 'Freight On Board') has a wider usage - the principle is the same, ie., seller has liability for goods, insurance and costs of transport until the goods are loaded (or delivered), but the point at which goods are 'FOB' is no longer likely to be just the port of export - it can be any place that it suits the buyer to stipulate. So, if you are an exporter, beware of buyers stipulating 'FOB destination' - it means the exporter is liable for the goods and pays transport costs up until delivery to the customer.

Focus list

A list of companies, recommended by an investment firm, whose shares are worth buying or selling.

Footer

In a report or document, a line or block of text that appears at the bottom of every page which is printed from a computer.

Footfall

The extent or measure of numbers of people who visit a business or shop or other retail/leisure/entertainment venue during a given period of time. Footfall is a crucial factor in retailing methods, and also in promotion and advertising which focuses on the physical presence on foot of consumers at a particular location.

Force field analysis

A tool, developed by social psychologist Kurt Lewin, which is used to analyze the opposing forces involved in causing/resisting any change. It is shown in balance sheet format with forces that will help (driving forces) listed on the left and forces that hinder (restraining forces) listed on the right.

Force majeure

A clause in a contract which exempts the contracting party (e.g., insurer) from liability in the event of an unforeseen intervention or catastrophe which prevents fulfilment of contractual obligations, such as war, act of God, etc. The term force majeure is French, meaning loosely 'superior strength'.

Forced ranking

Also known as a vitality curve, this is a system of work performance evaluation in which employees are compared against each other instead of against fixed standards. Based on the "20/80 Rule" idea, that 20 percent of employees do 80 percent of the meaningful, productive work, the top 20 percent of workers are rewarded and, oftentimes, the bottom 10 percent are fired.

Foreign exchange

Facilities' business across national boundaries, usually expressed in foreign currency bought or sold on the foreign exchange market.

Forex

Also called FX, refers to Foreign Exchange, in which foreign currencies are bought and sold.

Fortune 500

Published by Fortune magazine, an annual list of the 500 US corporations with the largest revenue.

Forward integration

A business strategy whereby a company takes control of its distributors, therefore guaranteeing the distribution of the controlling company's products.

Forward rates

A mechanism whereby the risk of changes in exchange rates can be covered by obtaining a new rate quote for a future exchange of currencies.

Forwarding company

Also called a 'freight forwarder', a company specialising in transfer of freight from businesses or individuals by finding an appropriate transporter of the goods.

Four-colour process

In printing, the use of four ink colours -yellow, magenta, cyan and black - which are combined together to produce the whole spectrum of colours.

Fractional ownership

An arrangement where a number of people or companies each buy a percentage of an expensive asset, such as a property. The individual owners then share the asset, and when it is sold the profits are distributed back to the owners.

Fragmentation

Ability to break up or identify various media that target specific audiences, allowing marketers to more effectively target segments and niches.

Franchise

An authorisation or license - effectively a business, which can be bought - enabling someone (franchisee) to use the franchisor's company name and trademarks to sell their products services, etc., and usually to receive certain support, in a particular area of a country. A franchise for a whole country is typically called a master franchise.

Free collective bargaining

A situation in which workers and union members meet with employers to discuss working conditions, pay, etc., in talks that are not limited by law or government.

Free enterprise

An economic system in which private businesses have the freedom to compete with each other for profit, with minimal interference from the government.

Free market

A market in which prices of goods and services are affected by supply and demand, rather than government regulation.

Free on board

Maritime trade term. The supplier delivers the goods to a ship at a specified port. The supplier then pays the shipping costs after obtaining official clearance. Once they have been put on board, the buyer is then responsible for the goods.

Free port

A port where goods can be brought and stored temporarily, without custom duties having to be paid, before being shipped to another country.

Free rider

A person or organisation that enjoys benefits and services provided by others, and doesn't pay their fair share of the costs.

Free zone

An area in a country where importers can store foreign goods, prior to further transportation, without having to pay customs duties or taxes on them.

Freeconomics

A situation in which companies provide certain goods and services for free, and those businesses who don't follow suit are likely to fail.

Freedom of association

The right of workers to join a union and to bargain collectively. This right is protected by the Universal Declaration of Human Rights and the Human Rights Act of 1993.

Freedom of association

The right of individuals to join together to form, or join an existing, group or organisation, including a union.

Freemium

(Combination of *free* and *premium*) When a product or service, such as a digital application for a smart phone or tablet, is provided free of charge, but a premium is charged for advanced features or functionality.

Freeware

Computer software that is copyrighted by the author and offered, usually on the Internet, free of charge.

Frequency

Number of times an advertising message is presented within a given time period. In general, number of times something occurs within a specified period of time. Frequency may refer to the issues of a periodical, the purchases made by a customer over time, or the number of times a commercial or an advertisement is aired or printed or reaches its audience.

Frequency distribution

An organization of data, usually in a chart, which depicts how often an different events occur. A histogram is one common type of frequency distribution, and a frequency polygon is another.

Frequency words

Terms use in marketing plans or proposals that contain bias—unless followed by data (numbers, percentages, indices, etc.). The following require data: usually, constantly, mostly, frequently, typically, generally, continually, sometimes, occasionally, sporadically, intermittently, rarely, seldom, hardly ever. The two exceptions: always (100%) and never (0%).

Frictional unemployment
Unemployment of people who are temporarily between jobs, changing careers, changing location, etc.

Fringe benefit
A benefit given to employees in addition to their salary, such as a company car, pension scheme, paid holidays, etc.

Front-end load
A fee charged for an investment, for example an insurance policy, limited partnership, mutual fund, etc. The fee is made with the initial payment, and subsequent payments are therefore lower.

Frontstage technology
Innovative advances embraced by consumers that provide convenience and confidence relative to usage and purchasing decisions. Example: 24/7 banking/ATMs at your fingertips (Internet). It's technology that makes it easier for consumers to satisfy needs.

FTSE
An abbreviation of the Financial Times Stock Exchange (Index), commonly referred to verbally as 'footsie'. There are various FTSE indices (indexes), including most notably the FTSE 100, which is the index of the top 100 shares on the London Stock Exchange, whose movement is regarded as an important indicator of national (and wider) economic health and buoyancy. The FTSE 100 represents about 80% of the market capitalization of all shares listed on the London Stock Exchange, which is interesting considering over 3,000 companies are listed in total.

Fulfilment
In the context of business and retailing, fulfilment refers to the processing of a (consumer or commercial) customer's purchase/order - i.e., a 'sale'. Fulfilment is generally considered to happen after the order is placed and usually payment is made, completing on confirmation of safe and correct delivery to the customer. Payment/ invoicing is generally separate from the fulfilment process/provider. In most cases fulfilment entails the warehousing, stock management, product 'picking', order assembly/ compiling, packaging and delivery, then confirmation of safe delivery, of products/orders for which payment has already been made. Fulfilment may be an internal activity of the selling organization, or may instead be contracted to an external provider of fulfilment services.

Fulfilment house
A provider of order-processing fulfilment services to a 'selling' company, typically processing sales/ orders of the selling company, through to the delivery of products to the purchaser. Specific activities of a fulfilment house generally include warehousing, stock control, order picking, packaging, distribution/ delivery to the customer (and confirmation thereof), and typically a degree of direct customer communications, and potentially handling returns.

Full-time contract
A permanent or ongoing contract of employment in which the employee works at least the standard number of hours in a working week, usually 35.

Full-time equivalent (FTE)

A value assigned to signify the number of full-time employees that could have been employed if the reported number of hours worked by part-time employees had been worked by full-time employees instead.

Functional job analysis

Developed by the U.S. Department of Labour, functional job analysis is a method of gathering specific and detailed job information. This information can be used to write job descriptions.

Fundamental analysis

An analysis of stocks based on fundamental factors, such as company earnings, growth potential, etc., to determine a company's worth, strength, and potential for growth.

Fungible

Fungible is the property of a good or a commodity whose individual units are capable of mutual substitution, such as sweet crude oil, shares in a company, bonds, precious metals, or currencies. It refers only to the equivalence of each unit of a commodity with other units of the same commodity.

Future

A legally binding contract to deliver/ take delivery on a specified date of a given quality and quantity of a commodity at an agreed price.

G

Gaffer

In the entertainment industry, a member of a film crew who handles the lighting equipment.

Gag clause

Refers to the employment contract restrictions used as a means of protecting the organization's trade secrets or proprietary information.

Gagging clause

An informal term which has become generally used in formal business/ employment language, a 'gagging clause' is a clause in an employment contract, or more commonly a termination contract, which prevents an employee from disclosing certain information about the company or employing organization (typically extending to related organizations/ interests) to the press, union officers, authorities, etc., and by implication also extending to the police. Often an employer agrees or enforces a payment with/upon the employee to secure the signature to the gagging clause or contract which contains it.

Gagging order

A legal order issued by a court to prevent the public reporting of a court case.

Gainsharing

Also called profit sharing. An incentive system which enables employees to have a share in a company's profits.

Game theory

Sometimes called Games Theory, this is a potentially highly complex branch of mathematics increasingly found in business which uses the analysis of competing strategies (of for example market participants) and their effects opon each other to predict and optimise outcomes and results. Relates strongly to cause and effect and chaos theory. Game Theory may also arise in military strategy.

Gamification

Use of gaming concepts to motivate or drive certain behaviors from a target audience. Much like continuity Programmes, organizations offer awards, points, and other specific offers when customers check in on their websites. It's an incentive, or reward, for multiple visits.

Gamification

Use of gaming concepts to motivate or drive certain behaviors from a target audience. Much like continuity Programmes, organizations offer awards, points, and other specific offers when customers check in on their websites. It's an incentive, or reward, for multiple visits.

Gantt chart

A bar chart that shows planned work and finished work in relation to time. Each task in a list has a bar corresponding to it. The length of the bar is used to indicate the expected or actual duration of the task.

Gap analysis

Enables a company to assess the gap between its actual performance and its potential performance, by comparing what skills, products, etc. are available to what is required to improve performance, output, etc.

Garden leave

Also called Gardening Leave. Term used when an employee's contract has been terminated but they are instructed by the company to stay away from work, on full pay, during their notice period. Often to prevent them from working for competitors during that time.

Garnish

To take part of someone's wages, by law, to pay their debts, e.g. child support, alimony.

Gatekeeper

A person in an organisation who controls access to the people in the organisation, and/or controls access to information or goods, or even a market. Microsoft could be described as a gatekeeper to the computer industry. Google could be described as a gatekeeper to the internet industry.

Gazelle

A US term for a fast growing company that creates a lot of job opportunities, and which has grown by at least 20% in the last four years.

Gazump

In selling and buying property, a term used to describe when a purchaser has an offer accepted by the vendor but is then gazumped because someone else makes the vendor a higher offer which the vendor then accepts instead of the first person's offer.

Gearing

The ratio of debt to equity, usually the relationship between long-term borrowings and shareholders' funds.

Geek speak

Technical language often used by computer experts which doesn't make sense to non-technical people.

General agents

General agents are middleman for carriers and brokers and usually focus on the 250 employee market. Usually an individual appointed by a life or health insurer to administer its business in a given territory. GAs are important for companies who sell to small employers or brokers e.g., benefits administration software providers.

General agreement on tariffs and trade (GATT)

An institutional framework producing a set of rules and principles with the intention of liberalising trade between member countries.

General creditor

A person or company that lends unsecured money, so that the creditor is unlikely to recover much of the loan if the debtor goes bankrupt or does not pay it back.

General strike

Widespread withdrawal of labour by a nation's workforce, which aims at bringing the country to a standstill because of a disagreement over pay and/or working conditions.

Generalist

A person who has a broad general knowledge at a high level, and/or many skills.

Generation I
The term used to describe children born after 1994 who are growing up in the Internet age.

Generation X
A term used for people born during the 1960s and 1970s, who are often described as disaffected and irresponsible.

Generation Y
The term used to describe individuals born between 1985 and the present.

Genetic-based Discrimination
The practice of requesting or requiring genetic testing information during the hiring process or using genetic testing information to base any other employment decisions or actions.

Geocentrism
A world orientation with world market strategies.

Geodemographics
Study of where potential customers live, their ages, income levels, education, and how it affects spending. Data are used to create clusters that help marketers identify and define potential target markets—those who might be intrigued to know more about their products.

Geographic information system (GIS)
demographic databases, digitized maps, and computer software designed to help marketers interpret data and define potential markets.. Ex: Metropolitan Life employs GIS to target customers and boost profits.

Geographical differential
The variance in pay established for same or comparable jobs based on variations in labour and costs of living among other geographic regions.

Geographical segmentation
a defined market segment defined or divided according to geographic units, such as nations, states, regions, counties, cities, or neighborhoods. McDonalds' burgers in India are made from lamb, and in Mexico, chili sauce is added to the beef.

Geotargeting
Ability to target a marketing or advertising campaign based on defined set of target customers within a defined geographic territory.

Gerontocracy
A government or political system which is ruled by old men.

Get all your ducks in a row
A term for getting organised, having everything in order and making sure all the small details are accounted for before embarking on a new project.

Get go
From the start, the earliest stage of something. Used in the phrase 'From the get go.'

Gift tax
A tax payable on gifts over a certain annual value made during the lifetime of the giver.

Giro
A system, used in some countries, of transferring money from one bank or post office account into another using a central computer.

Giveback
An agreement in which employees accept a wage reduction or fewer benefits as a gesture of goodwill, usually because of an economic

downturn. The employees are often offered wage rises and new benefits at a later date.

Glamour stock

A company's shares, which are very popular with investors, because they have performed well on the stock exchange.

Glamping

A portmanteau word meaning 'glamorous camping', for example staying in a posh serviced yurt (a large Mongolian-style nomadic tent) and eating luxury hamper foods.

Glass ceiling

An invisible barrier in the workplace which prevents women and minority groups from advancing to positions of leadership in a company, although some do manage to 'break through' the glass ceiling.

Glass wall

An imaginary barrier in the workplace which prevents women and minority groups from being employed in other sectors of business or industry.

Glitterati

Combination of Glitter and Literati. Glamorous, rich, famous people, often connected to show business.

Global environment

All semi or uncontrollable factors which a marketer has to account for in carrying out global operations.

Global evaluation

A four stage organisational development process evolving from first stage; domestic focus to a fourth stage; global marketing strategy of extension, adaptation and creation of market opportunities.

Global market

A universal market that can be viewed as a total global economy in which organizations target markets that extend beyond local borders; hence, globalization.

Global marketing

Marketing on a worldwide scale reconciling or taking commercial advantage of global operational differences, similarities and opportunities in order to meet global objectives.

Global products

Products designed to meet global market segments.

Global village

A term used to describe the whole world as a single community, connected by electronic communication systems, such as the Internet.

Globalisation

The process of integrating nations, economically and socially, through free trade, international business activities, technology (for example the Internet), etc.

Glocalisation

Global Localisation. A term used when an international company adapts its manufacturing methods, products or services to suit local conditions.

Goal setting

Assigning specific, attainable goals to a person, team or organization. Goal setting is a motivational technique, as workers often rise to the challenges given them.

Going public

An expression used to describe the first public selling of shares of an institution that previously sold shares privately.

Gold reserve
The amount of gold bullion or gold coins held by a country's central bank to support its currency and provide security for its international debts.

Golden handcuffs
Financial incentives or benefits given to a valued employee to ensure that they continue working for a company, and to discourage them from wanting to leave to work for another company.

Golden handshake
Usually offered to high-ranking executives in a large company. A clause in their contract which provides them with a large sum of money and/or other benefits in the event of them losing their job or retiring.

Golden parachute
A company's agreement with an employee, usually a top executive, which promises a significant amount of money and/or benefits if the employee is forced to leave their job, usually because of a change of company ownership, outside of the control of the original employer company.

Gone to the wall
Describes a business which has failed.

Good faith bargaining
A requirement of the Employment Relations Act of 2000 that all parties to a contract conduct negotiations with a willingness to reach an agreement on new contract terms.

Goodwill
The difference or premium which a purchaser pays, or which a seller asks, for a business or company compared to the 'book value' of its assets, typically representing intangibles such as brand value, intellectual property, talent, market relationships, etc., and which tend to reflect the overall value and appeal with which the purchaser regards the target acquisition. Over-estimating goodwill value, sometimes to an extraordinarily stupid degree, is a surprisingly common downfall of many big corporate takeover deals, when arrogance and blindness to market trends of the acquiring CEO and takeover team can lead to a reckless waste of shareholder funds and ruthless cost-cutting, post-acquisition, when performance, synergies and return on investment fail to reach required levels.

Googlewhack
Two proper words (found in a dictionary) which together produce just a single result from a normal Google search. A googlewhack tends not to retain its status indefinitely, and sometimes only fleetingly, because due to the strange popularity of the effect, googlewhacks are likely to be published on the web when discovered, which immediately produces a second occurrence.

Grace
A period of time given to a debtor to enable them to pay an overdue bill or loan, or extra time given in a contract for a piece of work to be finished.

Grandfather clause
A provision in a new law which allows the person or business already engaged in the activity, which may have been made illegal, to continue to be so engaged.

Graphology
The study of handwriting, often used as a way of analysing a person's character.

Grass roots

The ordinary people in a business or organisation, rather than the management or the decision-makers.

Gratis

Gratis is the quality of an action where the action is willingly provided without any requirement by the provider for compensation or monetary remuneration. It is often referred to in English as free of charge (FOC), complimentary, or on the house.

Graveyard market

A term used on the Stock Exchange to describe a Bear Market in which share owners are reluctant to sell because they face substantial losses, and buyers are reluctant to buy because the financial outlook is poor. Those who are in it can't get out, and those who are on the outside have no desire to get in.

Gravy train

A business activity which makes a large profit for an individual or an organisation without much effort. To have it easy.

Green audit

Also called Environmental Audit. An official assessment which shows the effect that an organisation or a company has on the environment.

Green card

In the US, a legal document which allows an immigrant to become a permanent resident, to work legally and to become eligible for citizenship.

Green marketing

Promotional activities aimed at reflecting the level of its concern for renewable/recycled resources and well-being of the community. For example, Nestle Waters is touting its Eco-Shape bottle as one of the lightest half-liter plastic bottles available.

Green taxes

Also called Ecotax. Taxes which are levied on companies, businesses, etc., to discourage activities which will harm the environment.

Greenback

An informal term for US paper money, i.e., the dollar, derived from the colour of the money.

Greenwashing

Organizations that spend more time and money claiming to be "green" through promotional Programmes than actually implementing business practices that minimize environmental impact. Ex: Hotels that ask guests to reuse sheets or towels; this does little to reduce water and energy.

Grey knight

A third person, or company, who makes an unsolicited bid in a corporate takeover, and who takes advantage of any problems which arise between the first bidder (White Knight) and the company being acquired.

Grey market/gray market

In marketing and business a grey market (gray market in US-English) is the supply of official goods through unofficial channels, for example the availability of branded consumer products on the internet from unauthorized stockists. Also called a parallel market orproduct diversion. These terms do not refer to counterfeit goods. The reference is to the unofficial, sometimes illegal, distribution and availability of official branded original goods. The term alludes to the older expression 'black market', and is used or analysed most commonly from the standpoint of manufacturers, who generally regard grey markets as threatening to their marketing distribution and pricing strategies. The term grey market extends widely and includes notably the substantial availability of products which have been diverted from one international marketing territory to another.

Grey swan

a marketing/economics/probability expression about random events with big consequences, a 'grey swan' refers to a major predicted or known event of national or more usually international significance, which has uncertain outcomes and unquantifiable effects on society, economics, etc.

Grievance

a complaint by an employee due to an alleged violation of law or collective bargaining or dissatisfaction with work conditions.

Grip

In the film and TV industry, a member of the film crew who makes sure that the lighting is right for a scene. They also move scenery and set up large pieces of equipment.

Gross domestic product

Commonly abbreviated to GDP, Gross Domestic Product is a very frequently used term in business and economics, and basically refers to a nation's total production at market values. GDP is however not easily explained or understood at a detailed and precise level. GDP may be calculated in different ways. Each method requires some qualification of precise definition, and then comprises quite complex formulae, mainly to ensure there is no double-counting, and no ommissions. The main methods seem to be as follows, although each nation has its own rules, and various institutional bodies produce other rules and standards for calculations and definitions. Ordinary people can reasonably regard fully detailed definitions of GDP very confusing. Lots of experts do too.

Gross misconduct

An action so serious that it calls for the immediate dismissal of an employee. Examples include fighting, drunkenness, harassment of others and theft.

Gross national product (GNP)

The market value of all goods and services outputted by residents of a country in one year including income from aboard.

Gross profit

Sales less cost of goods or services sold. Also referred to as gross profit margin, or gross profit, and often abbreviated to simply 'margin'.

Gross profit margin

Expressed as a percentage, what is left from a company's sales after cost of goods sold is paid out. Gross profit margin is obtained by dividing gross income by net sales.

Group dynamics

The way that people interact within a group that determines how it functions and how effective the group is.

Growth strategy

Strategy aimed at winning larger market share, even at the expense of short-termearnings, such as diversification, product development, market penetration, and market development (from the Marketing Opportunity Grid).

Guerrilla marketing

Unconventional methods of performing marketing activities (primarily promotion) on a low budget. It is up to the "guerrilla marketer" to be creative to generate product publicity. It can take many forms, such as social media (pop-up ads on Facebook and Twitter or video clips on YouTube). These tactics are utilized by both small and large-scale companies.

Guru

An influential teacher or an expert in a particular subject who shares their knowledge, often by writing books.

H

Hacker

Nowadays the word hacker commmonly refers to a person who breaks into or 'hacks' into the secure computer systems of an organization, especially websites and online systems, using online connection, often just as a technical challenge, or potentially with intent to steal, destroy, vandalise information, websites, etc. Originally however the terms hack and hacker referred to a person who enjoyed exploring and experimenting- perfectly legitimately and legally - with computer code and related computing systems, out of curiosity or for purposes of technical challenge and improvement, discovery, etc. This is an example of how language and meanings evolve over time, particularly when a term becomes distorted for dramatic effect by mass media. Be aware in this case therefore, that some people - especially original 'old-school' hackers and computer code enthusiasts could be offended and unjustly maligned by the criminal implication of the common illicit hacking interpretation. Incidentally among coding enthusiasts the original technical term for a criminal 'hacker' was a 'cracker'.

Haggle

Negotiate with someone over the price of something until an agreeably mutual price is reached.

Haircut

A percentage subtraction from the market value of an asset, typically on a large scale, enforced by a powerful institution or authority in response to debt/liabilities incurred by the asset owners/investors, producing an effective devaluation of the asset. The 'haircut' term became a more general description for a tax or levy imposed on ordinary savings accounts with reference to the EU-imposed tax on Cyprus bank deposits in 2013, although the underpinning principle/ cause was consistent with the technical meaning of the term.

Hall test

A term used when a group of people are gathered together at a particular location and asked to take part in market research.

Halo effect

Where the image or reputation of a person (or group or organization or brand or other entity) is enhanced by influence from or association with the quality of another situation. A halo effect typically refers to an unreliable indicator of good quality (ethics, goodness, honesty, value, benevolence, etc) but might rarely instead refer to an unreliable indicator of negative quality.

Handbill

A small printed advertisement, usually on one sheet, often given out to people by hand.

Hands-free
Term used when a telephone can be used without having to be held in the hand.

Hands-off
A term often applied to managers who do not directly participate when dealing with a situation in the workplace by letting the people involved decide what they want to do.

Hard selling
An aggressive type of selling which puts a lot of pressure on a prospective customer to buy a product or a service.

Harvesting
A term used when a product is still being sold, although it is no longer being invested in, prior to being withdrawn from the market.

Hashtag
A type of tag (here a prefix used with a word/term/reference/etc via electronic keypads, computing, smartphones, etc) in the social networking website Twitter and similar short messaging systems, so that a word preceded by the hash symbol (#) may be found subsequently or otherwise organized, analyzed, displayed, etc. The symbol is generally called the pound sign in the US, since it is used commonly instead of the traditional British £ symbol in referring to sterling currency.

Hawthorne effect
The theory that organizations can motivate their employees as much or more by expressing concern for problems as by actually improving their work conditions. This personal interest results in increased performance, according to the observations of productivity researcher George Elton Mayo.

Hawthorne effect
Specifically the inclination of a group of workers to change their behaviour positively because they were being studied, irrespective of whether they were subjected to 'positive' or 'negative' conditions. First observed in studies by Elton Mayo at the Western Electric plant in Chicago, beginning 1928. The Hawthorne Effect basically established that attitude was more influenced by emotional rather than economic factors.

Headhunt
To find a person who is specialised in a particular job, usually for a senior position in a company, and then persuade them to leave their present employment.

Health and safety
Concerned with the protection of employees from risks and dangers in the workplace.

Health care flexible spending account (FSA)
A benefit plan designed to allow employees to set aside pre-tax dollars to pay for eligible medically related expenses, such as medical, vision or dental exams, copays and deductibles, as well as other out-of-pocket expenses.

Health savings accounts (HSA)
A tax-free account that can be used by employees to pay for qualified medical expenses. To be eligible for a Health Savings Account, an individual must be covered by a High Deductible Health Plan (HDHP), must not be covered by other health insurance, is not eligible for Medicare and can't be claimed as a dependent on someone else's tax return.

Heat map
Graphic representation of data where varying degrees of a single metric appear by color, such as tracking clicks on a marketer's website.

Heatseeker
A person who, without fail, always buys the most up to date version of an existing product as soon as it comes onto the market.

Heavy-up
Short period of concentrated advertising in a media schedule. Advantageous when a product is more likely to be used at one specific time. Ex: With an approaching summer, Water Babies Sun Screen will be touting its protection when families will soon be lounging at the beach.

Hedge fund
A type of investment fund, which is unregulated and usually very high risk, used by individuals and organisations (not the general public) with large amounts of money to invest.

Hedging
A mechanism to avoid the risk of a decline in the future market of a commodity, usually by entering into futures markets.

Heterogeneous markets or products
Geographic markets or products the marketer or customer sees as different. This term also applies to markets, in that a heterogeneous market is unique or different from others. As regards the need for winter snow blower equipment, Minneapolis and Houston would be heterogeneous (dissimilar winter weather).

Hierarchy of effects
Series of 7 steps that prospective customers move through, from initial product awareness to trial. These steps are divided into cognitive (knowledge about), affective (feelings about), and conative (action tendencies towards purchase) dimensions.

Hierarchy of needs
The ordering of a person's needs into hierarchy of relative potency such that as lower order needs are fulfilled higher, unfulfilled order needs emerge, which require fulfillment.

High context culture
Minimum reliance on explicit verbal or written conversations, more on the "implied".

Hire purchase
HP. A contract between a buyer and seller in which the buyer takes possession of an item and then pays for it in regular instalments, usually monthly, and does not become the owner of the item until the final payment has been made. Also referred to as 'Buying on the never-never'.

Histogram
A specialized bar chart showing the distribution of measurement data. It will pictorially reveal the amount and type of variation within a process.

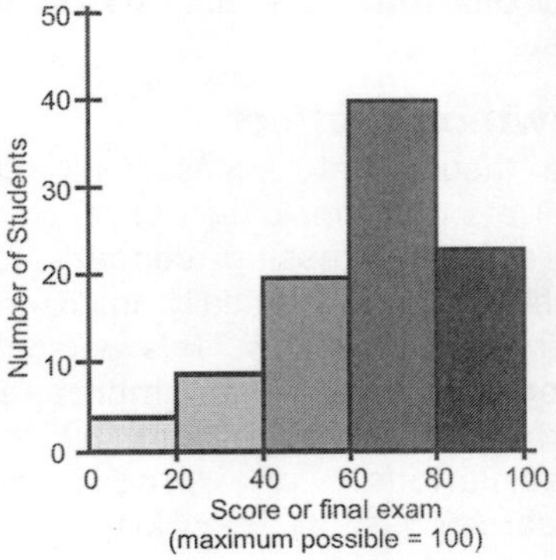

Holding company
A company which is formed for owning and holding controlling shares in other companies.

Holding period return/yield
The yield calculated by dividing the income plus price appreciation during a specified time period by the cost of the investment.

Hole in the wall
An informal term for a cash dispensing machine, also called an ATM (automated teller machine).

Homeostasis/homoeostasis
Homeostasis is a powerful and illuminating concept. Technically, yet somewhat unhelpfully, the OED (Oxford English Dictionary) defines homeostasis as "The tendency towards a relatively stable equilibrium between interdependent elements, especially as maintained by physiological processes". Homeostasis is perhaps more easily understood initially via its Greek roots, meaning 'similar' and 'standing still'. Homeostasis refers scientifically to the act of 'self-balancing' or 'internally self-compensating' in ecological/ biological systems.

Homogeneous markets or products
Geographic markets or products the customer sees is basically the same (sharing similar attributes, or easily substitutable products). Homogeneous markets share similar traits or conditions. As regards the need for winter snow blower equipment, Minneapolis and Cleveland would be homogeneous.

Horizontal integration
Distribution strategy in which one company establishes ownership or control of another company's production, transportation, manufacturing, distribution, or retail outlet. Ex: .Most guitar companies do not manufacture their own low-end guitars. They contract Samick Guitars, the largest guitar manufacturer in the world (Indonesia). Samick can produce them much cheaper than these companies can produce themselves. Samick controls the low-end production channel for these products.

Horizontal integration
The joining together of businesses which produce similar goods or offer similar services, or are involved in the same stage of activities, such as production or selling.

Horizontal sector/horizontal market
Horizontal market sector-Often called simply a 'horizontal'-this refers to products/services which can be supplied to or 'across' a number of 'vertical' sectors, for example, office cleaning services to various industries (verticals), or transport services to different industries (verticals).

Hoshin kanri
Japanese term for hoshin planning, a form of interactive strategic planning which aids the flow of information up and down the organizational layers in a systematic, productive way.

Hoshin planning
A method of strategic planning for quality. It helps executives integrate quality improvement into the organization's long-range plan. According to the GOAL/QPC Health Care Application Research Committee, "Hoshin Planning is a method used to ensure that the mission, vision, goals, and annual

objectives of an organization are communicated to and implemented by everyone, from the executive level to the 'front line' level."

Hot desking

In an office, the practise of having a pool of desks, which are usually equipped with phone and computer links, so that workers can use them when they are required, rather than having their own individual desk.

Hothouse/hothousing

Informal term for an intense development environment or method, or the verb equivalent, typically applied to training people or developing ideas or ventures; a metaphor alluding to a heated greenhouse for growing plants.

HR audit

A periodic measurement of human resources effectiveness, conducted by internal staff or with the use of an HR audit system.

HR generalist

An individual who is able to perform more than one diversified human resources function, rather then specializing in one specific function.

HTML banner ad

Form of Internet promotion featuring information or special offers for products and services. These small space "banners" are interactive: when clicked, they open another website where a sales can be finalized. The hosting website of the banner ad often earns money each time someone clicks on the banner ad.

Human capital

The collective skills, knowledge and competencies of an organization's people that enables them to create economic value.

Human capital management

The challenge of recruiting and retaining qualified candidates, and helping new employees fit into an organization. The goal is to keep employees contributing to the organizations intellectual capital by offering competitive salary, benefits and development opportunities. The major functions of human capital management include Recruitment, Compensation, Benefits and Training.

Human resource information system (HRIS)

Business software systems that assist in the management of human resource data (e.g. payroll, job title, candidate contact information). Some of the larger HRIS platforms include SAP and Peoplesoft.

Human resource outsourcing (HRO)

A contractual agreement between an employer and an external third-party provider whereby the employer transfers responsibility and management for certain HR, benefit or training-related functions or services to the external provider.

Human resources

HR. The people who are employed by and operate a business or organisation. The department within a company which deals with recruitment, training, employee benefit, etc.

Hunt and peck

Inexpert slow typing on a keyboard using only one or two fingers.

Hush money

A bribe or payment, which is often illegal, given to someone to stop them from disclosing information, usually to prevent bad publicity or to hide a crime.

Hushmail

An internet service offering encypted email, file storage, etc.

Hyperbole

(Pronounced 'hy-per-bollee' - emphasis on the 'per' syllable)- Hyperbole is an extreme and figurative exaggeration or overstatement, which in strict grammatical terms is not generally expected to be taken seriously or interpreted literally, for example, "I've been waiting for ever for a bus," and yet where hyperbole is used for motivational or persuasive effect in business or politics, the technique very often intends to convey maximum impact on an audience, for example, "You'll never have another opportunity like this..." The word derives ultimately from the Greek root words: huper, over, and ballein, to throw.

Hyperinflation

An extraordinarily high rate of economic inflation during which a country's prices rise and currency loses its value uncontrollably in a vicious cycle, usually occurring during severe political instability or war. Normally inflation is measured in terms of a few percentage points increase per year-typically below 10% and sometimes approaching 20%. By contrast hyperinflation may be at a rates of tens of percentage points increase per month, and in extreme rare cases hundreds of percentage points per month. In this event, where prices can be doubling and currency values halving every few weeks (or days, in very rare situations), a country is forced to issue new banknote denominations of ludicrously high values, and within living memory news stories have featured workers collecting their wages in wheelbarrows.

I

Idea showers
Usually called Brainstorming. A method of problem solving involving members of a group meeting and sharing ideas.

Identity theft
A crime in which someone obtains another person's personal information, such as passport, credit card details, etc., and poses as that person in order to steal money, get benefits, make purchases, etc.

Ideology
An individual's organisation or country's political belief.

Idle time
The time that a piece of equipment or a machine, such a as computer, is available, but is not being used.

Image advertising
Attempt to create a favourable mental picture of a product or firm in mind of consumers to associate the advertised product or firm with certain lifestyles or values. Ex: In some markets, McDonalds' golden arches image is being changed to appear more upscale.

Impeach
To charge somebody, usually a government official, with serious misconduct. To cast somebody out of public office, for example a president or courtroom judge because of a serious crime or misdemeanor.

Imperfect market
A market in which buyers do not have access to enough information about prices and products, and where buyers or sellers can have an influence over the quantity and price of goods sold.

Import duty
A tax charged on certain goods which are brought into a country.

Impound
To seize and hold property, funds, etc., in custody (typically by a state-empowered authority), often during legal dispute.

Impression
Singlular display or viewing of a particular ad or web page. Some search engine ad fees are based on the number of impressions; others are PPC (number of clicks).

Impression
Singlular display or viewing of a particular ad or web page. Some search engine ad fees are based on the number of impressions; others are PPC (number of clicks).

Inbound marketing
(where the customer comes to you) Passive sales technique the relies on

the customer to find a product (as opposed to marketer-directed promotional efforts to communicate with potential customers). Achieved through website content personalization, media monitoring, and lead nurturing.

Inbound marketing

(where the customer comes to you) Passive sales technique the relies on the customer to find a product (as opposed to marketer-directed promotional efforts to communicate with potential customers). Achieved through website content personalization, media monitoring, and lead nurturing.

Incapacity benefit

A state benefit in the UK which is paid to people below pensionable age who have made National Insurance contributions, and who are too ill or disabled to work.

Incentive marketing

The offering of rewards or gifts to sales people as an incentive to get more orders from dealers or customers. To offer customers rewards for buying products or services.

Incentive pay

Additional compensation used as a motivational tool to exceed specified work goals.

Incidence rate

Indicates the number of workplace injuries/illnesses and the number of lost work days per 100 employees.

Income elasticity measurements

A description of the relationship between the demand for goods and changes in income.

Income fund

An investment fund with high returns which pays the owners a regular income.

Income per capita

The market value of all goods and services outputted by a country divided by the total number of residents of that country.

Income statement

The financial statement of a firm that presents both revenues and expenses during a specified time period.

Income tax

A tax paid by individuals to the government, the amount of which is dependent on how much a person earns from their salary and/or other sources of income.

Incubator

An organisation or company which provides support to new businesses to help them develop and grow.

Indemnify

To insure and offer financial protection against loss, damage or liability.

Independent contractor

A self-employed person who works for another person or organization on a contract basis.

Independent financial advisor

(IFA) Someone who works independently, i.e., not for a particular company, and offers people advice about financial matters and recommends where to invest their money.

Index

A quantity whose variation represents market fluctuation (The Standard & Poor's 500 index measures the overall change in the value of 500 stocks of the largest firms in the US.).

Index-linked

Concerning salaries, pensions, investments, etc. If they are Index-Linked it means that the payments or income from these may vary according to the rate of inflation.

Indicator

Quantitative measure of performance. Indicators are usually ratios comparing the number of occurrences a certain phenomenon and the number of times the phenomenon could have occurred.

Indict

To formally charge someone with a crime.

Indirect compensation

Compensation that is not paid directly to an employee and is calculated in addition to base salary and incentive pay (i.e., health/dental/vision insurance, vacation, retirement benefits, educational benefits, relocation expenses, etc.).

Indirect materials

In accounting, products or services, such as electricity, cleaning materials, chemicals, etc., which are used in the production of goods but are not part of the end product.

Individual employment agreement

A written document that describes the legal relationship between an employer and employee.

Induction

The introduction and training of a member of staff in a new job or position in a company.

Industrial action

Also called a strike in the UK. Known in the US as Job Action. A protest by employees during which they refuse to work, usually because they want better wages and/or better working conditions.

Industrial psychology

Applied psychology concerned with the study of human behavior in the workplace and how to efficiently manage an industrial labour force and problems encountered by employees.

Industrial relations

A field of study that examines the relationship between employer and employees, particularly groups of workers in unions.

Industrial tribunal

An independent judicial body which deals with disputes between employers and employees.

Industrialist

A person who owns or runs a large industrial enterprise. They are often referred to as a Business Magnate.

Industry rank

Value Line's ranking of a company within its own industry.

Inflation

Normally referring to the economy of a country, inflation is the gradual increase in the price of goods and/or services, and the consequential devaluing of the national currency. Inflation is typically up to 10%, or more unusually approaching 20% per year. Minimising inflation is normally a high priority within national fiscal policy since higher levels of inflation cause a variety of economic and business problems.

Inflation risk

The uncertainty of the future real (after-inflation and -tax) value of an investment.

Inflection point

In business, when important significant changes take place in an organisation.

Infomediary

An agent who works on behalf of a business, collecting information on, and developing profiles of, individual customers.

Infomercial

Information Commercial. A long television commercial presented in the form of a documentary or TV Programme. This format is used so that it does not appear to be selling a product or service.

Information superhighway

Communications network, notably the Internet, which provides high speed access to information in the form of sound, text, images, etc.

Information system

A system for gathering, analysing and reporting data aimed at reducing uncertainty in business decision making.

Information technology

Information technology (IT) is the application of computers and telecommunications equipment to store, retrieve, transmit and manipulate data, often in the context of a business or other enterprise. The term is commonly used as a synonym for computers and computer networks, but it also encompasses other information distribution technologies such as television and telephones. Several industries are associated with information technology, such as computer hardware, software, electronics, semiconductors, internet, telecom equipment, e-commerce and computer services.

Inheritance tax

Also called Death Duty in the UK. Known as Death Tax in the US. A tax imposed by the government which much be paid on the total value of the estate of a deceased person.

Initial public offering

An Initial Public Offering (IPO being the Stock Exchange and corporate acronym) is the first sale of privately owned equity (stock or shares) in a company via the issue of shares to the public and other investing institutions. In other words an IPO is the first sale of stock by a private company to the public. IPOs typically involve small, young companies raising capital to finance growth. For investors IPOs can risky as it is difficult to predict the value of the stock (shares) when they open for trading. An IPO is effectively 'going public' or 'taking a company public'.

Injunction

An official court order which demands that someone must refrain from carrying out certain actions.

Innovation

The introduction of new ideas, goods, etc., or new methods of production. A new way of doing something.

Inorganic

A term used to describe the growth of a business from mergers or takeovers, rather than from the increase in productivity or activity of the company's own business.

Inside information
Information about a company which is known only by the owners, management and/or employees, and not the general public. The use of Inside Information for the buying and selling of shares is usually illegal.

Inside track
An advantageous position in a company or organisation. To know about something before others get to hear about it.

Insolvency
Not having enough finances or assets available to pay all your debts.

Instant access account
A bank or building society account which allows you have instant access to your money without any penalties.

Institutional advertising
Promotional messages aimed at creating, improving, or reinforcing an organization's image: reputation enhancement, goodwill, advocating ideas. Such efforts are not intended to promote sales; rather, it's a form a corporate advertising, often aimed at vested publics with an interest in how the organization conducts business (stockholders, elected officials).

Insurance adjuster
Also known as a Claims Adjuster. An independent person who investigates insurance claims for an insurance company and evaluates the damage caused and decides whether the claims are valid, and if they are, how much should be paid in settlement to the insured party.

Intangible asset
A company's assets which do not physically exist, such as brand name, trademarks, copyrights, etc.

Intangible rewards
A subjective benefit that has no monetary value, such as praise for excellent performance.

Integrated marketing
Strategy aimed at unifying different marketing mix elements/tactics, such asmass marketing, one-to-one marketing, and direct marketing. It complements and reinforces themarket impact of each method in product development, pricing, distribution, promotional Programmes, and customer service.

Intellectual capital
The skills and knowledge of a company's employees, which can be used to make the company more successful than its competitors.

Intellectual property
Commonly abbreviated to IP, an idea or creation, e.g., artwork, writing, etc., that belongs to an individual or organisation, which has commercial value and therefore cannot be copied or sold without the owner's permission.

Intensive distribution
Selling a product through all responsible and suitable wholesalers or retailers who will stock or sell the product.

Intentional destruction
Situation or circumstances requiring organizations to break down the existing structure of its operations to properly research future potential and restructure itself to face the realities of a dynamic marketplace. Generally brought on by advancements in technology and innovation.

Inter alia
Latin for 'among other things' - a traditional term which typically

precedes a list of examples, and is found in official or formal text or various sorts. Inter alios means 'among other people', but is much less used.

Interactive plans

A planning system whereby headquarters sets a policy and framework and subsidiaries interpret these under local conditions.

Interest rate

A fee which is charged for borrowing money, e.g., a loan from a bank or financial institution, lease arrangement, goods bought through hire purchase, etc.

Intermediary

A mediator or agent who negotiates between two parties who are unable or unwilling to reach an agreement by themselves.

Intermediate good

Physical resources applied to or used in the creation of a final product. For example, sugar may be consumed directly or used in the manufacturing of ice cream. (Changing the shape or form of a resource in the creation of another product is call a transformation.

Internal customer

Someone within your organization, further downstream in a process, who receives the output of your work.

Internal equity

In a company or organisation, ensures the pay each employee receives is determined fairly by the type of job they do.

International monetary fund

A fund, with world wide country membership, (united nations) which lends money to countries on a short term basis to assist them balance of payments problems.

International organisation for standardization

ISO. A non-government organisation with over 150 member nations, which promotes international standards in trade, technology, science, economy, etc.

International product life cycle

A model which suggest that products go through a cycle whereby high income, mass consumption countries go through a cycle of exporting, loss of exports to final importers of products.

International products

Goods or services seen as having extended potential into other markets.

Internesia

Relating to the Internet. Being unable to locate a particular website which you found interesting or on which you saw a useful piece of information.

Internet cafe

Also called a Cybercafe. A public place where people can use a computer, usually for a fee, to check e-mail, access the Internet, etc. These places often sell drink and food, like a regular cafe.

Intervention price

A guaranteed minimum price set by a government for a product, usually farm produce. If the price falls below this then the government, or agency, will buy the produce at the Intervention Price.

Interventionism

The policy of a government to intervene and manipulate a country's (often its own) affairs and/or economy.

Intestate
Without leaving a will, as used in the phrase, 'to die intestate'.

Intrapreneur
A person employed by a large company to work independently to develop new projects and business within the company.

Intrinsic value
The actual or real value of a business, commodity, asset, etc., rather than the market value or share price.

Invention
A new device, process, product, etc., which has been created and developed by an individual or a group.

Investment
Money or capital that is invested in a business or in an account with a financial institution in order to make a profit or earn interest.

Investment adviser
A professional who, for a fee, manages an investment portfolio.

Investment boutique
A small company which offers specialist advice about investments and business.

Invisibles
'Invisible' services of a country, such as banking, tourism, insurance, etc, of which the buying and selling are from international trade.

Involuntary liquidation
When a company is forced into bankruptcy by its creditors, so that its debts can be paid.

Ishikawa diagram
Another name for the cause & effect diagram, after its inventor, Kaoru Ishikawa.

Ishikawa, kaoru
One of Japan's quality control pioneers. He developed the cause & effect diagram (Ishikawa diagram) in 1943 and published many books addressing quality control. In addition to his work at Kawasaki, Ishikawa was a long-standing member of the Union of Japanese Scientists and Engineers and an assistant professor at the University of Tokyo.

Island position
An advertisement or commercial which is surrounded by text, or placed between TV Programmes, with no other advertisements, so it has no competition.

Iso 9000
A set of internationally-accepted standards, created by the International Organization for Standardization, for quality management and quality assurance. These standards apply uniformly across all industries and company size. Companies can receive ISO 9000 certification for meeting these standards.

Iso 9001, 9004
Developed by the International Organization for Standardization (ISO), it is a set of standards for quality management systems that is accepted around the world. Organizations that conform to these standards can receive ISO 9000 certification. The standard intended for quality management system assessment and registration is ISO 9001.

Issue price
On the Stock Exchange, the price at which a new share, stock, etc., is offered to the public.

Issuer
One who under writes (issues) and distributes a company's securities.

J

Jasdaq
Japanese Association of Securities Dealers Automated System. Japanese securities exchange, the headquarters of which are situated in Tokyo.

Jingle
A short song used in a promotional announcement, usually mentioning a brand name

Job accommodation network (JAN)
A service provided by the US Department of Labour's Office of Disability Employment Policy (ODEP), JAN's mission is to facilitate the employment and retention of workers with disabilities by providing employers and people with disabilities with information on job accommodations, entrepreneurship, and related subjects.

Job analysis
The process of gathering information about the requirements and necessary skills of a job in order to create a job description.

Job board
An online location that provides an up-to-date listing of current job vacancies in various industries. Applicants are able to apply for employment through the job board itself. Many job boards have a variety of additional services to help job seekers manage their careers and their ongoing job search processes.

Job classification
A method of evaluation used for job comparisons, which groups jobs into a prearranged number of grades, each having a class description and a specified pay range.

Job costing
A system of calculating the cost of each individual job or project carried out by a business, includes time, labour, materials, etc.

Job description
A written statement that explains the responsibilities and qualifications of a given job, based on a job analysis. The job description usually includes specific required tasks as well as an overview of the position and whom the employee reports to.

Job evaluation
A comparison of one job with other jobs in a company for the purpose of assessing fair compensation.

Job lock
A situation in which a person feels they cannot leave their job because they are afraid of losing benefits connected to the job.

Job protected leave
Allows people to officially take time off from their work for a longer period

without the fear of losing their job, often because of illness or pregnancy.

Job sharing

A work schedule in which two or more people voluntary do one full-time job, sharing the work and dividing the hours between them.

Johari window

A leadership disclosure and feedback model used primarily in self-help groups and corporate settings as a heuristic exercise which can be used in performance measurement and features the four quadrants (windows) of “knowing.”

Joint consultation

An organisational decision-making process in the UK, where managers and employees representatives, usually from unions, meet to discuss matters relating to the employees working conditions, etc.

Joint stock company

A company or organisation owned by joint shareholders, which is a type of corporation and partnership. The stockholders run the company and share its profits and debts.

Joint ventures

An enterprise in which two or more investors share ownership and control over property rights and operations.

Jumble display

Mixture of often dissimilar products on a single display—usually promoted as clearance items.

Junk bond

Also known as High Yield Bonds. A high risk bond with a high interest rate, often used by companies to raise finances in order to take over other companies.

Just-in-time

JIT. A manufacturing system in which materials and components are delivered immediately before they are required, in order to increase efficiency, reduce waste and minimise storage costs.

Just-in-time instruction

Training given as needed for immediate application, without lag time and the usual loss of retention.

K

Kaizen
Japanese for 'improvement'. When implemented in the workplace, kaizen activities help to improve the running of a business.

Kanban
Japanese for 'visible record'. In industry, a manufacturing system which is regulated by the use of cards or boards which contain specifications and instructions for the production process of goods.

Keiretsu
In Japan, an alliance of companies or organisations which own shares in one another as a means of security, but each individual company operates independently.

Kerb market
In the US, the buying and selling of shares in companies which are not listed on the stock exchange. In the UK, the buying and selling of stocks and shares outside official trading hours.

Kettling
Term which is used to describe the police tactic of penning protesters into an area by forming a barrier around them and refusing to let them out.

Key account
In business, a company's main client or customer, who represents a large percentage of the company's income.

Key performance indicators (KPIS)
Tasks that are central to the success of a business and show, when measured, whether the business is advancing toward its strategic goals.

Keyword advertising
Used on the Internet. When a user types in a particular 'keyword', an advertisement which is linked to a business relevant to that word, is displayed alongside the search engine results.

Keyword effectiveness index
Compares the number of searches for a key word, providing Internet marketers the ability to include these terms/words on their websites.

Keyword effectiveness index
Compares the number of searches for a key word, providing Internet marketers the ability to include these terms/words on their websites.

Kickback
A bribe or illegal payment made to someone in exchange for a successful referral for a job or transaction.

Kidult
An adult who enjoys films, games, TV, clothes, etc., which are deemed more suitable for children or much younger people.

Killer app
Short for Killer Application. Derives from the computer industry. A new product or service which is the first in its category and therefore dominates that particular market, creating huge returns on the initial investment.

Kitemark
In the UK, the official mark of approval by the British Standards Institution, to show that a product or service is safe, reliable and of good quality.

KJ method
Another name for the affinity diagram, after its inventor, Kawakita Jiro.

Knocking copy
In advertising, the criticism or attacking of a competitor or a rival product.

Knock-off
An unauthorised copy of a product, usually designer clothing.

Knowledge
A customer's understanding or relationship with an notion or idea. This applies to facts or ideas acquired by study, investigation, observation, or experience, not assumptions or opinions.

Knowledge base
A knowledge base or knowledgebase (also KB or kb) is a special kind of database for knowledge management. A knowledge base is an information repository that provides a means for information to be collected, organized, shared, searched and utilized. It can be either machine-readable or intended for human use.

Knowledge worker
Also known as an Intellectual Worker. A person who is employed by a company to use their brain and intellect to work with information, rather than performing manual tasks.

Ksas
The Knowledge, Skills and Abilities an employee needs to meet the requirements of a job.

Kudos
Common management term meaning positive recognition, praise or fame- from the Greek word kydos, meaning glory.

L

Labeling
Description, instructions, and warnings printed on products and packaging as required by law or as an aide to the consumer.

Labour certification
Labour certification is a statement from the U.S. Department of Labor (DOL) that a particular position at a particular company is "open." It is the first step in the process of obtaining a green card.

Labour force participation rate
The ratio between the labour force (all those currently employed or seeking work) and the nation's total working-age population.

Labour intensive
A job requiring a lot of work, and often a lot of workers, in comparison to the costs of materials, equipment, etc.

Labour law
Also known as Employment Law. Legislation which defines the legal rights and obligations of employees in the workplace.

Labour law posting
Federal and state regulations requiring employers to post in conspicuous places a variety of labour law posters with information regarding employee rights

Labour market
A geographical region (local, national or international) in which labour transactions occur—employers find workers and workers find work.

Lading
Freight or cargo carried by a large vehicle. The act of loading cargo onto a ship.

Laffer curve
Named after US economist Arther Laffer (b.1940), the Laffer Curve refers graphically to notional/optimal government revenues according to changing levels levels of taxation, on the basis that at each extreme, i.e., 0% and 100% taxation, government revenues are zero, and that somewhere in between, a certain taxation % level (for which no general standard exists or can be applied) will produce optimal government revenues.

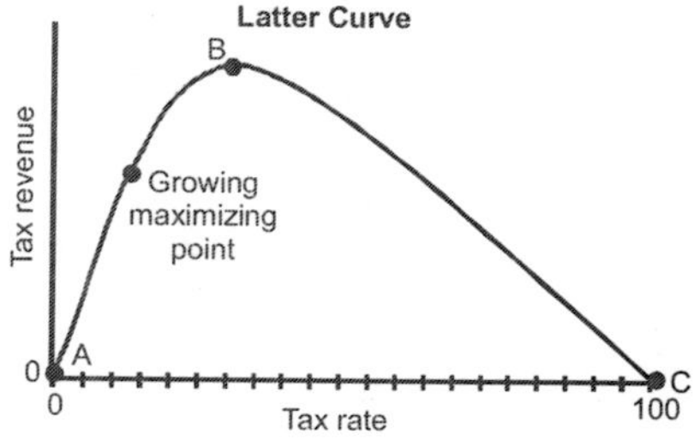

The expression was popularized in the mid-1970s after discussions between Laffer and government officals Don Rumsfeld and Dick Cheney, seemingly to advance Laffer's counter-intuitive argument that lower taxation would increase tax revenues. Laffer attributed the underpinning curve concept theory to Ibn Khaldun and John Maynard Keynes.

Lagniappe (native to Southern Louisiana and Southeast Texas: pronounced "lan-yap")
A little something extra; an unexpected surprise; gifts given to customers at the time of purchase. Ex: It's getting your car washed and vacuumed at no charge when taking it for service at the dealership. Or the chocolate chip cookie at check-in at Doubletree hotels.

Laicisation
The defrocking of a minister or priest. The changing to lay status.

Laid-off
In industry, etc., when workers lose their jobs, sometimes temporarily, because there is no work for them.

Laity
Usage is typically 'the laity' ('lay-ity'), an old traditional alternative word for lay people/members, typically used in relation to church organization and council, but applicable widely to ordinary people, as distinct from professional or qualified folk.

Landing page
A website page used to collect relevant data from those interested in the content featured on that page. Also known as Lead-capture page. Often used for invitation-only and special offer promotional Programmes that feature exclusive offers or discounts. A unique method to evaluate effectiveness of Internet marketing Programmes.

Larceny
The crime of unlawfully taking someone else's property or money. Theft.

Large cap
On the Stock Exchange, a company that has a large market capitalisation, i.e., a high total value of shares.

Law of one price
The rule that without trade barriers and transportations costs, identical products would cost the same worldwide using the appropriate exchange rate of currency.

Lay (people/person/member)
Also layman, or laywoman. Lay means non-professional, non-expert-ordinary member(s), of the public or of an organization, typically referring to religious communities, often relating to professions such as law and medicine, but potentially in any situation where non-professionals/ experts are differentiated from qualified/professionals. The term may have an arrogant or patronising implication where expert, qualified, learned professionals discuss the general public or members who lack expertise.

Layaway
Often referred to as Lay-By. A means of purchasing an item by paying a small deposit to reserve it and then paying the balance in installments. When the total purchase price has been paid the customer can then take delivery of the goods.

Lead user
Term introduced by economist Eric von Hippel in 1986. Lead users are

individuals or companies who greatly benefit from being the first to use or adapt a product for a particular need, often months or years before the general public or other businesses are aware of the need for the product.

Leader
Someone who leads, sets example, inspires, motivates, etc-technically having the personal qualities which attract followers for given situations.

Leadership
A person or number of people responsible for leading a team or group of people, usually in some sort of organized body or company, or the direction of a smaller team in a specific project or situation.

Leadership development
Activities, whether formal or informal, that enhance leadership qualities

Leading indicator
A particular measure of a country's economic activity, used to predict near future economic trends.

Lean
Also known as the Toyota Production System or Just-In-Time Production. A system used in management, production, manufacturing, etc., to decrease waste and increase efficiency, especially with the use of automated assembly lines in the motor industry.

Learning curve
A graph depicting the rate at which a person learns a new skill. A steep learning curve shows that a person is learning quickly, and a shallow learning curve means that a person is slower and taking more time to learn.

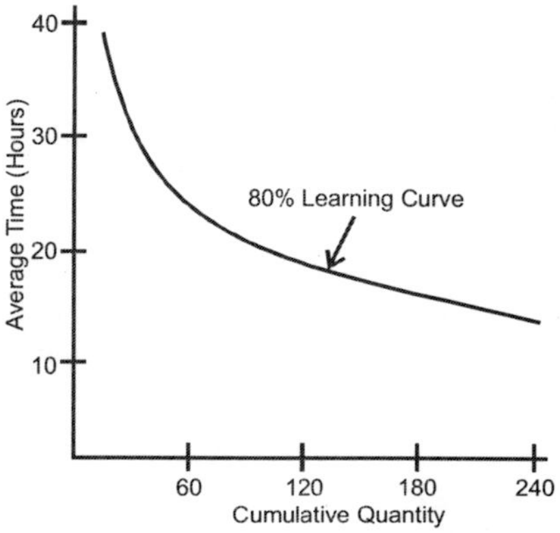

Learning management software and systems
A software platform for businesses and organizations designed to train and educate employees. Components typically include content delivery and other tools needed to administer, measure, track, and report / analyze the effectiveness of a company's training initiatives. Modern learning management systems (LMS) are often cloud-based solutions, allowing access to training and other LMS content & features online using a standard web browser.

Learning style
Learning styles are overall patterns that provide direction to learning and teaching. They involve educating methods, particular to an individual, that are presumed to allow that individual to learn best.

Lease purchase
A finance agreement in which an item, usually a car, is leased for a certain period of time with an option to purchase at the end of the contract.

Leaseback
An arrangement between a purchaser of a property and the vendor in which

the vendor immediately leases the property back from the purchaser.

Leave of absence

The period of time which a person is permitted by their employer to be absent from their job.

Leave-behind

A premium left with prospective customers by a sales person to remind them of the product or service being sold.

Legal aid

Legal assistance provided , usually by the state, for people or organisations who cannot afford to pay for solicitors or legal advice.

Legal entity

An individual or organisation who has the legal right to enter into a contract or an agreement, is responsuble for its actions, and can sue or be sued if the terms of the contract are broken.

Legal reserve

The minimum amount of money, required by law, that a bank, insurance company, etc., must set aside in order to be able to operate.

Legal tender

In day-to-day language the term generally refers to coinage or banknotes which have not been withdrawn or demonetised by the Bank of England and so are valid, but technically the term the UK refers to forms of currency which by law must be accepted by a creditor in payment of a debt.

Lemon

A defective product which is poor quality and fails to function as promised. Particularly used in the automotive industry, specifically for a poor-quality second-hand car, or a sub-standard new vehicle.

Lender of last resort

A country's central bank which loans money to other banks or financial institutions which cannot borrow money from anywhere else and do not have enough reserves to cover cash withdrawals by their customers.

Letter of comfort

A letter of approval written to a bank by a parent company on behalf of a subsidiary company which needs financial backing.

Letter of indemnity

A document in which an individual, company, etc., guarantees to protect another from costs, liability, etc., as a result of certain actions which may be carried out.

Letters of credit

These mechanisms are used by exporters and importers, and usually provided by the importing company's bank to the exporter to safeguard the contractual expectations and particularly financial exposure of the exporter of the goods or services. (Also called 'export letters of credit, and 'import letters of credit'.) When an exporter agrees to supply a customer in another country, the exporter needs to know that the goods will be paid for. The common system, which has been in use for many years, is for the customer's bank to issue a 'letter of credit' at the request of the buyer, to the seller. The letter of credit essentially guarantees that the bank will pay the seller's invoice (using the customer's money of course) provided the goods or services are supplied in accordance with the terms stipulated in the letter, which should obviously reflect the agreement between the seller and buyer. This gives the supplier an assurance that their invoice will be paid, beyond any other assurances or contracts made with the customer. Letters of credit are often complex documents that require careful drafting to protect the interests of buyer and seller. The customer's bank charges a fee to issue a letter of credit, and the customer pays this cost. The seller should also approve the wording of the buyer's letter of credit, and often should seek professional advice and guarantees to this effect from their own financial services provider. In short, a letter of credit is a guarantee from the issuing bank's to the seller that if compliant documents are presented by the seller to the buyer's bank, then the buyer's bank will pay the seller the amount due. The 'compliance' of the seller's documentation covers not only the goods or services supplied, but also the timescales involved, method for, format of and place at which the documents are presented. It is common for exporters to experience delays in obtaining payment against letters of credit because they have either failed to understand the terms within the letter of credit, failed to meet the terms, or both. It is important therefore for sellers to understand all aspects of letters of credit and to ensure letters of credit are properly drafted, checked, approved and their conditions met. It is also important for sellers to use appropriate professional services to validate the authenticity of any unknown bank issuing a letter of credit.

Letters of guarantee

There are many types of letters of guarantee. These types of letters of guarantee are concerned with providing safeguards to buyers that suppliers will meet their obligations or vice-versa, and are issued by the supplier's or customer's bank depending on which party seeks the guarantee. While a letter of credit essentially guarantees payment to the exporter, a letter of guarantee provides safeguard that other aspects of the supplier's or customer's obligations will be met. The supplier's or customer's bank is effectively giving a direct guarantee on behalf of the supplier or customer that the supplier's or customer's obligations will be met, and in the event of the supplier's or customer's failure to meet obligations to the other party then the bank undertakes the responsibility for those obligations. Typical obligations covered by letters of guarantee are concerned with: 1. Tender Guarantees (Bid Bonds) - whereby the bank assures the buyer that the supplier will not refuse a contract if awarded. 2. Performance Guarantee - This guarantees that the goods or services are delivered in accordance with contract terms and timescales. 3. Advance Payment Guarantee - This guarantees that any advance payment received by the supplier will be used by the supplier in accordance with the terms of contract between seller and buyer. There are other types of letters of guarantee, including obligations concerning customs and tax, etc, and as with letters of credit, these are complex documents with extremely serious implications. For this reasons suppliers and customers alike must check and obtain necessary validation of any issued letters of guarantee.

Levy

A tax imposed by government, to meet a specific objective.

Liabilities

General term for what the business owes. Liabilities are long-term loans of the type used to finance the business and short-term debts or money owing as a result of trading activities to date . Long term liabilities, along with Share Capital and Reserves make up one side of the balance sheet equation showing where the money came from. The other side of the balance sheet will show Current Liabilities along with various Assets, showing where the money is now.

Libertarian/libertine

A person who believes in the freedom of speech and thought, and that people should be able to do whatever-within reason-they wish with minimal interference from government. The words derive from the Latin root liber, meaning free, like the word liberty, meaning freedom.

Licensing

A method of foreign operation cooperation whereby an organisation in one country agrees to permit a firm in another country to use the manufacturing, processing, trademark, know-how or some other skill provided by the licensor.

Lien

A legal right to take and keep another persons property until a debt has been paid by the property owner.

Life tables

Also called Mortality Tables. Tables which show peoples life expectancy, depending on their age, lifestyle, etc., often used by insurance companies.

Lifeboat

An emergency loan offered to a company or bank which is in financial trouble.

Lifestyle business

A business set up and run so as to fit with the wider life needs of the business owner(s) which might be called 'life balance', or happiness or wellbeing. Typically this will mean that the business can be established and operated with very simple, relatively small-scale, and easily manageable: infrastructure, overheads, inbound supply-chain (if any), premises (typically in a home), legal issues, administration products/ services range, ambition, marketing and advertising, technology and ICT, staffing, and demands on workload, time, and generally work pressures. Given these criteria, certain types of businesses do not make naturally good lifestyle businesses, because they imply/require a more burdensome degree for one or a number of the features listed above. Businesses that do not naturally make good lifestyle businesses would be for example: manufacturing.

Lifo (last in, first out)

A method of determining who should be laid off in which the most recent hires are laid off first.

Lightning strike

A sudden strike by workers, with little or no warning. These strikes are often short in duration and usually without official union backing.

Like-gate

Online barrier that requires a user to first "Like" a brand's page before being able to access specific content that could include special limited time offerings, special sales, and other promotions, thus allowing the brand marketer to stay in touch with target customers.

Likeonomics
Phenomena that consumers buy products from companies they like. Underlying principle: The more people like you, the more they will buy from you, and thus the more profit the company makes (attributed to Advertising Guru David Ogilvy).

Limit order
An order to buy stock once the price has dropped below the price limit.

Limited company
In the UK, a company that has a name ending in 'Ltd.' The owners of these companies have limited liability if the company gets into debt.

Limited liability
In law, the owners and/or shareholders of a limited company only lose the amount they have invested if the company gets into debt.

Linchpin
The most important person or thing in a business or organisation.

Line authority
In business, the power given to management allowing them to give orders and to control subordinates.

Liquidate
The closing down of a business by selling its assets to pay its debts.

Liquidated damages
The fixed amount agreed upon by parties to a contract, to be paid to one party in the case of a breach of contract by the other party.

Liquidity
The ability or ease with which assets can be converted into cash; also the degree to which one can obtain the full cash value of an investment.

Liquidity ratio
Indicates the company's ability to pay its short term debts, by measuring the relationship between current assets (ie those which can be turned into cash) against the short-term debt value. (current assets/current liabilities) Also referred to as the Current Ratio.

List price
Known as 'Sticker Price' in the US. The advertised or recommended retail price (RRP) of a product.

List rental
The renting, from an organisation, of a mailing list which has potential customer names and addresses, for a one-off mailing.

Litigant
A person or party who is involved in a court action or lawsuit.

Litigate
To legally settle a dispute in, or take a claim to, a court of law.

Litigious
To routinely or enthusiastically take legal action to settle disputes.

Litotes
A language term referring to understatement, used for emphasis, often ironically, in which the negative-opposite is used instead of the positive expression, for example, "It wasn't the best presentation I've ever given," when the speaker means that they considered it to have been a particularly poor one. Another example is the commonly used "Not bad," or "Not half Bad," when referring to something very good. The word litotes comes from Greek, litos, meaning single, simple or meagre.

Living trust
A trust created in which assets can be transferred to someone while the grantor (the person who owns the assets) is still alive. Living Trusts avoid dealing with the legalities of a will.

Loan shark
A loan shark is a person or body that offers loans at extremely high interest rates. The term usually refers to illegal activity, but may also refer to predatory lending with extremely high interest rates such as payday or title loans. Loan sharks sometimes enforce repayment by blackmail or threats of violence. Historically, many moneylenders skirted between legal and extra-legal activity. In the recent western world, loan sharks have been a feature of the criminal underworld.

Local content measure
Where a business or investor is required to purchase a certain amount of locally sourced materials to be used in the manufacturing, etc., of their product.

Local products
Goods or services seen only suitable in one single market.

Lockout
A term used during an industrial dispute, when management closes down a workplace and bars employees from entering until they agree to certain terms and conditions.

Locus standi
(Latin-place of standing) The right or capacity of a litigant to be heard or to bring an action in court.

Logistics
Process of planning, implementing, and controlling the efficient and effective flow and storage of goods, services, and related information from point of origin to point of consumption for the purpose of conforming to customer requirements, internal, and external movements, and return of materials for environmental purposes.

Logotype (logo)
Graphic element used to identify a company, or its products and services. Typically trademarked to legally protect ownership and usage rights so others cannot use it.

Long grass
To 'Kick something into the long grass' means to push a problem aside in the hope that it will be ignored or forgotten.

Long position
A situation in which an investor or dealer holds onto shares, etc., which they have purchased, expecting them to rise in value in the future.

Long term liability
Taxes, leases, loans, etc., which are payable over a period greater than one year.

Long-term care insurance
Helps provide for the cost of long-term care beyond a predetermined period, and is generally not covered by health insurance, Medicare, or Medicaid.

Long-term debt
A debt owed over a relatively long period of time.

Loophole
An unintentional mistake in a contract or a law which allows people to evade an obligation in the contract, or to get round the law without actually breaking it.

Looping
In films, TV Programmes, etc., the process of dubbing the original film footage by synching (lining it up) with new or replacement dialogue.

Loss leader
Products sold at or below cost to stimulate other profitable sales. Often, popular items are priced below cost to entice customer visits to a retailer's store of website. Can be highly profitable, should customers purchase several other items at the same time.

Loss leader
In retail, a product which is offered at a very low price to attract customers who will then buy other goods which will produce more profit for the retailer.

Low context culture
High reliance on explicit verbal or written communications or other explicit format.

Low hanging fruit
A term used in business for something which is easily obtainable and highly visible, and provides a quick easy way to making a profit.

Low yield
A term used to describe investments which are low risk and do not produce a high level of income.

Loyalty card
A card given to customers by a retailer which gives the customer points, etc., every time they shop there. These points convert into vouchers which the customer can spend at the store at a later date.

Luddite
A derogatory term for someone who opposes or disapproves of new technology and/or new methods of working, often because the changes threaten jobs. From the Luddite rioters of 1811-16, who in defence of labourers' jobs in early industrial Britain wrecked new manufacturing machinery.

Lump sum payment
A single large payment given to an employee, usually instead of more and smaller pay increases.

M

Machine code
Also known as Machine Language. A computer language, which consists only of numbers, that can be read and interpreted by a computer's central processing unit (CPU).

Macro
In a computer, a single instruction which results in a complete series of more detailed instructions being put into effect.

Macromarketing
Study of marketing processes, activities, institutions, and results from a broad perspective such as a nation, in which cultural, political, and social interaction are investigated. It is marketing in a larger context than any one firm: the delivery of a standard of living.

Magalog
A catalogue which appears to be a magazine, used for marketing purposes.

Magic bullet
A simple effective solution to a serious or complex problem, especially in medicine, for example a cure for a disease. The simplicity is for users, not necessarily for the developers.

Magnetic media
Disks and tapes which are used to record and store computer data.

Mail merge
The process of automatically personalising a customised letter or document by using a list of individual names and addresses, so the same letter can be sent to many people.

Mail order
The purchasing or selling of goods over the Internet, telephone, from catalogues, etc., which are delivered to the customer by mail.

Mainframe
Also known as 'Big Iron'. A large powerful central computer to which a network of smaller computers are connected, used commonly by large organisations.

Mainstream
A term applied to activities, ideas, products/services, etc., that are used/followed/supported by most people. Mainstream basically means 'commonly used by people'. Mainstream as a marketing term is the opposite to 'niche' or specialised. Interestingly while 'mainstream' seems like a relatively modern word, it's actually existed in this sense since about 1830.

Majority interest
Owning more than 50% of the total shares in a company, and therefore more than 50% of the voting interest.

Make to stock
In manufacturing, products which are made and stocked before customers orders have been received.

Makegood
In advertising, a free advertising slot given to a company by a TV station, magazine, etc., if the company's advert was previously run incorrectly.

Maladministration
In business or government, the act of incompetence or running a system in a dishonest way.

Managed care
A health care system in which the provider manages the care of the individual for a fixed fee. The opposite of this preventive intervention (or, population-based) approach is fee-for-service. Managed care emphasizes wellness and prevention.

Managed economy
An economy in which goods, allocation of resources and prices are determined by the government.

Managed hosting
A type of Internet hosting in which the hosting supplier deals with technical issues and problems related to the website, in addition to the basic hosting of the website.

Management buy-in
When a management team from outside a company acquires more than 50% of the company, so they become the majority shareholders, and then manage the company themselves.

Management buy-out
MBO. The purchase of all or part of a company by the company's existing managers.

Management by exception
A management style in which managers give employees the authority to run projects, etc., by themselves and managers only become involved if the employees fail to meet certain criteria or standards.

Management by objective (MBO)
A process of defining objectives within an organization so that management and employees agree on the overall goals and objectives for the organization. The employees determine and set goals for themselves based on the overall goals and objectives for the organization.

Manager
A person who is in charge of a project, department, group, team, etc.

Mandate
Technically a legal or official document giving an order or instruction. More loosely it refers to a permission or approval. In politics or democratic situations such as trade unions it refers to an authorisation for leadership to act based on election or vote. Derived from Latin mandatum meaning 'something commanded', from manus (hand) and dare (give). Mandate is also a verb, meaning to empower someone to take action.

Mandatory convertible bond
Bonds that must be redeemed in shares by the company which issues them, usually by a specified date.

Margin
The difference in the price of producing a product and the price it sells for, calculated as a percentage, i.e., profit margin.

Margin account
An account held by an investor with a broker in which the broker lends the investor money to purchase shares, etc., which are then used as collateral against the loan.

Margin call
A demand by a broker for an investor to bring his margin account up to the minimum level required by depositing additional money, shares, securities, etc.

Marginal productivity
The additional output of a product, etc., which is produced as a result of adding one unit of a resource, for example labour input, in the production process.

Markatainment (marketing + entertainment)
Using other goods and services to entertain customers at the point of purchase. Ex: Best Buy stores a free outdoor screening of the as-yet-unreleased Harry Potter movie for those waiting in line for doors to open for Black Friday sales. This is a form of publicity and sales promotion.

Market
Economic system bringing together the forces of supply and demand for a particular good or service. A market consists of customers, suppliers, and channels of distribution, and mechanisms for establishing prices and effecting transactions where exchanges take place. Often, marketers will define primary, secondary, and even tertiary markets to help it allocate its limited resources in the most effective and efficient manner.

Market basket
A way of measuring the cost of living. A collection of products or services which consumers buy on a regular basis, and the prices which are paid for them.

Market capitalization
The value found by multiplying the number of outstanding common stock shares by the share price; indicates firm size and total value held in stock.

Market clearing price
The price of a product or service at which the level of demand equals the level of supply.

Market control
A situation in which the quantity and/or price of goods or services is influenced by buyers or sellers.

Market development
Addition of new geographic markets in which to offer the existing mix of products and services—those NOT currently served by a firm.

Market economy
A situation in which businesses operate in a free market, i.e., they are in competition with each other and are not under government control.

Market entry
The way in which an organisation enters foreign markets either by direct or indirect export or production in a foreign country.

Market forces
Influences, such as the availability of raw materials for the production of goods, or customer numbers, which affect supply, demand and prices of products and services.

Market holding price
The charging of a price at what the market can bear in order to hold market share.

Market leader

A company or brand which has the highest sales of a particular product. A best-selling product.

Market order

An order to purchase or sell stock at a current price.

Market orientation

A business strategy whereby a company focuses on meeting the customers needs and wants regarding products and services.

Market penetration price

A low price at which a new product is offered when it first comes onto the market, in order to attract customers, after which the price is usually increased.

Market positioning

The adoption of a specific market stance, either leader, challenger, follower, flanker or adopter, vis a vis competition.

Market research

The process of gathering and analysing information about customers, competitors, etc., in order to make decisions and solve problems connected with selling products or services.

Market risk

The movement of a stock price relative to the overall market; indicated by beta.

Market saturation

The point at which a market is no longer generating new demand for a firm's products, due to competition, decreased need, obsolescence, or other uncontrollable variables.

Market sector

Competing businesses which produce or buy similar goods and/or services. The customers for which certain goods and services are marketed.

Market segment

A subgroup within a larger market in which people share certain characteristics and require similar products or services.

Market segmentation

Targeted market or audience for a given product is divided into categories (segments) based on geographic, demographic, or psychographic variables, such as demographic segmentation, geographic segmentation, and psychographic (behavioral) segmentation.

Market share

Percentage of sales volume captured by a brand, product, or firm in a given market.

Market test

The testing of a product or service in several areas of the country to see if customers will like it and want to buy it.

Market testing

Risk-reduction effort based on planning and executing a regional or local marketing strategy before rolling out nationally. Markets are selected based on demographics that mirror the total potential target market. Also used to test awareness and recall of advertising messages.

Market timing

The selecting of the best time for leaving or reentering the market in order to achieve the maximum result.

Marketing

Planning, executing and controlling the conception, pricing, promotion and distribution of ideas, goods and services in order to build lasting, mutually profitable exchange relationships satisfying individual and organisational objectives.

Marketing analytics

scientific process for identifying patterns and relationships in survey data that will increase effectiveness of marketing activities. For example, after more than 40 years the GAP changed its logo, which set off negative postings on various blogs. So much so that the company went back to its original logo. When companies change parts of their strategy without consulting long-time faithful fans, it can cause an uproar and loss of loyalty by loyal customers. (Of course, the other side of this action is that the GAP received lots of free publicity.)

Marketing blitz

Intensive fast-paced campaign (attack), designed to build up business clients. Examples include face-to-face campaigning and intensive media ad spending. Several books on the topic: check out Guerilla Marketing by

Marketing channels

Connected system of exchange relationships of wholesalers and retailers, developed to build lasting bridges between buyers and sellers. It is based on their ability to perform marketing activities more effectively and efficiently than the producer.

Marketing concept

Goal-oriented risk-reducing integrated philosophy practiced by producers of goods and services that focuses efforts on satisfying the needs of consumers by allocating resources to satisfy that need, and making a profit by doing so. For example, a successful marketing concept in the perfume industry is about selling dreams, sex, and romance the benefits derived from perfume, not the perfume itself (its ingredients and packaging).

Marketing environment

Range of uncontrollable variables related to competitive, economic, political/legal, technological, and social/cultural variables that impact the target market and marketing mix.

Marketing hyperopia

Condition or situation when consumer willpower against acquiring a product or service is overshadowed or exaggerated by desire, pleasure, or indulgence to have it—often apart from the expense or actual need fulfillment. Often occurring in Maslow's Belonging and Esteem need levels.

Marketing mix

Combination of marketing elements used in the sale of a particular product, sometimes called the 4 Ps: product, price, place, and promotion.

Marketing myopia

When a business is being shortsighted regarding the needs of its customers, only focusing on its products or short range goals and missing marketing opportunities.

Marketing objectives

What an organization wishes to achieve (the end result). They focus on existing products in existing markets, new products for existing markets, existing products for new markets and new products for new markets (Marketing Opportunity Grid). Most importantly, they can be measured in terms of sales volume, sales value, market share, profit, percentage of penetration outlets, awareness and esteem. Savvy marketers also add timelines and assign responsibilities to individuals to assure accountability.

Marketing plan
Set of specific goals (measurable), timelines (when goals are to achieved), and actions required (assignment of responsibility) to successfully implement a marketing strategy.

Marketing PR
Marketing PR is the combining of what are traditionally two separate departments, public relations and marketing, to one integrated front whereby all marketing and PR activities focus on reaching buyers directly. Marketing PR incorporates both traditional marketing and PR tactics with social media and other Internet-based initiatives that support the measurable goals of online publicity, increased web site traffic, search-optimization (SEO) and, lead generation. A key difference between traditional PR and Marketing PR is the use of a press release. Traditional PR writes and distributes a press release for the sole purpose of securing media placements. Marketing PR does this as well but also uses the press release to enhance website SEO, increase web site traffic and generate qualified sales leads.

Marketing research
Process of gathering, analyzing, and interpreting information (data) about a market, product, or service; or about past, present and potential customers' characteristics, such as pricing, spending habits, location, and needs; or about the industry as a whole and its competitors.

Marketing scorecard
A reporting approach that aligns marketing outcomes with objectives. Allows organizations to set, monitor, and adjust results to reduce risk. EX: Some oil companies use a scorecard to evaluate effectives of their service suppliers. During the life of a project, the supplier is graded on any number of factors; an overall score at the end may well determine whether it will be asked to bid on a future project.

Marketing strategy
Plan allowing the organization to concentrate its limited resources on the greatest opportunities to increase sales and achieve a sustainable competitive advantage. It is comprised of a target market and marketing mix.

Marketing-oriented company
An organization that aligns or adjusts the allocation of its resources to product development, distribution, pricing, and promotional message channeling as dictated by the demands, interests, and needs of its target market. This approach reduces risk and enhances sustainability of the organization.

Market-to-market
The process of valuing a security, share, etc., on a daily basis to assess its current price, rather than its acquisition price or book value.

Mark-up
Dollar amount added to the cost of products to get the selling price (can include incentives such as discounts and allowances), expressed as a percentage of the new selling price. Applies to each channel member.

Mark-up chain
Sequence of mark-ups used at different stages in a channel to help

determine the price structure among all channel members. This is helpful to marketers when analyzing the profitability of a new product or service.

Marque
A brand name or model of a well-known manufactured product, especially an expensive car.

Mass customization
Extension of one-to-one marketing exposure for customizing products and services on a mass scale via personalizing buying interactions for each customer.

Mass market
Describes products or services which have mass appeal and are aimed at large numbers of people or a whole population.

Mass marketing
Broad unfocussed attempts to appeal to an entire geographic market with one basicmarketing strategy utilizing mass distribution and mass media. Also called undifferentiated marketing.

Master franchise
Allows companies or individuals the right to purchase a sub-franchise business which can be developed in a particular area or country.

Material requirements planning
The use of computer software to plan and manage a production process, for example the amount of materials or parts required, calculation of workload, delivery schedules, etc.

Maternity leave
The time a pregnant employee is entitled to take off from her job before and after the birth of her baby. Entitlement to Maternity Leave depends on how long the woman has been with her employer.

Maternity pay
An employee benefit paid to pregnant women when they take time off from their job to have their baby. Entitlement to Maternity Pay depends on how long they have worked for their employer and varies from country to country.

Mates rates
To sell a product or service to a friend or family member at a discounted or reduced rate on the normal price.

Matrix management
Also known as Dotted Line Responsibility. A system of management in which people from different departments in an organisation work together, so that each individual employee has two bosses, one functional and one operational. This is common in project management.

Matrix organisation
A complex form of organisational structure bringing together the competencies of geographic knowledge, product knowledge and know how, and functional competencies - financial, production and marketing - and a knowledge of the customer, industry and its needs.

Matrix organization
Used primarily in the management of large projects, a horizontal authority structure in which teams are created from various departments and report to more than one boss.

Maven
An expert, often self-proclaimed, in a particular field.

Maverick
An independent thinker who does not conform to accepted opinion on certain matters and takes a stand from other people.

Mean
The average of a group of measurement values. Mean is determined by dividing the sum of the values by the number of values in the group.

Mean wage
The average wage for a worker in a specified position or occupation, which may be skewed up or down if there are a few extreme examples in the sample.

Media
Any paid for communication channel including television, radio, posters etc..

Media scheduling
A timetable for the allocation of advertising messages in the media over a given time horizon.

Mediagenic
A tendency (for a person or activity, etc) to convey a favourable impression when reported by the media.

Median
The middle of a group of measurement values when arranged in numerical order. For example, in the group (32, 45, 78, 79, 101), 78 is the median. If the group contains an even number of values, the median is the average of the two middle values.

Median wage
The margin between the highest paid 50 percent and the lowest paid 50 percent of workers in a specific position or occupation. It is often more representative of the average wage than a mean would be, as it can account for extreme outliers.

Mediation services
The use of a trained third party to settle an employment dispute. The third party has no legal authority and so must use persuasion to settle the dispute.

Medical savings account (MSA)
A savings account funded by employees in which tax-deferred deposits can be made for use as medical expenses, co-payments, or deductibles.

Meltdown
A situation in which something, or someone, suddenly dramatically ceases to function properly.

Meme
Originally a biological term referring to a behavioural characteristic which transfers non-genetically between people, meme increasingly refers more widely to other non-human characterstics or examples which arise as imitations of or variations on a particular theme.

Memo
Usually used for communication within an organisation. Memos can be formal letters or informal notes to colleagues.

Memorandum and articles of association
A legal document drawn up when a company is formed containing details such as company name, type, objectives, and number and value of shares, etc.

Memorandum of understanding
A sometimes informal written agreement between two or more parties which establishes each party's responsibilities and requirements.

Menial (work, job, task)
Unskilled typically poorly paid work.

Mentor
Someone who is experienced and gives guidance and support to a person less experienced to help them develop and grow and achieve their goals.

Mentoring
An informal training process between a more experienced person and a junior employee.

Menu bar
On a computer screen, the strip at the top of each open window that contains pull down menus with functions, for example file, edit, etc.

Mercantile
Relating to trade or commerce.

Mercantilism
A nationalist doctrine of one nation prospering at the expense of another nation.

Merchandising
The practice of promoting and selling goods. Commercial products which are associated with a film, pop group, TV show, celebrity, etc., such as toys, clothing, food products, household items, etc.

Merchant bank
Known in the US as an Investment Bank. A financial institution which offers financial advice and services to large businesses and wealthy individuals.

Merge-purge
The process of combining two or more lists or files of names and addresses etc., typically databases, and removing duplicated and/or unwanted items, to produce one new clean list or database.

Merger
Buying or combining companies financially using cash and/or stocks. Ex: Bank One and JPMorgan Chase bank form one strategic brand that builds on brand loyalty, and helps both lower risk and obtain more control over financial markets.

Merit pay
Performance-related pay which provides bonuses or base pay increases for workers who perform their jobs effectively, according to measurable criteria.

Meritocracy
In business, a system in which people advance because of their abilities rather than their connections or wealth, etc.

Merlin
TV/Movie term for a visual mistake in a film or TV show, derived from the accidental inclusion of a beer can in a TV drama scene featuring Merlin, in the days of King Arthur and the Knights of the Round Table.

Mesne profits
Compensation or penalty charges instead of, or 'in lieu' of, rent claimed by a landlord against a person illegally occupying land or property and subsequently evicted, commonly arising from a court order.

Message
An informative communication about a product or service placed in a communication channel.

Meta/metatags/metadata

Meta means an additional useful part of the whole thing, usually data or communication of some sort, and usually hidden or underlying and coded. The original sense is from the Greek word meta, loosely meaning 'with' and arises now commonly as a prefix in computing and communications terminology, for example referring to meta tags (increasingly 'metatags') within website or computer code, which are typically hidden in normal use but which carry useful or vital information about the material or functionality concerned-specifically useful for computerised automated functions and analysis, data search, retrieval, organization and display, etc. The similar term meta data (increasingly 'metadata') refers more generally to information or code which is usually hidden in normal use or communications but which carries important meaning towards understanding or using the whole message or instruction, or other form of data.

Metacraftsmanship

Metacraftsmanship is a term used to tie together the many ideas shared by quality improvement, reengineering, management, leadership, and customer-driven production. Although these theories have much in common, they are often treated as separate and disparate approaches to improving a business. Metacraftsmanship focuses on overcoming the losses to society which are engendered by specialization, and suggests ways of getting complex organizations to work the way a single craftsman would.

Metamarkets

Markets that are similarly associated with a product or service. They can also be different products spread across different industries, but are closely related in the minds of consumers.

Mezzanine finance

A high interest, usually unsecured, loan in which the lender often has the right to obtain shares in the business which has acquired the loan. Sometimes used in management buy-outs.

Microblogging

A type of blogging allowing users to post or broadcast pictures and/or short messages or articles typically in the range of 140-200 characters.

Microcap

In the US, small companies on the stock exchange that have shares which are very low in total value.

Microcredit

The loaning of very small sums of money to entrepreneurs, especially in the developing world, typically enabling the start-up of small business activities, especially social enterprise.

Microeconomics

A branch of economics which studies individual parts of the economy, such as households, industries and businesses, and how they make decisions about spending money, use of goods and services, etc.

Micromarketing

Practice of tailoring products and marketing Programmes to the needs and wants of specific individuals and local customer groups.

Microsite

A small separate part of a larger website which is designed to be used for a particular purpose, e.g., advertising or selling. Often co-branded or 'white label', i.e., run by a larger website organisation for a smaller website acting as an agent or affiliate.

Middle management
In organisations and business, managers who are in charge of small departments and groups of people while reporting to upper management.

Middleman
Any person or business entity that plays a marketing role between producer and consumer in a distribution system (buying, selling, transportation, storing, sorting/ assorting, grading, financing, research/data sharing). Examples include real estate brokers, banks, insurance companies, trucking/ warehouse firms, and auto dealers.

Midsession
On the stock exchange, the middle period of trading during the day, usually around noon.

Milk round
In the UK, a term used when large companies visit universities each year to advertise job opportunities to students.

Mindshare
In advertising, the development of consumer awareness of a product or brand.

Minimax strategy
In Game Theory and strategy generally, a method which seeks to minimise the maximum potential losses, which usually equates to 'playing safe'.

Minimum wage
The lowest amount an employer can pay an hourly employee. This rate is set by the federal government.

Minimum wage
The legal lowest wage an employee can be paid by an employer.

Minion
A low-ranking loyal and often favoured servant or worker.

Minister without portfolio
A government minister who has not been appointed to any specific department, and who has no specific departmental responsibilities. Also refers metaphorically to an executive or director or manager in an organization who has authority and rank but no responsibility for specific activity.

Minority business enterprise
A business which is at least 51% owned, operated and controlled on a daily basis by one or more African American, Asian American, Hispanic American, or Native American citizens.

Mirror site
On the Internet, an exact copy of a popular website. This is done so that some of the traffic can be diverted from the original website to the Mirror Site when the original site becomes very busy. Alternatively a copy website whose purpose is to attract and direct additional visitors towards the original site, regarded as unacceptable SEO (search engine optimisation) or 'cheating' by most search engines.

Misery index
Created by economist Arthur Okun, an economic indicator of a country which adds the inflation rate to the unemployment rate.

Mission creep
Originally applied to military operations, a gradual expansion of a project that goes beyond original aims,

so things turn out differently than planned, often resulting in undesirable consequences.

Mission statement

A written declaration of the purpose of an organization or project team. Organizational mission or vision statements often include an organizational vision for the future, goals, and values.

Mitigate

To make something less severe or dangerous, e.g., using 'Mitigating Circumstances' as an excuse to try to make an offence seem less serious than it appears.

Mixed economy

A country's economic system which has both private and state owned enterprises in operation.

Mnemonic

A technique or mechanism for helping to remember something, such as an acronym or rhyme.

Mob

A crowd of people-usually unruly and agitated. Mob is actually a shortened version of the full Latin phrase, mobile vulgus, meaning excitable crowd. The term was abbreviated in English first as 'mobile', in the 1600s. In more recent times the meaning of mob has become much wider-notably slang for gangsters (hence 'mobsters'), and in modern times to expressions such as 'flash mob', whose full technical meaning (aside from its earliest underworld meaning) is a secretly planned, surprising and quickly-formed excitable crowd.

Mobile marketing

Use of mobile technology (iPhone, iPads, netbooks/notebooks) for promotional purposes. A way for companies to connect with customers—anytime and anyplace. The concept is a fairly new form of permission marketing.

Mobile recruiting

Using mobile technologies to find and connect with people (candidates) who use mobile devices (e.g., phone).

Mode

The most frequently occurring value in a group of measurements.

Modem

From MOdulate and DEModulate. An electronic device which is used to connect computer systems using a telephone line for transmitting data.

Moderator

An arbitrator or mediator. Someone who presides over a debate. On the Internet a person who presides over a website forum to make sure that rules and guidelines are adhered to.

Mogul

Also called a tycoon. A very rich, powerful business person.

Mondeo man

A derogatory term used to describe the average British man, who is depicted as boring, living in a semi-detached house in Kent with a wife and two children. Also used to describe travelling salesmen, a large number of who drive Mondeo cars.

Monetary base

Also known as Narrow Money in the UK. The total amount of a country's currency which is in circulation, for example, coins, notes, etc. held by individuals and in bank deposits.

Money at call

A loan or debt which must be paid upon demand.

Money spinner
A product or project that generates a lot of earnings.

Money-market fund
A type of mutual fund that invests in short-term securities such as Certificates of Deposits and Treasury Bills.

Monopoly
A situation in which one company or organisation has complete control of all, or nearly all, of the market for a particular type of product or service.

Monopsony
Also known as Buyers Monopoly, a market in which there is only one customer for a product or service being sold by several sellers.

Mooc
Acronym for 'Massive Open Online Course' conceivably the future of most higher/further education globally.

Moore's law
Founder of Intel Gordon Moore's theory that the power of computing has the potential to double every two years (often quoted as every 18 months).

Moppers
Mobile shoppers who use cell phones and other devices such as iPads to browse on-line stores, comparison shop, and get recommendations from friends.

Moppers
Mobile shoppers who use cell phones and other devices such as iPads to browse on-line stores, comparison shop, and get recommendations from friends.

Moral hazard
The situation in businesses and organisations when people are protected, e.g. by insurance cover, so they are more likely to take risks.

Mortgage
A loan acquired from a bank, building society, etc., with which to buy property or land, usually to be paid back with interest over a specified number of years at regular monthly intervals. To borrow money from a bank, etc., using your property as collateral, giving the lender the right to own your property if the loan is not repaid.

Mothball
In business, to stop using a piece of equipment or building, etc., for a period of time, but keep it in good condition for when work can resume.

Motherboard
Also known as the Logic Board. The main circuit board of a computer which has all the components to make everything in the computer work together, such as the monitor, keyboard, mouse, DVD drive, etc.

Motivation
Implies an emotion or desire that causes the customer to think and act. It's a driving force arising from personal temperament or constitution that can be stimulated through incentives applied to an external influence (as an expected reward) inciting action. In marketing, it's the energy/fuel that drives the thought process, designed to result in a specific action by the consumer (purchase).

Motivational research
A type of market research used to investigate the reasons why people buy specific products or brands.

Motivational theories

Psychological models that attempt to explain what motivates people. These theories can help employers design incentive strategies.

Mountweazel

A fictitious entry in a reference source or listing, traditionally an act of mischief, but also used to catch copyright cheats or those who obtain and use a database without a licence or a fee. Logically mountweazel entries are removed from legitimate authorized versions. Mountweazel is supposedly named after a false entry Lillian Virginia Mountweazel in the 1975 New Columbia Encyclopedia. Also called a nihilartikel, from the Latin nihil meaning nothing, and the German word artikel. A fictitious 'trap street' is the equivalent used to combat map copyright theft.

Mousetrapping

Use of Internet browser tricks to keep a visitor captive at a site, often by disabling the "Back" button or generating pop-up windows (not too marketing-oriented, for sure).

Msa

Metropolitan Statistical Area – City > 50k population, or urban center with 100k population.

Mulct

A fine or financial penalty, or the verb form, to cheat or swindle someone out of money or penalize someone by imposing a fine, from the Latin word multare, to fine.

Multichannel distribution

Occurs when a producer uses several competing channels to reach the same target market, perhaps using several middlemen to sell directly (sometimes called dual distribution).

Multinational corporation

MNC. Also known as Transnational Corporation. A company which operates in several countries outside the country in which it is based.

Multinational products

Goods or services adapted to the perceived unique characteristics of national markets.

Multiple factor indices

A measure of potential demand indirectly using, as proxies, variables that either intuition or statistical analysis suggest can be closely correlated with the potential demand for the product under view.

Multivariate testing

Research method of analyzing effect of multiple variables in a controlled situation/scenario. Example: Inputting relevant factors that a home buyer might debate when choosing a financial institution for his loan. This enables marketers to quickly identify an appropriate marketing strategy for the home buyer.

Murketing

Blurring the lines between branding and everyday life. Ex: Axe body care products promote an "effect" (socialization) rather than a means of hygiene.

Murphy's law

Humorous saying: Anything that can possibly go wrong will go wrong.

Mutual company

A type of organisation, business, etc., which is owned by members and has no shareholders. The members usually have a share of the profits.

Myers-briggs type indicator

(MBTI) A psychometric questionnaire or personality test in which people answer questions about themselves, which helps identify strengths and personal behavioural/behavioral preferences.

Mystery shopper

A person hired by market research companies or manufacturers, etc., to visit or telephone shops or service providers anonymously in order to assess the quality of goods, helpfulness of staff, layout of premises.

N

Nagware

Also known as Begware. Computer shareware that periodically displays messages on your computer screen prompting you to register for a product and/or pay a fee.

NAICS (North American Industrial Classification System)

Standard used by Federal statistical agencies in classifying business establishments for the purpose of collecting, analyzing, and publishing statistical data related to the U.S. business economy. A complete and valid NAICS code contains six digits and applies to businesses in the United States, Canada, and Mexico each to have country-specific detail. The first two digits designate the economic sector, the third digit designates the subsector, the fourth digit designates the industry group, the fifth digit designates the NAICS industry, and the sixth digit designates the national industry.

Naked debenture

Also known as Uncovered Debenture. A company's loan or debt which is not backed by any security, i.e., the company's assets.

Narrow branding

Ways/methods by which brands present themselves differently to different customer segments (a more customer-centric approach to marketing). Ex: Food companies that address those who "live to cook" (affinity in the belonging and esteem needs), and those who "cook to live" (basic physiological or safety/security need set).

Narrow money

Also called M1. A country's money supply which can be exchanged, for example coins, bank notes, bank cheques, travellers cheques, etc.

National association of securities dealers automated quotations system (NASDAQ)

A "virtual stock exchange"—that is, a stock market without a trading floor whose orders are made through a computer network.

National brand

A brand or product which is available nationwide rather than a local brand which is available in only one area of the country.

National debt

The total amount of money owed by a nation's government.

Nationalism

The assertion of indigenous culture by an individual, organisation or country.

Natural wastage
In business, the process of reducing the number of employees by not replacing those who have left their jobs, rather than by redundancy or dismissal.

Needs
Basic forces that motivate a person to think about and do something/take action. In marketing, they help explain the benefit or satisfaction derived from a product or service, generally falling into the physical (air > water > food > sleep > sex > safety/security) or psychological (belonging > esteem > self-actualization > synergy) subsets of Maslow's Hierarchy of Needs. A mouthwash or toothpaste might be used to rid the mouth of germs (safety/ security), or combat bad breath and yellow teeth (esteem).

Negative certificate of origin
A document which states that goods, or any part of the goods, were not produced in a country from which the buyer refuses to accept goods or produce.

Negative equity
A term commonly used in the property market during a recession when a property is worth less in value than the outstanding balance of the loan with which it was purchased. This usually only affects the borrower if they need to sell the property during this time.

Negative growth
A term used to describe a recession. The opposite of economic growth.

Negative inventory
A situation where a mistake in the ordering system or transactions of a business shows the stock to be less than zero. Sometimes this is done deliberately to reduce costs.

Negotiating table
Describes formal discussions where agreements are trying to be reached.

Negotiation
Bargaining between two or more parties with the goal of reaching consensus or resolving a problem.

Neologism
A word or expression which has been newly invented but is not yet in common use, or an old word which has a new meaning. There are a few in this very dictionary listing.

Nepotism
In business and organizations, nepotism refers to those in power showing favouritism towards friends and family, for example by giving them jobs because of their relationship rather than their abilities. The word came into English from French in the mid-1600s and originally derives from the Italian nipote, nephew, and the tradition of giving privileges to the 'nephews' of popes, who were typically actually illigitimate sons.

Nest egg
A sum of money which someone has saved for the future.

Net assets
Total assets (fixed and current) less current liabilities and long-term liabilities that have not been capitalised (eg, short-term loans).

Net current assets
Current Assets less Current Liabilities

Net lending
The total amount of funds lent by a bank or building society over a certain period, minus any repayments made by borrowers.

Net present value (NPV)

NPV is a significant measurement in business investment decisions. NPV is essentially a measurement of all future cashflow (revenues minus costs, also referred to as net benefits) that will be derived from a particular investment (whether in the form of a project, a new product line, a proposition, or an entire business), minus the cost of the investment. Logically if a proposition has a positive NPV then it is profitable and is worthy of consideration. If negative then it's unprofitable and should not be pursued. While there are many other factors besides a positive NPV which influence investment decisions; NPV provides a consistent method of comparing propositions and investment opportunities from a simple capital/investment/profit perspective. There are different and complex ways to construct NPV formulae, largely due to the interpretation of the 'discount rate' used in the calculations to enable future values to be shown as a present value. Corporations generally develop their own rules for NPV calculations, including discount rate.

Net price

The price payable for goods or services after any deductions, discounts, etc., have been taken off.

Net profit

Net profit can mean different things so it always needs clarifying. Net strictly means 'after all deductions' (as opposed to just certain deductions used to arrive at a gross profit or margin). Net profit normally refers to profit after deduction of all operating expenses, notably after deduction of fixed costs or fixed overheads. This contrasts with the term 'gross profit' which normally refers to the difference between sales and direct cost of product or service sold (also referred to as gross margin or gross profit margin) and certainly before the deduction of operating costs or overheads. Net profit normally refers to the profit figure before deduction of corporation tax, in which case the term is often extended to 'net profit before tax' or PBT.

Net profit margin

A measure of a company's profitability and efficiency, calculated by dividing a measure of net profits (operating profit minus depreciation and income taxes) by sales.

Net sales

Amount of sales found by subtracting returns and allowances from money collected for goods and services.

Net worth

Value found by subtracting all liabilities from all assets.

Net yield

The profit from an investment after taxes, costs and all other expenses have been deducted.

Net-centric

Activities, communities, services, information, etc., interconnected by the Internet.

Netiquette

Proposed code of proper behaviour when communicating via the Internet, not only with email, but for comments posted on social networking sites. Of concern to those whose postings might be judged by employers, customers, and suppliers.

Networker

A person who meets and builds relationships with other people in order to make business or social contacts.

New issue
On the Stock Market, a share or bond which is offered to the public for the first time.

New product
"New" means substantially changed or altered in form. Technically, "new" has a shelf life of 6 months before it has to be removed (or the product altered again). Simply changing the packaging does not constitute the word "new" being placed on the product, other than to say "New Packaging."

New York stock exchange (NYSE)
The largest stock exchange in the U.S. located in New York City (Also known as "Wall Street," this stock exchange carries stocks of well-established companies on its trading floor.).

New York stock exchange index
A market-value-weighted measure that indicates stock market changes for all NYSE stocks.

Newbie
A newcomer or novice at something, especially on the Internet.

Next-generation
Term used to describe a product or technology which has been improved or upgraded so that the newest version is much more advanced than previous versions.

Niche
Particular specialty in which a firm has garnered a large market share. Often, the market will be small enough so that the firm will not attract much competition. For example, a company that makes a line of specialty chemicals for exclusive use by the petroleum industry is said to have a niche in the chemical industry.

Niche market
A specialised market in which a specific product is sold to a particular type or group of customers. A product or service for which there is sometimes little demand and often little or no competition.

Nielsen rating
In the US, a system which measures TV audiences, i.e., which Programmemes are watched by which type of person. Companies use this information to decide when to advertise their products, and TV companies use this information to set prices for advertisement slots.

Nih syndrome
Not Invented Here. A term used for companies who reject ideas or products which are not theirs because they originated from outside the company.

Nikkei index
A share price index for the 225 stocks traded on the Tokyo Stock Exchange in Japan.

Noise
In the context of quality management, noise is essentially variability. For example, if you are making ketchup, noise in the process comes from variations in the quality of incoming tomatoes, in changes in ambient temperature and humidity, in variations in machinery performance, in variations in the quality of human factors, etc.

No-load fund

A fund which does not impose a sales or commission fee on the investor for the buying and selling of stocks and shares.

Nominal group technique

Technique used to encourage creative thinking and new ideas, but is more controlled than brainstorming. Each member of a group writes down his or her ideas and then contributes one to the group pool. All contributed ideas are then discussed and prioritized.

Non tariff barriers

Measures, public or private that cause intentionally traded goods or services to be allocated in such a way as to reduce potential real world income.

Non-callable

Also known as Bulletbond. A bond or stock which cannot be redeemed by the issuer before a particular date or until maturity.

Non-compliance

Failure or refusal to obey or comply with a rule, regulation or standard, which can commonly result in serious action by an inspector or ombudsman.

Non-departmental public body

Also known as Quangos (Quasi-Autonomous Non-Governmental Organisations) In the UK, organisations which are not government departments but are accountable to Parliament and are financed by the government to deal with public matters, e.g., Health Trusts.

Non-disclosure

A signed formal agreement in which one party agrees to keep certain information secret. Often used in business when products or projects are being developed.

Non-executive

In business, a member of a board of directors or a consultant who is not an employee of a company but who gives independent advice.

Non-executive director

Also called Outside Director. A person who is an independent member of a company's board of directors, i.e., they are not an employee of the company and are therefore not responsible for the day to day operations of the company but monitor the activities of the full time executives.

Nonfeasance

Failure to perform a duty or carry out an act when under legal obligation.

Nonprofit marketing

Marketing of a product or service in which the offer itself is not intended to make a monetary profit for the marketer.

Non-recourse debt

A type of loan or debt in which the borrower is not personally liable to the lender. If the borrower fails to make repayments the lender can only take back what was bought with the loan and none of the borrowers other assets.

Non-tariff barrier

(NTB) A type of non-tax trade restriction on imported goods which is used to make it difficult for certain goods to be taken into a country.

Nosedive

A sudden drop or plunge in prices, values, etc.

Not enough bandwidth
Term which is used when there are not enough people and/or enough time to get a job done.

Notary
A notary is a lawyer or person with legal training who is licensed by the state to perform acts in legal affairs, in particular witnessing signatures on documents. The form that the notarial profession takes varies with local legal systems.

Notebook
A very small portable computer.

Notice of deficiency
In the US, an official document sent to a taxpayer which shows that they owe more tax than has been declared on their tax form.

Notice period
The period of time during which an employee must work between resigning from and leaving their place of work.

Not-spot
An area of poor or lack of coverage in cellphone service or similar communications technology.

No-win no-fee
Conditional Fee Agreement. An agreement with your solicitor in which you don't have to pay their fee if your court case is not successful.

Np chart
A control chart indicating the number of defective units in a given sample.

Number cruncher
An accountant or person who's job is working with numbers, and who is able to do large calculations. A computer which can perform complex calculations in a short time.

Numbered account
Often called a Swiss Bank Account. An account, offered by certain banks, which can only be identified by a number, so the account holder is known only to a restricted number of the bank's employees.

O

O*net (occupational information network)

A free online database that contains thousands of occupational definitions to help match job seekers with jobs, which is administered and sponsored by the U.S. Department of Labour's Employment and Training Administration.

Objects clause

A section in a company's Memorandum Of Association which sets out the objectives of the company.

Observation interview

A method of assessing job requirements and skills by observing the employee at work, followed by an interview with the employee for further assessment and insight.

Obsolescence

The state of becoming obsolete or out of date. Old-fashioned.

Occam's razor/ockham's razor

A guiding principle or maxim for theorists, writers, communicators, etc., which asserts that the most effective (and arguably most reliable) explanations and theories employ minimal assumptions. In other words, in choosing between competing theories or explanations for uncertain things, the most reliable theory will be that which entails the least use of assumptions and other unknowns. More generally the term is used in reminding/guiding us of a need for prudence, economy and simplicity in describing, justifying, or explaining ideas and concepts, etc. The 'razor' term seems first named and recorded by Sir William Hamilton in 1852, after the 14th-century English logician and Franciscan friar Father William of Ockham (c.1285-1349), who was a notable early advocate of the principle. Philosophers and scientists throughout history (including Einstein, Russell, Newton) have described similar and basically supportive versions of the Occam's Razor principle, moreover many great thinkers have also demonstrably put the principle into practice in their own work, from which we can derive a reasonable degree of confidence in the validity of the concept itself. It's a very memorable and teachable idea the theme itself, its Ockham derivation, and the metaphorical allusion to 'shaving' away unnecessary or unsubstantiated aspects of a written or spoken theory or explanation.

Occupational hazard

Aspects of a job which can be dangerous or pose a high risk of injury.

Occupational psychology

Also called Organisational Psychology. The study of peoples behaviour at work, covering personal relations, mental health, employee selection and training, safety, etc.

Ochlocracy

Mob rule. Also known as Mobocracy. Ocholocratic groups are typically prone to extreme actions and not very clever decisions, which may be a reflection of vengeful motivation, weak intelligence, lack of organization, or any/all of these. An ochlocracy is usually an example of ineffective democracy, and of the so called 'wisdom of crowds' not working very well. Often mob rule results from a reaction against oppressive leadership. A popular metaphor which criticizes mob rule is: 'the lunatics have taken over the asylum'. Ochlocracy derives from the Greek word okhlos meaning mob. An ochlocrat is one who advocates or participates in mob rule.

Odd lot

A lot that is less than 100 shares, or less than a round lot.

Off-balance sheet

(OBS) Refers to items such as assets or debts which are not recorded on a company's balance sheet.

Offer by prospectus

A description of a company, for example financial structure, prospects, aims, etc., used when new shares are offered to the public, or when the company is for sale.

Offer document

A document which a prospective buyer of a company sends to the company's shareholders giving details of the offer in the hope of persuading them to sell their shares.

Office of fair trading

(OFT) In the UK, a non-ministerial government organisation, established in 1973, to protect consumers and ensure that competing businesses deal fairly, and to prohibit cartels, rogue trading, etc.

Official strike

A work stoppage by employees that has the backing and approval of a union.

Offline

Refers to a computer which is not connected to the Internet.

Off-market

Refers to the buying and selling of shares outside the Stock Market.

Off-peak

A time period when a service, e.g. phone network, travel, electricity, gas, etc., is being used less frequently by consumers, therefore prices and rates are cheaper at this time.

Offshore

Refers to accounts, investments, banks, etc., which are in countries where there are lower taxes and/or little government control.

Offshoring

The act of moving work to an overseas location to take advantage of lower labour costs. Offshoring usually involves manufacturing; information technology and back-office services like call centers and bill processing. Companies can build its own work center abroad, establish a foreign division, or create a subsidiary in remote locations.

Off-the-books

A payment which is not officially recorded, usually to avoid tax.

Off-the-charts
Something way below or way above normal expectations.

Off-the-grid
A person who does not wish to be in 'the system' (for example has no bank account, employment or tax identification, no fixed address, etc). May instead refer to a person who lives self-suffiently in terms of gas, electric, water, sewerage services, etc. Or someone not connected to the internet.

Off-the-peg
Known in the US as Off-the-Rack. Describes merchandise, usually clothing, which is made in standard designs and sizes, rather than made-to-measure, and is available in stock at retail outlets.

Oligarchy
A small, elite group of usually wealthy people or families who control a government or organisation, and who are unwilling to share their power.

Oligopoly
Condition/situation in which a market is controlled by a small group of firms (at least 2 different organizations, as opposed to monopoly in which there is only one firm).. Ex: In many cities, airlines or mass merchandisers compete against each other for sales. It's all about exerting control over a large part of a defined market.

Ombudsman
A government official who investigates complaints from the general public about companies, government officials, the media, etc.

Omnishambles
Severe chaos, typically in several areas of organizational responsibility, and typically where a person or organization is expected to be well-organized.

Onboarding
The process of moving a new hire from applicant to employee status ensuring that paperwork is done, benefits administration is underway, and orientation is completed. One of the great quality gurus, and, like Deming, an early student of the work of Walter Shewhart at Western Electric. His work has specialized in linking management to quality engineering. Dr. Juran is the founder of the Juran Institute which has long been the vehicle of his work in quality management and is well-known for espousing "the quality trilogy" of quality planning, quality control, and quality improvement. Juran has authored many books and other works in an effort to spread awareness of quality management ideas and applications.

One-stop
Describes a retail establishment which provides an extensive range of goods and services, so the customer can purchase everything they need without having to go elsewhere.

One-to-one marketing
Personalized customer management approach employed by organizations desiring to tailor its offerings based on individual customer needs, often accomplished through private/ personalized counseling and customized on-line offerings.

Online
Refers to a service or product which is available to use or buy on the Internet. A computer which is connected to the Internet.

Onshore accounts

Bank accounts or investments held in countries which have normal rates of tax and strict government control.

Open account

An arrangement between a vendor and buyer in which the vendor allows the buyer to pay at a later date for goods received.

Open border

A border which allows the flow of unrestricted goods and people between countries.

Open cheque

Also known as an Uncrossed Cheque. A cheque which does not have to be paid into an account, and can be cashed at the bank of the person who wrote it. Also means a cheque which has been signed but no amount has been filled in.

Open communication

In business, a situation in which employees have full information about the organisation, and are encouraged to exchange ideas and objectives with management.

Open market

A market which operates without restrictions, in which anyone can buy and sell.

Open offer

Also known as Entitlement Issue. An offer to existing share holders of a company, which entitles them to purchase new shares at a fixed price, usually lower than the current market price, in order to raise money for the company.

Open shop

A business or factory which does not require employees to be members of a trade union.

Open source

Describes computer software for which the original source code is freely accessible to everyone, so that anyone can modify or copy the Programme without paying a fee.

Open-book management

A management strategy emphasizing employee empowerment and individual impact on the success of the company by making the organization's financial data available to all employees so they can make better decisions as workers.

Open-ended investment companies

Limited investment companies which manage mutual investment funds. An OEIC can issue more shares if there is a demand from investors. The fund reduces if investors sell their shares back to the company.

Operating costs and expenses

The costs and expenses necessary to operate a company; includes manufacturing, marketing, research and development operating costs.

Operating income

The income derived after subtracting operating costs and expenses from net sales.

Operating lease

An arrangement in which a business leases equipment, cars, buildings, etc., for a period of time which is less than the expected useful life of the asset.

Operating margin

A measure of a company's profitability and efficiency, calculated by dividing a measure of operating profit (sales minus cost of producing goods and operating expenses) by sales.

Operation process chart

Used in manufacturing, a chart which shows each stage of a production process, including when materials are needed, how much time is to be allocated for each job, how many people are required to carry out the work, etc.

Opinion leader

A high-profile, influential public figure, such as a celebrity or business person, whose opinions and tastes are respected and/or copied by the general public.

Opportunism

The practice of exploiting and taking advantage of opportunities which present themselves, with no regard for other people or eventual consequences.

Opportunity cost

Term which refers to the value or benefit of something which will be lost in order to achieve or pursue something else.

Optimise

To get the most out of something. To use something in the best possible way.

Option

A bilateral contract giving its holder the right, but not the obligation to buy or sell a specified asset at a specific price, at or up to, a specific date.

Ordinary capital

The amount of capital invested in a company by shareholders.

Ordinary creditor

A creditor who has no priority or security if a company which owes them money goes bankrupt. Therefore, they will be paid only after other creditors have been paid.

Ordinary interest

Interest paid which is calculated based on a 360 day year, or 12 months of 30 days.

Ordinary resolution

A resolution accepted and passed by a company's shareholders by a simple majority, i.e., more than 50%, at a shareholders meeting or by a signed postal resolution which has been sent to the shareholders.

Ordinary share

Also called Common Stock. A share in a company which entitles the owner to a share in the company's profits, and the right to vote at shareholders meetings.

Organic growth

Describes when a company develops and expands by increasing output and/or sales through its own activities, rather than by a merger or acquisitions (buying other companies).

Organic search results

Search results returned by search engines that are based purely on the content of the pages and page popularity. Organic search results are not categorized directory results, or pay-per-click advertising results. According to MarketingSherpa.com, total money spent on search engine optimization represents only 12% of what is spent on pay-for-click advertising (PPC). What makes this statistic so startling is that it is that organic search engine results (those that show up in natural "free" listings) are better noticed, read, and clicked on than the paid listings.

Organigram
Also called Organisation Chart. A diagram which shows the structure of a business or organisation, showing connections between departments, jobs, etc.

Organised labour
Employees who are members of a Trade Union.

Organizational culture
The values, attitudes, beliefs and behaviors that characterize an organization. It is the unwritten workplace ethos that is picked up by new employees.

Organizational development
A planned organization-wide effort to improve and increase the organizations effectiveness, productivity, return on investment and overall employee job satisfaction through planned interventions in the organization's processes.

Orientation
Introducing new hires to the organization and its policies, benefits and culture. Training and familiarization with each department are sometimes included.

Orphan product
In medicine, a test, device, drug, etc., which may be useful for certain rare diseases or disorders but is not financially viable, so is therefore not developed for commercial use.

Orphaned technology
A term which refers to computer products, Programmes, etc., which have been abandoned or not marketed by their developers.

Osha
The Occupation Safety and Health Administration, an agency of the U.S. Department of Labour. The agency's goal is to promote health and reduce accidents, injury and death in the workplace.

Outbid
To offer more money than a rival for something, especially at an auction.

Outbound telemarketing
When a company calls prospective customers on the phone in order to sell them goods or services, compared to Inbound Telemarketing where the customer calls a company for assistance or to purchase goods.

Outdoor advertising
Out-of-home advertising (or outdoor advertising) is made up of more than 100 different formats. Outdoor advertising is essentially any type of advertising that reaches the consumer while he or she is outside the home.

Outgoings
Term used in the UK to describe money being paid out on a regular basis by an individual or a company.

Outlay
The total amount of money which has to be spent to acquire an asset or start a project, including costs, taxes, delivery charges, etc.

Outplacement
A benefit offered by a downsizing employer to assist former employees in re-entering the job market. Assistance can include job training, resume workshops, interview practice and career counseling.

Output tax
In the UK, the amount of VAT (Value Added Tax) a company or business adds to the price of its products or services.

Outside shareholder
A shareholder who doesn't own more than 50% of a company's shares.

Outsourcing
Contracting out non-core functions, such as payroll, benefits administration or manufacturing, to save money and focus on what the company does best.

Outstanding shares
Also called Outstanding Stock. A company's ordinary shares which have been issued and are owned by investors.

Outward investment
Investments which are made abroad.

Overage
A company's surplus, such as money or goods, which is available but exceeds the amount needed or required.

Overallotment
On the Stock Market, the offering for sale of more shares, etc., than are actually available, in the anticipation that some orders will be cancelled.

Overbought
On the Stock Market. a situation in which there has been too much buying of shares, etc., which has therefore caused prices to rise too high.

Overcapitalised
Refers to a business which has been provided with more money than it needs. To overestimate the capital value of a business.

Overdraft
Refers to the amount of money that is owed to a bank because withdrawals from an account exceed deposits. An arrangement in which a bank extends credit to a customer, usually up to a maximum amount.

Overhead
An expense that cannot be attributed to any one single part of the company's activities.

Overmanned
A situation in which there are more workers than are needed for a job.

Overproduction
Overproduction, oversupply or excess of supply refers to excess of supply over demand of products being offered to the market. This leads to lower prices and/or unsold goods along with the possibility of unemployment. The demand side equivalent is underconsumption; some consider supply and demand two sides to the same coin – excess supply is only relative to a given demand, and insufficient demand is only relative to a given supply – and thus consider overproduction and under consumption equivalent.

Overproduction is often attributed as due to previous overinvestment – creation of excess productive capacity, which must then either lie idle (or under capacity), which is unprofitable, or produce an excess supply.

Overriding commission
A commission paid to an agency office manager based on business created by agents who work at that office.

Over-the-counter market
A communications network, supervised by the National Association of Securities Dealers (NASD), which trades bonds, non-listed stocks, and other securities.

Overtime

Overtime is the amount of time someone works beyond normal working hours. Normal hours may be determined in several ways:

1. by custom (what is considered healthy or reasonable by society),
2. by practices of a given trade or profession,
3. by legislation,
4. by agreement between employers and workers or their representatives.

Overtrading

A situation which occurs when a company expands its business too quickly and does not have enough capital to pay expenses, such as debts, wages, etc., which often results in liquidation.

Own brand

Known as House Brands in the US and Home Brands in Australia. Products which are sold by a retailer under the retailer's own name, rather than the name of the manufacturer.

Owner-operator

A self-employed commercial truck or lorry driver who uses their own vehicle to run a business.

P

P and P (P&P)

Postage and Packing. In the UK, The cost of packing and sending goods, usually added to the price of mail-order goods.

P/E ratio (price per earnings)

The P/E ratio is an important indicator as to how the investing market views the health, performance, prospects and investment risk of a public company listed on a stock exchange (a listed company). The P/E ratio is also a highly complex concept - it's a guide to use alongside other indicators, not an absolute measure to rely on by itself. The P/E ratio is arrived at by dividing the stock or share price by the earnings per share (profit after tax and interest divided by the number of ordinary shares in issue). As earnings per share are a yearly total, the P/E ratio is also an expression of how many years it will take for earnings to cover the stock price investment. P/E ratios are best viewed over time so that they can be seen as a trend. A steadily increasing P/E ratio is seen by the investors as increasingly speculative (high risk) because it takes longer for earnings to cover the stock price. Obviously whenever the stock price changes, so does the P/E ratio. More meaningful P/E analysis is conducted by looking at earnings over a period of several years. P/E ratios should also be compared over time, with other company's P/E ratios in the same market sector, and with the market as a whole. Step by step, to calculate the P/E ratio:

1. Establish total profit after tax and interest for the past year.
2. Divide this by the number of shares issued.
3. This gives you the earnings per share.
4. Divide the price of the stock or share by the earnings per share.
5. This gives the Price/Earnings or P/E ratio.

Package deal

A set of several products which are offered for sale and must be bought in a combined package.

Packaging

Promoting the product on the shelf and protecting the product during shipment. Designing a package also includes consideration or size and weight to make transportation and storage more effective and efficient (as in sizing containers to fit neatly onto pallets).

Page break

On a computer screen, a mark which indicates where a new page will be printed in a document.

Page traffic

In computing, the number of times a web page has been visited.

Paid-up capital
The total amount of money which has actually been paid in full by shareholders for their shares.

Paid-up policy
An insurance policy on which no more premiums are required, and the policy is considered paid in full and still remains in force.

Paid-up share
A share for which the shareholder has paid the full amount, as stated in the contract.

Palm top
A small computer which fits into the palm of the hand.

Pan-european
Relating to all, or most of, the countries in Europe.

Pants
Street slang now mainstream, referring to anything of very poor quality. Interestingly the term first appeared in the late 1800s, based on the word 'knickers' as an expression of contempt or ridicule.

Paper loss
In business, a loss which has occurred and appears in a company's accounts, but has not yet been realised until a transaction has been made, e.g. the sale of an asset which has lost value.

Paper profit
A profit which has been made but has not yet been realised until a share, etc., has been sold.

Paper-pusher
An office worker who has a boring job dealing with paperwork all day.

Par value (bond)
The face value of a bond, usually $1,000 for corporate bonds, and generally higher denominations for many government bonds.

Paradigm
A way of thinking about a given subject that defines how one views events, relationships, ideas, etc. within the boundaries of that subject.

Paradigm shift
Term first used by Thomas Kuhn in 1962 to describe when an important or significant change occurs in the perception of things. A sudden change in point of view.

Paralegal
A legal assistant who is not a qualified lawyer, but who is trained to work in or with the law.

Parallel market
A country's separate market which deals in goods and currencies outside the country's normal official government controls.

Parastatal
In certain countries, a company or organisation which is partially or fully owned and controlled by the government.

Parent company
A company or organisation which owns more than 50% of the voting shares in another company, therefore the Parent Company controls management and operations in the other (subsidiary) company.

Pareto chart
A quality assurance tool that ranks information, like reasons for certain problems, in descending order. The goal is to identify the most serious

problems so improvements can be made.

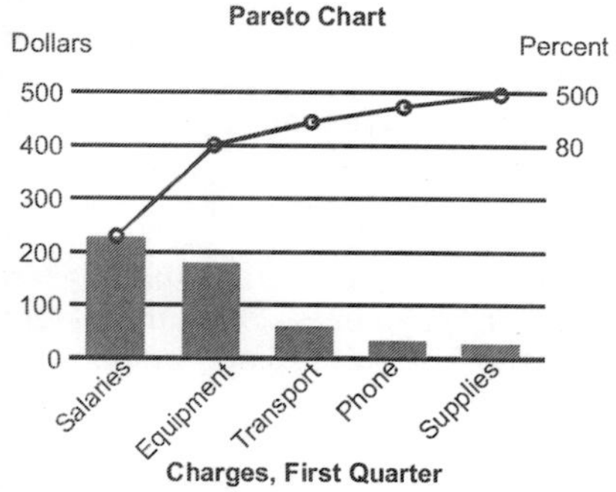

Pareto principle

The idea that a few root problems are responsible for the large majority of consequences. The Pareto principle is derived from the work of Vilfredo Pareto, a turn-of-the-century Italian economist who studied the distributions of wealth in different countries. He concluded that a fairly consistent minority, about 20% of people, controlled the large majority, about 80% of a society's wealth. This same distribution has been observed in other areas and has been termed the Pareto principle. It is defined by J.M. Juran as the idea that 80% of all effects are produced by only 20% of the possible causes.

Parkinson's law

A humorous and generally true observation by Cyril Northcote Parkinson (British historian 1909-1993) that capacity or time is inevitably filled, for example: 'Work will expand so as to fill the time available for its completion'.

Part exchange

Known in the US as Trade-In. A payment method, usually when purchasing a car, in which the buyer gives something they own, for example a car, as part payment to the vendor for the more expensive item. The balance is usually paid in cash or with a loan.

Participating performance share

A type of share/stock which gives a company's shareholder the right to receive dividends and also extra payments relating to the company's profits.

Partnership

A business which is owned by two or more people, all sharing the profits and responsibility for managing the business.

Part-time worker

Someone who works less hours than a full time employee on a permanent basis for a company, usually for a set number of hours a week.

Party plan

Also called Party Selling. A method of marketing in which agents host parties, usually at someone's home, to demonstrate and sell products to invited potential customers.

Pascal

A computer language which is used to write Programmes, also used in teaching Programmeming.

Passing trade

Describes customers who go into a shop, public house, etc., because they notice it as they are passing by.

Passive exporter

An organisation which awaits orders or comes across them by choice.

Patent

An official document which grants an inventor or manufacturer sole rights to an invention or product.

Patent pending
A phrase sometimes printed on goods to show that a patent has been applied for but not yet granted.

Paternity leave
The right of male employees, to take time off from his job following the birth of his baby. Entitlement to Paternity Leave depends on how long they have been with their employer.

Paternity pay
An employee benefit paid to husband of pregnant women so that he can take time off from his job after the birth of the baby to give support to the mother. Entitlement to Paternity Pay depends on how long the person has been with his employer.

Patron
A person who purchases goods or services, often on a regular basis, from a shop or company. A benefactor or sponsor who supports and/or gives money to an individual or an organisation, such as a charity.

Pawnbroker
A money lender who lends cash at a high rate of interest in exchange for the borrowers personal possessions, such as jewellery, as security, which is returned when the loan is fully paid. If the loan is not repaid the Pawnbroker sells the item.

Payable to bearer
A cheque, security, etc., which can be exchanged for money by the person in possession.

Pay-as-you-go
Refers to a method of paying for a service as you use it, such as mobile phone credit. Also can be used to pay debts as they are incurred.

Paye
Pay As You Earn. In the UK, a system of paying income tax, which is deducted from an employees salary by an employer and paid to the government.

Paying agent
An agent, usually a bank, that makes dividend payments to shareholders on behalf of the issuing company.

Payment by results
A system of paying employees according to the amount of work they do. Therefore, the bigger the volume of work output, the bigger the salary.

Payout ratio
The ratio found by dividing the dividends per share by earnings per share (Shows how well earnings support dividends, or how secure the dividend is. The lower the ratio, the more secure the dividend.).

Pay-per-click
Internet ad model used to direct traffic to websites. Advertisers pay the website owner when the ad is clicked. Search engines provide advertisers the opportunity to bid on keyword phrases relevant to their target market.

Pay-per-click
Online advertising payment model in which payment is based on qualifying click-throughs. A typical PPC agreement has the advertiser paying for clicks to the destination site based on a prearranged per-click rate. Popular PPC advertising options include search engines (right sidebar on Google). Paying per click is different than paying per impression which generates lower-quality traffic/ leads.

Pay-per-impression

Online advertising payment mode in which payment is based on how often the "publisher" (e.g., web site where you purchase a banner ad) shows your banner ad on their web site (e.g., an "impression"). Typically, prices are set per one thousand exposures.

Payroll

Documentation created and maintained by the employer containing such information as hours worked, salaries, wages, commissions, bonuses, vacation/sick pay, contributions to qualified health and pension plans, net pay and deductions.

PDA

Personal Digital Assistant. A small hand-held electronic device that is used for storing information and can serve as a telephone, diary, alarm clock, fax, etc.

Pecking order

The hierarchy in businesses, organisations, etc, i.e., the order of people at different ranks.

Pecuniary

Relating to, or involving money.

Peer appraisal

A performance assessment given by an employee's peers who have observed the employee's job performance.

Peer group

A social group of equals, for example, in age, social class, education, etc. A group of products or businesses which are similar.

Peer-to-peer

Computer systems which act as servers and are connected to each other via the Internet, allowing people to share share files, so there is no need for a central computer.

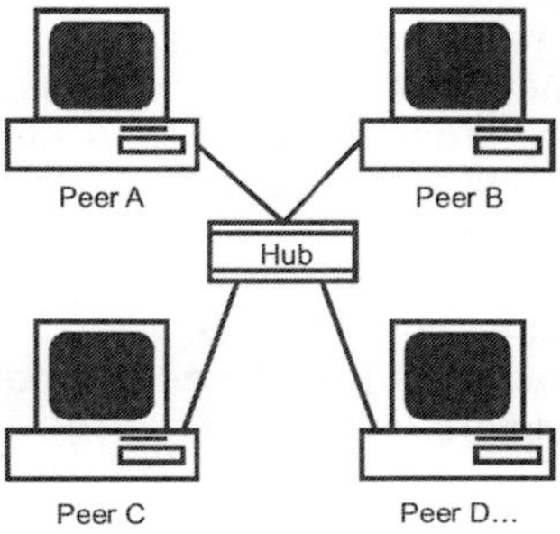

Pen portrait

A description of a person, a 'character sketch in words', now commonly a person-profile used for audience targeting purposes (marketing, recruitment, etc), although the expression dates back to the 1800s, originally referring to a description of a person, so as to produce a picture in the mind. 'Pen Picture' was an early alternative term.

Penalty clause

A clause in a contract which states that a specified sum of money must be paid by the party who breaks the contract.

Penetration

Process by which the marketers attempts to increase sales of an existing product in existing markets, thus minimizing risk. It's also a pricing strategy designed to price a product or service at the lowest potential price to break into a market. Often, it's slightly below that of the lowest-price competitor's product, or at a level that's perceived as low.

Penetration price

The charging of a low price in order to gain volume sales conducted under conditions of little product uniqueness and elastic demand patterns.

Penetration pricing
The practice of charging a low price for a new product for a short period of time in order to establish a market share and attract customers.

Penny share
Describes shares which have a very low value and therefore appeal to speculators.

Pen-pusher
An employee with a boring job whose work consists of dealing with unimportant documents, paperwork, etc.

Pension
A private or government fund from which regular payments are made to a person who has retired from work, or who is considered too ill to carry on working.

Pension fund
A fund set up to collect money on a regular basis from employers and employees, which pays the employees pension when they retire from work.

Peppercorn rent
In the UK, a very low or nominal payment, which was originally a single peppercorn, made to secure a lease.

Per capita
For each person in the population.

Per diem
Latin for 'Per Day'. Often refers to money paid to employees for daily expenses or reimbursements.

Percent chart (p chart)
A control chart that determines the stability of a process by finding what percentage of total units in a sample are defective.

Perception (perceptual process)
A process by which consumers make sense of stimuli they get from not only marketer's promotional messages, but also unmet needs (such as a growling stomach to remind them to eat). There are 3 steps in the process: sensing (getting the attention of the customer), selecting (deciding to figure out what it means), and interpreting (assignment meaning and whether to take action).

Perfect competition
Describes a market in which no one can influence prices because there is enough information about a product to prevent control by an individual or a single organisation.

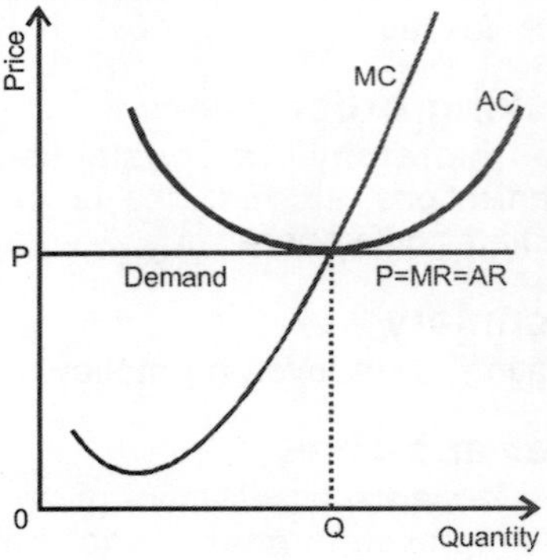

Perfect storm
Coincidentally arising circumstances combining to produce a disastrous effect. This is an allusion to weather factors, commonly applied to economic or trading situations, but applicable to any disaster or chaotic outcome resulting from forces or effects whose combination and timing has not been thought likely or anticipated at all.

Performance Evaluation Review Technique (PERT)

A management scheduling tool which charts the tasks involved in a project, showing the sequence of the work, the time needed for each task, etc.

Performance appraisal

A periodic review and evaluation of an individual's job performance.

Performance improvement

A plan to improve an employee's performance in which the performance problem is identified, modified and monitored.

Performance management

The process of maintaining or improving employee job performance through the use of performance assessment tools, coaching and counseling. The ultimate goal is to better meet organizational objectives.

Performance planning

An organization-wide plan to manage employees and their performance wherein goals are set for employees, departments and the organization as a whole.

Performance-related pay

A scheme set up in the workplace in which the employees get paid according to how well they perform in their job.

Peripatetic

Working or travelling from place to place, staying at different locations for a short period, such as, and especially as a teacher does, in working at more than one school. The teacher analogy is apt since the word derives from the Greek peripatetikos, and the earlier peripatein, which referred specifically to the teaching style of Aristotle (384-322 BC, Greek philosopher, student of Plato, teacher of Alexander the Great), who walked about while he talked. The ancient Greek prefix peri means around, or round, and patein means to tread.

Perishability

products and services that worsen in quality over time, thus reducing their value. In addition to fresh vegetables, fruits, bread, and milk, consider airline ticket fare promotions with an expiration/ending date.

Perishables

Describes food, such as fruit, meat, fish, dairy products, etc., which will decay or spoil rapidly.

Perjury

The criminal offence of knowingly telling a lie (with intent to influence the outcome of the hearing) in a court of law after having taken an oath or affirmation. It closely relates to and is often implicit within the offence of perverting the course of justice, which in the UK technically carries a maximum penalty of life imprisonment. The word perjury derives from Latin perjurium, meaning false oath, similar to jury which comes from jurare, meaning to swear.

Permatemp

A person who works for an organisation on a long-term contractual basis, but who is not a permanent employee.

Permission marketing

Building an ongoing relationship of increasing depth with customers based on approval to send or receive email newsletters, catalogs, and other promotional incentives to gain brand recognition and status. Mostly used by on-line marketers to invite consumers to take part in defining the range of services to be offered.

Permission marketing

Building an ongoing relationship of increasing depth with customers based on approval to send or receive email newsletters, catalougs, and other promotional incentives to gain brand recognition and status. Mostly used by on-line marketers to invite consumers to take part in defining the range of services to be offered.

Personal action

A type of court case in which an individual claims damages for personal injury, damage to his property, etc.

Personal allowance

Known as Personal Exemption in the US. The amount of income an individual can earn in a year before paying tax.

Personal assistant

PA. A person who works for one person, often an executive, in an organisation, performing secretarial and administrative duties.

Personal day

When an employee is permitted to have time off work to deal with personal matters.

Personal development

Also called Self-Development. Acquiring abilities, skills, knowledge, etc., in order to enhance one's performance and self-perception.

Personal information manager

Computer software which handles personal information, such as names, addresses, memos, lists, e-mails, etc.

Personal liability

An individual's legal responsibility in the event of injury to someone, damage to property and/or the debts of their own company.

Personnel

The people who work for a business or organisation. An administrative department in an organisation which deals with employees and often liaises between departments.

Persuasion/The three modes of Persuasion

Aristotle's 2,300 years-old three principles model for communications which successfully move an audience to action or change: 1 Ethos: The integrity of the communicator. 2. Pathos:The emotional effect (of communicator and message) on the listener/reader/audience. 3. Logos: The relevance and strength of the message content.

Pest analysis

Political Economical Social and Technological Analysis. A business tool which is used in strategic planning and helps to understand the environmental influences on a business or orgasnisation.

Peter principle

Formulated by Canadian author Laurence J Peter (1919-1990): 'In a hierarchy, every employee tends to rise to his level of incompetence'. The theory that employees rise in rank in an organisation until they are finally promoted to a level, and remain there, at which they do not have the ability to do their job.

Petrodollar

Term coined by professor of economics Ibrahim Oweiss in the 1970s which describes the large amounts of money earned by oil production in OPEC

(Organisation of the Petroleum Exporting Countries) countries.

Petty cash
A small amount of cash kept by a business to pay for small purchases.

Phablet
A tablet computer that is also a phone. Or a phone that is also a tablet computer. This term emerged in 2012/13 with the launch of the technology to which it refers. A word formed like this (i.e., a combination of parts of the two words/things it refers to - in this case, phone and a tablet) is called a phablet.

Pharmaceutical
Relating to or engaged in the process of making and selling medicinal drugs.

Philanthropy/philanthropist
Promotion of the welfare of others, typically through financial provision (a philanthorpist is one who does this). From the Greek philanthropos, meaning man-loving.

Philology
The branch of knowledge which deals with the study of the history of language and literature. Historical linguistics.

Phishing
A type of fraud carried out on the internet by sending people legitimate-looking e-mails asking for their personal information, such as bank account details, passwords, etc., and using them to steal their money.

Photocall
A planned and announced occasion during which celebrities, politicians, products launches, etc., have photographs taken by the press and other media for publicity purposes.

Physical capital
Refers to a company's assets which are used in a production process, such as machinery, buildings, materials, etc.

Physical distribution
Transporting and storing of goods as a part of the commercialization schedule. This is not to be confused with Exposure, which is where the customer wants/expects the product to be available for possession utility

Picket
A person, or persons, posted at the entrance of a place of work which is affected by a strike, in order to stop people entering the premises.

Pictogram
Also called a Pictograph. A graphic symbol or diagram which represents a concept, an amount, an activity, etc., in pictures.

Pie chart
A chart that compares groups of data to the whole data set by showing each group as a "slice" of the entire "pie." Pie charts are particularly useful for investigating what percentage each group represents.

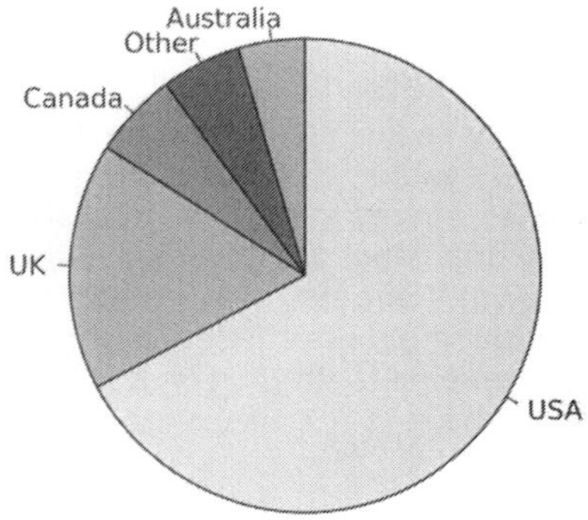

Piece rate
A payment system in which employees are paid a fixed rate for each item they produce.

Piecework
Work in which payment is based on the amount of work done regardless of the time it takes to do it.

Piggyback
A system which rides on the back of an existing system, e.g. a loan or mortgage or an advertising campaign.

Pin
Personal Identification Number. A number given by a bank to a customer so the customer can access their bank account using an ATM (cash machine), or use their credit/debit card in retail outlets.

Ping
Packet INternet Groper. An Internet Programme which is used to check if another computer on a network is working. To contact someone on a computer.

Pink collar
Describes jobs which were once traditionally done by women, such as nursing, secretarial, teaching, etc.

Pink sheets
Formally known as Pink Quote. In the US, a system displaying over-the-counter shares, which is published every day. Most companies listed on the Pink Sheets are very small and do not meet the minimum requirements for trading on the Stock Exchange.

Pink slip
In the US, an official notice of job termination given to an employee.

Pinning
Every time an individual pins an article or image, it gets shared with others that have chosen to follow that account. Followers can then "like" a pin and continue sharing.

Piracy
The unauthorised copying of CDs, DVDs, computer Programmes, etc., in order to sell them or give them away.

Pixel
Short for Picture Element. The smallest element of an image displayed on a computer screen. The quality of the image depends on the number of pixels per square inch, i.e., the more pixels the higher the resolution.

Place mix
Those activities involving distribution (moving the product from producer to consumer through channel members called wholesalers and retailers) and exposure (researching and delivering the product where the customers wants or expects it to be available). Marketers enroll channel members based on their ability to perform marketing activities more effectively and efficiently than they can.

Plain language
Represented notably by the Plain Language Movement, and the Plain Language Information and Action Network (PLAIN), in the late 1900s Plain Language became a generally recognized technical term for the advocation and use of clear explanations, descriptions, instructions, etc., in official documents and other communications, which frequently use goobledegook or 'officialese', i.e., language which is overly complex and/or containing confusing jargon and abbreviations,

etc.

Plaintiff

A person who brings a lawsuit against someone else in a court of law.

Plan sponsor

An entity that has adopted and has maintained an employee-benefit plan. The plan sponsor is often an employer, but may be a union or a professional association. The Plan Sponsor is responsible for determining employee participation and the amount of benefits involved.

Plan-Do-Check-Act (PDCA) cycle

A four-step improvement process originally conceived of by Walter A. Shewhart. The first step involves planning for the necessary improvement; the second step is the implementation of the plan; the third step is to check the results of the plan; the last step is to act upon the results of the plan. It is also known as the Shewhart cycle, the Deming cycle, and the PDCA cycle.

Planned economy

A country's economic system controlled by the government, which makes all the decisions about production, distribution and consumption of goods and services.

Planogram

In retailing, a drawing or diagram which shows when and how products should be displayed in a store.

Plasma

Interestingly, in physics, plasma is the often overlooked fourth state of matter, aside from solid, liquid and gas. Plasma is ionized gas containing free electrons, making it responsive to electromagnetism, and conductive of electricity, in turn enabling it to take a very visible physical shape unlike other forms of gas. The stars are made of plasma; so is lightening and the Northen Lights (Aurora Borealis). Plasma display screens also basically employ this effect.

Plenary/Plenary session

Plenary essentially means full or complete. In the context of formal organized gatherings it means fully attended by everyone together. The term 'plenary session' is very commonly used in business and management to refer to a session which all attendees attend at a conferences or other event, notably to differentiate from smaller sessions of sub-groups concerened with different topics and held in different locations/ rooms. Separately plenary refers to something or someone having a complete or absolute quality, such as an official with plenary (full and complete) power.

Plimsoll

Named after merchant Samuel Plimsoll. International Load line or Waterline on the hull of every cargo ship, which indicates the maximum depth to which a ship can be safely loaded with cargo.

Plutocracy

A government which is controlled by wealthy people.

PMI

Purchasing Managers Index. Published every month, an economic measure relating to manufacturing. A PMI over 50 indicates industry is expanding.

Poison pill

A business strategy used by a company to avoid being taken over by another company, e.g., the selling of assets, shares, etc., to make the company look less attractive to the potential buyer.

Poisoned chalice
A job or situation which seems good at first but soon becomes unpleasant or harmful.

Policy deployment
Another name for hoshin planning.

Political correctness
The practice of not using words, expressions, actions, etc., which could cause offence to minority groups. PC could also stand for Political Claptrappers - People who insist on political correctness from everyone at all times, even in their private lives.

Polycentrism
A host country orientation on a subsidiary basis.

Polymath
A person of great knowledge and varied learning. Loosely from Greek poly, many, and manthanein, learn.

Ponzi scheme
Named after Charles Ponzi, a fraudulent investment scheme, similar to a Pyramid Scheme, in which people are offered high returns, while their money is used to pay earlier investors, so that later investors often end up with little or no return because new investors can't be found.

Poorgeoisie
People who are rich but pretend they don't have much money.

Population
Total set of items from which a sample set is taken.

Pop-under
On a computer, an advertisement, etc., which comes up on the screen behind the web page which is being viewed, and does not appear until the page is closed.

Pop-up
On a computer screen, a small window containing an advertisement, etc., which appears on a page on top of the content which is being viewed.

Pork barrel
A US political term used when government funds are used for projects which benefit certain local groups or constituents, and show their political representative in a good light.

Port of entry
A place in a country where people and/or goods can officially leave or enter.

Portal
On the Internet, a website, which is the point of entry to other websites, and offers services such as e-mail, news, shopping, etc.

Porter's generic strategies
Named after economist Michael Porter. Describes strategies used by companies to achieve a strong advantage against competitors.

Portfolio
A collection of investments, such as shares, bonds, etc., which are owned by an individual or organisation.

Portfolio career
Concept attributed to guru Charles Handy in the 1990s. A career in which a person pursues several jobs at the same time, rather than working full-time for one particular company.

Portmanteau word
A word formed from parts of two separate words, whose combination

generally produces the meaning also. Many new management and business words, especially slang and jargon, enter the language in this way, and some become popular and well-established.

Pos

Point of Sale or POP (point of purchase) – Business or market where products and services are transacted. Also used to convey temporary displays used by marketers to showcase products. Soda companies use POP/POS in advance of sporting or holiday events to feature their products in other parts of the store or warehouse. Another example is gas station pump toppers that advertise daily food or drink specials inside the store.

Positioning

Term used to describe the way a company, product, service, etc., is marketed in order to make it stand out from the competition by choosing a niche according to brand, price, packaging, etc.

Positioning (or Framing)

How potential buyers see the product, relative to the position of competitors. It happens in the minds of the target market. It is the aggregate perception the market has of a particular company, product, or service in relation to their perceptions of the competitors. Repositioning involves changing the identity of a product, relative to the identity of competing products, in the collective minds of the target market. It's also physical product placement/location in stores.

Positive language

Art of using words or phrases to create a positive image about a product, service, or organization. It tells customers what you CAN do rather than can't do.

Positive sum game

A win-win situation in which both sides involved in a business transaction, etc., can profit.

Postage and packing

Called Postage and Handling in the US. The cost of wrapping an item and sending it by post. Often used for mail order goods.

Post-date

To insert a future date on a cheque or document at the time of writing, so it becomes effective at that later date.

Post-fordism

Also called Flexible Modernity. An industrial production system which has changed from mass production in large factories, such as Ford Motors, and moved towards smaller flexible, more specialised manufacturing systems.

Power brand

A brand of goods, etc., which is well known and has a large share of the consumer market for a long period of time.

Power lunch

A business meeting held over lunch in which important decisions may be made, or high level discussions carried out.

Power nap

A short nap. usually lasting about 20 minutes, taken during the day, that refreshes a person so they can carry on working.

Prairie dogging

This occurs when someone who works in an open office, which is divided into cubicles, drops something or shouts and everyone else pops their heads above the dividing walls to see what is happening.

Precedent

A past act or decision which is used as an example to decide the outcome of similar subsequent acts.

Predatory lending

The often illegal practice of lending money to people who the lender knows are unable to pay back the loan, such as low-income house-owners, who subsequently may lose their homes which they have used as security against the loan.

Predatory pricing

Occurs when a firm charges extremely low prices for a product with the intent of driving competition out of business or out of a specific market. Prices then tend to return to normal once the competitor has been eliminated. While illegal and unethical, it's difficult to prove in court.

Predatory pricing

Also known as Destroyer Pricing. A situation where a company charges very low prices for goods or services in order to put its competitors out of business, after which prices will be raised.

Preemptive marketing

Building relationships with consumers/ clients BEFORE they need your services. This can include introducing an organization's products/services towards building preference, loyalty, even conviction of not having to search for alternatives when the need arises.

Preference share

Also called Preferred Shares. A type of share which pays the owner a fixed dividend before other share owners are paid their dividends. Preference Shareholders do not usually have the right to vote at shareholders meetings.

Preferential creditor

A creditor who has the right to receive payment of debts, before other creditors, from a bankrupt company.

Preferred stock

Stock whose holders have precedence over common stock in claiming dividends and assets.

Pre-market

On the Stock Market, trading which takes place between members before the official opening time.

Premium bond

A bond whose value is greater than its face value.

Premium income

The revenue recieved by an insurance company from its customers.

Premium only plan (POP)

Section 125 is part of the IRS Code that allows employees to convert a taxable cash benefit (salary) into non-taxable benefits, so they may pay for qualified benefit premiums before any taxes are deducted from their paychecks. The Premium only plan allows for certain employee paid group insurance premiums to be paid with pre-tax dollars.

Present value

The amount invested at a certain interest rate.

Presenteeism
The opposite of Absenteeism. A situation where employees work very long hours or come to work when they are ill and their performance is below standard, which can have a negative effect on the business.

Press agent
A person employed to arrange publicity for an individual or organisation, for example in newspapers, on television, etc.

Press conference
Called A News Conference in the US. A meeting held by a business, organisation, individual, etc., to which journalists are invited to hear a public announcement, and usually to ask questions.

Pressure group
An organised group of people, or lobbyists, who campaign to influence businesses, governments, etc., to change their policies.

Prestige pricing
Setting a high price based on the quality and the demand for which consumers are willing to spend. For example: Starbucks gives a feeling of a high end product by its packaging, delivery and product promise, based on years or consistent promotion in its iconic coffee houses as "creating a product of excellence."

Price
The amount of money required to purchase something or to bribe someone. The amount agreed upon between the buyer and seller in a commercial transaction.

Price bundling
Selling 2 or more goods or services as a single package, as in Taco Bell offers 2 hard tacos, a burrito, and a drink in a package for 1 price (usually a saving if you add up the pricesof each individual item).

Price ceiling
The maximum price which can be charged bearing in mind competition and what the market can bear.

Price control
Maximum and minimum price limitations, often during periods of inflation, which a government puts on essential goods and/or services.

Price discrimination
The practice of a provider to charge different prices for the same product to different customers.

Price escalation
The difference between the domestic price and the target price in foreign markets due to the application of duties, dealer margins and/or other transaction costs.

Price fixing
The, often illegal, practice of prices being fixed, by agreement, by competing companies who provide the same goods or services as each other.

Price floor
The minimum price which can be charged bounded by product cost.

Price gouging
Controversial strategy that sellers sometimes use to charge higher than normal prices for products and services, especially when there is little or no competition.

Price mechanism
Describes the way prices for goods and services are influenced by the

changes in supply and demand. Shortages cause a rise in prices, surpluses cause a fall in prices.

Price mix
Those objectives and strategies marketers apply to setting and managing profits for itself and each channel member. Pricing policies vary among organizations based on internal goals, ROI(return on investment), cost of goods, etc.

Price support
A system in which a minimum price is set by a government, and sometimes subsidised, for a product or commodity.

Price tactic
Justifying the use of low price as the principle reason why consumers will buy a product, as opposed to sustainable features or benefits. A short term remedy vs. strategy.

Price taker
A company or individual whose selling or buying of goods and services has little or no influence over prices.

Price-earnings ratio (P/E)
The ratio found by dividing market price per share by earnings per share (This ratio indicates what investors think of the firm's earnings' growth and risk prospects.).

Price-earnings ratio to earnings per share growth
The ratio found by dividing a stock's price-earnings ratio by its earnings per share growth rate, indicating the company's profits relative to investors' expectations.

Price-earnings relative
The relative amount found by dividing a stock's price-earnings ratio by that of the market as given by a widespread market yardstick such as the S&P 500 or the Value Line index (This relative suggests to the investor whether his investment's price is reasonable compared to the market. Also can be used for historical comparison with P/E relatives of recent years.).

Price-to-book ratio
The ratio found by dividing a stock's market price per share by its book value (defined as being assets minus all liabilities) per share (This ratio measures the stock's value relative to its net assets. A high ratio, for instance, might suggest that a stock is overvalued.).

Price-to-cash-flow ratio
The ratio found by dividing a stock's price per share by its cash flow per share (This ratio, similar in type to the price-earnings ratio, serves as a measure of investors' expectations on a firm's future financial success.).

Pricing
To evaluate the price of a product by taking into account the cost of production, the price of similar competing products, market situation, etc.

Primary data
Data which is collected by a company, business, etc., itself for its own use, using questionnaires, case studies, interviews, etc., rather than using other sources to collect the data.

Primary demand
Consumers demand for a generic product rather than a particular brand.

Primary market
Group of consumers targeted to receive the major share of a marketer's

attention, resources, and media expenditures.

Primary research
Also called Field Research. The collection of new or primary data through questionnaires, telephone interviews, etc., for a specific purpose.

Prime cost
In manufacturing, etc., the cost of direct materials and labour required to make a product.

Principal
In finance, principal (the principal, or the principal sum/amount) refers to an amount of money loaned or borrowed. The term is used particularly when differentiating or clarifying an amount of money (loaned/borrowed/invested) excluding interest payments. Separately, more generally, in business the term 'the principal' refers to the owner of a business or brand, as distinct from an agent or representative, such as a franchisee.

Private brand
Also called House Brand. A product which is owned by a retailer, and therefore has its own brand label on it, rather than the manufacturer or producer.

Private company
Called A Private Corporation in the US. A company whose shares are not offered to the general public on the open market.

Private corporation
A corporation which does not offer stock for public sale (Private corporations are not required by law to provide information about their financial conditions.).

Private equity
Describes companies shares which are not available for investors to buy and sell on the Stock Market, because the company is unlisted.

Private sector
The part of a country's economy which is owned and run for profit by private businesses rather than being government controlled.

Privatise/privatize
(UK/US English spelling) To change or sell a government controlled business or industry to privately owned companies.

Privity
A legal relationship between two parties in a contract.

Pro
Public Relations Officer. Also known as a Chief Communications Officer. A person whose job is to promote and establish a good relationship between their client- an organisation or an individual - and the public.

Pro bono
Short for Pro Bono Publico (Latin for 'The Public Good'). Work carried out in the public interest for no fee or compensation, e.g. by a lawyer.

Pro forma invoice
An invoice prepared by a supplier describing goods, price, quantity, etc., which is sent to the buyer before the goods are supplied.

Pro rata
In proportion to. Refers to the division of costs, profits, income, etc., depending on the size of each persons share in the whole amount.

Pro tem
Temporarily. For the time being.

Probation
A trial period during which an individual's suitability for a job or membership to a club, etc., is tested.

Probationary arrangement
An agreement between an employer and employee that the employee will work for a set amount of time on a trial or probationary period.

Probity
Complete integrity. Having strong moral principals and total honesty.

Process capability
1. A statistical measure indicating the inherent variation for a given event in a stable process, usually defined as the process width divided by 6 sigma.
2. Competence of the process, based on tested performance, to achieve certain results.

Process capability index
Measurement indicating the ability of a process to produce specified results. Cp and Cpk are two process capability indices.

Proctor
Someone who supervises students, etc., taking exams to prevent cheating. Also a person or agent employed to manage the affairs of another person.

Procurement
Process (acquisition) of obtaining goods (materials) and services (expertise) from middlemen/suppliers. This is a major component of the "Marketing Concept: define customers" unmet needs; allocate resources; make a profit.

Product
Whatever the customer thinks, feels, or expects from an item or idea. From a "marketing-oriented" perspective, products should be defined by what they satisfy, contribute, or deliver vs. what they do or the form utility involved in their development. Ex: A dishwasher cleans dishes but it's what the consumer does with the time savings that matters most.

Product adoption curve
Explains that product and services are first purchased and evaluated by innovators and early adopters, after which by early and late majority, and finally laggards.

Product development
Creation of products with new or different characteristics than those already offered. This may involve modification of an existing product or formulation of an entirely new product that satisfies a newly-defined set of customer wants or desires.

Product differentiation
Attributes/qualities that make one product stand apart from both competitors and easily-substitutable alternatives. These may not always be favorable, as in the choice of how to finance a purchase or select a course of treatment for a disease. A major component of a marketer's product mix, usually focusing on a product's unique feature.

Product evangelist
A person who is committed to a promoting a product through demonstrations, talks, blogging, etc.

Product liability
Area of the law in which a manufacturer or retailer is legally responsible for

any damage or injury caused by a defective product.

Product life cycle

The normal stages that a product passes through from development to decline until it becomes obsolete, usually because it has saturated the market because everyone who wants it has purchased it.

Product mix

All of the products or product lines offered by a firm. Some companies have a wide product mix geared toward a diverse consumer group. For example, Procter & Gamble has a product mix that includes detergents, toothpaste, Procter bar soap, deodorants, disposable diapers, coffee, household paper goods, and food products. Some companies have a narrow product mix geared toward a particular market segment, such as the Williams Sonoma catalog that sells gourmet cooking accessories. A product mix is also one of the 4 Ps or the marketing strategy. It includes the product idea (features, accessories, installation, warranty, and product lines), packaging, and labeling.

Product organisation

A form of international organisational structure whereby executives in functional areas are given global responsibility.

Product placement

Also called Embedded Marketing. A type of advertising where a company pays a fee to have one or more of its products used as props in a film or television show.

Product portfolio

A variety of products which are manufactured or distributed by a company or organisation.

Product strategy

A set of decisions regarding alternatives to the target market and the marketing mix given a set of market conditions.

Productivity

The rate at which goods are produced based on how long it takes, how many workers are required, how much capital and equipment is needed, etc.

Professional employer organization (peo)

A staffing service that is contracted to assume the employers responsibilities and risk for his/her workforce. Employees are legally co-employed by the PEO. The PEO is responsible for such actions as the preparation of accurate payroll checks, the remittance of payroll taxes to federal and state jurisdictions and the preparation of various tax information.

Professional liability

The legal liability of a professional, such as a doctor, accountant, lawyer, etc., who causes loss, harm or injury to their clients while performing their professional duties.

Profit

What remains after all costs (direct & indirect) have been covered from the initial selling price.

Profit and loss account (P&L)

One of the three principal business reporting and measuring tools (along with the balance sheet and cashflow statement). The P&L is essentially a trading account for a period, usually a year, but also can be monthly and cumulative. It shows profit performance, which often has little to do with cash, stocks and assets (which must be viewed from a separate perspective using balance sheet and cashflow statement). The P&L typically shows sales revenues, cost of sales/ cost of goods sold, generally a gross profit margin (sometimes called 'contribution'), fixed overheads and or operating expenses, and then a profit before tax figure (PBT). A fully detailed P&L can be highly complex, but only because of all the weird and wonderful policies and conventions that the company employs. Basically the P&L shows how well the company has performed in its trading activities.

Profit margin

The margin found by dividing a firm's post-tax net earnings by sales (Profit margin measures how well a firm can earn money from sales relative to others.).

Profit sharing

An incentive scheme in which a business shares some of its profit , usually in cash or shares, with its employees.

Profit squeeze

A situation in which a company or business makes less profit over a period of time because of rising costs and/or falling prices.

Profit-centre

A business division or department or unit which is responsible for producing a profit, for example a shop unit within a chain of shops, or a branch within a network dealerships. Significantly a Profit-centre business unit will use a 'Profit and Loss Account' as a means of managing and reporting the business. A profit centre is involved in selling to customers.

Profiteer

An organisation or individual who makes excessive profits by charging very high prices for goods which are in short supply.

Programme trading

On the Stock Market, the buying and selling of large amounts of shares by computer, the Programme of which is triggered when trading reaches a certain level of volume.

Prohibitive

Preventing or discouraging something, for example people are discouraged from buying a product because the price is prohibitive, i.e., too high.

Project

A very general term for a task or objective of some complexity and duration, such that it needs properly planning, organizing, resourcing and managing. A small project can easily be part of a person's usual work duties. A large project can be as big as starting a new business, or constructing a skyscraper, or putting a spacecraft on Mars. Typically large projects are established as being separate to usual operational duties and responsibilities of workers, although any job can at any time be extended to include responsibility for the management of a project within it. A project differs from conventional 'work' mainly in being far more firmly structured, scheduled, resourced, and proactive, etc., whereas conventional 'work' is less predictable and tends to be of a more passive, responsive, reactive and flexible nature. Projects may be opportunistic and proactive (such as new product developments, or building something new, or some sort of exploratory research), or a necessary response/reaction to problems, emergencies, failures, etc., (for example a product recall, or a disaster recovery or investigation, or a re-training requirement). Large projects almost inevitably involve a degree of people-management.

Project management

The process of managing and planning a successful project from start to finish, which includes controlling, organizing, managing resources, people, budgets, etc.

Project manager

A person responsible for planning and delivering a large stand-alone task, objective, venture, etc., (a large and complex 'project') or a professional who is skilled in doing this, which generally includes using suitable project management tools and systems, and people-management skills where appropriate. N.B. A person who is instructed to plan and manage a project within his/her conventional work duties is not necessarily, in the usual meaning of the term, a 'project manager'. The term 'project manager' usually refers to a person whose primary responsibility is to manage a stand-alone project which by definition falls outside of conventional and normal operational work duties.

Project sponsor

A person in an organization who instigates or proposes a project, and creates/establishes/agrees the necessary executive approval, funding, resourcing, etc., typically extending to the appointment of the project manager. A project sponsor is usually and crucially responsible for developing and presenting the financial justification for the project, which generally entails outcomes and timescales, and assuming personal accountability for the success of the project.

Prom

Programmemable Read Only Memory. In a computer, a permanent memory chip which can only be recorded on once, by the computer user, not the manufacturer, after which the data is stored and cannot be changed.

PROM

A promotional broadcast on television, radio, etc., advertising a product, TV show, film, etc.

Promotion

The use of marketing and/or advertising to bring attention to a product, brand, service, company, etc., usually in order to increase sales. The raising of an employee to a higher rank in an organisation.

Promotional mix

Combination of one or more promotional elements that a firm uses to communicate with customers: often a mix of personal selling, mass selling (advertising, public relations, and publicity), sales promotion, and direct marketing.

Prompt note

A document sent to someone to remind them when a payment is due on a purchase.

Proof copy

The printed pages of a book, magazine, etc., which is read and corrected (e.g. spelling mistakes) by a Proof Reader before the final printing of all the copies.

Propaganda

Politically motivated publication or writing designed to influence thinking or action, usually in a misleading way.

When carried out by a government or other authority this may also be referred to in more modern terms as 'spin'. The word derives from the Latin name of a Roman Catholic committee responsible for 'propagation of the faith' in the 1600s.

Proprietary trading
The buying and selling of shares, bonds, etc., by a securities firm with its own money for its own profit, rather than for its customers.

Proptype
An original design or working model of something, often used in demonstrations.

Prosecute
To bring a criminal charge against someone in a court of law.

Prospectus
A document published by a company which is offering its shares for sale, disclosing information such as the company's activities, objectives, finances, etc. A book published by a university or school containing information about courses, etc.

Prosumer
Profession/Producer Consumer. A consumer who is involved in the specification of products, or has professional tools and is involved in the the design and manufacture of products.

Protectionism
The policy of a country protecting its own industries against foreign competition by imposing taxes, etc., on imported goods.

Protocol
In computing, a set of rules which determine the way data is transmitted between computers. The code of conduct in an organisation, etc.

Provident fund
A form of retirement savings. An employer and employee pay regular, usually equal, amounts into an investment fund, which is then paid to the employee upon retirement, often in a lump sum.

Proviso
A clause in a contract which makes a condition or stipulation.

Proxy
A person who has been given the authority to act for another person.

Prudence
Aside from its usual general meaning of carefulness in judgment and decision-making, prudence particularly refers to caution in commercial/financial/economic risk-taking, and to the typically great caution exercised by financial folk (accountants and bankers notably) in planning, budgeting, forecasting, granting loans, extending credit, defining standards and policies, and accounting practice as a whole, etc.

Pseudo
Pronounced 'sudo', this is a prefix which can be put before many different words to represent a fake or false quality which often attempts to imitate or behave as the real thing. From Greek pseudos, meaning falsehood.

Pseudonym
a false name, commonly adopted by a writer seeking to hide their true identity.

Psychographic segmentation
The process of identifying and dividing consumers into groups according to

their interests, attitudes, social class, values, personality, etc.

Psychographics

Criteria for segmenting consumers by lifestyle, attitudes, beliefs, values, personality, buying motives, and/or extent of product usage—in essence: activities, interests, and opinions. For example, the market for shampoo may consist of various psychographic segments described by their primary purchase motives (beauty, health, grooming), usage styles (daily, weekly, salon-only), or lifestyle (frequent travelers, parents with young children, empty-nesters). Research studies might focus on what magazines they read, which TV shows they view, and their opinions on the importance of "good grooming."

Psychological contract

Usually expressed as 'the Psychological Contract', this is the understanding between employee(s) and employer as to their mutual expectations arising from the employment relationship. The expectations involve a complex balance of inputs and rewards, including contractually clear elements such as hours and pay, and extend to implications and assumptions about security, loyalty, and other highly subjective factors. The Psychological Contract is a two-way notional agreement between employee and employer, typically analysed from the employee perspective.

Psychological pricing (price ending)

Practice based on a theory that the display of certain types of prices impact retail sales. Often expressed as "odd/even," prices ending in 99-cents drive greater demand to non-rational consumers.

Psychometric test

A test which measures a person's personality, mental ability, knowledge, etc., often used to ascertain whether a potential employee is suitable for a job.

Public company

A company whose shares are traded on the Stock Market.

Public corporation

A corporation which offers stock for public sale (Public corporations are required by law to provide information about their financial condition, operations, and such.).

Public debt

Also known as National Debt. The total amount of money owed by a country's national and local governments.

Public domain

Something that is not protected by copyright and is openly available for anyone to use, look at, etc.

Public employee

A person employed by the government.

Public enterprise

A business or economic activity owned and controlled by the government.

Public issue

When a company offers shares for sale to the public for the first time.

Public liability

When the owner of a business, etc., is responsible for any injury or harm inflicted on a member of the public because of negligence or unsafe products, etc., against which an insurance policy can be obtained by the business.

Public relations

Form of communication that is primarily directed toward gaining understanding and acceptance by vested groups of what the marketer is doing. It often tends to deal with issues rather than specifically with products or services. PR also cannot be controlled by the organization because it is not purchasing the time or space in the media, but it offers legitimacy that advertising cannot claim. The practice of PR is used to build rapport with the various (vested) publics a company, individual, or organization may have (employees, customers, stockholders, voters, competitors, or the general population). Publicity releases, employee-training seminars, and company-produced newsletters, (house organs) are examples of instruments used in public relations.

Public works
Buildings and structures constructed by the government for public use, such as roads, bridges, schools, hospitals, etc.

Publicist
A publicity or press agent who publicises organisations, people, etc.

Publicity
Involves supplying information that is factual, interesting, and newsworthy to media not controlled by the organization (radio, television, magazines, newspapers, and trade journals). It is an uncontrolled method of placing messages in the media because the source does not pay the media for placement. Publicity typically generated from an organization's public relations department and its goal is to gain media coverage. Examples of newsworthy events that may receive media coverage, or publicity, include ground-breaking ceremonies, press conferences, organized protests, or ceremonial appointments or awards. PR/publicity is "doing good — and getting caught."

Puff
In advertising, to exaggerate the qualities of a product, etc., without actually breaking the law.

Pull strategy
Used in marketing to create a demand for a product by means of advertising and promoting to the end consumer, rather than through the marketing channel. To 'pull' the product through from distributor to final consumer.

Pump and dump
The illegal practice of artificially boosting share prices by false and misleading statements in order to sell the originally cheap shares at much higher prices.

Punitive
Inflicting or concerned with punishment, for example punitive taxes, punitive justice.

Punitive damages
Damages awarded, over and above general damages, by a court of law against a defendant who has committed a malicious act which has resulted in injury to a person or damage to property, in order to deter the defendant from committing similar acts in future.

Purchase ledger
A record of a company's accounts which shows amounts owed to suppliers for items purchased on credit.

Purchasing officer
A company employee who is responsible for the purchasing of equipment, materials and services from suppliers and contractors.

Purchasing power
Also called spending power, the amount of goods or services which can be purchased with a particular currency, or more generally, the amount of money a person or group has available to spend on goods and services. The term may also emphasise a group or organization's ability to achieve heavily discounted prices or rates due to the high buying volumes.

Purchasing power parity
The rate at which one unit of currency will purchase the same amount of goods and services as it bought in an equilibrium period, despite differential rates of inflation.

Pure play
Term that relates to a company which deals in one specific line of business, rather than a range of products, services, etc.

Purpose-based marketing (pro-social movement)
Marketing efforts designed to communicate social responsibility ideas that are shared between an organization and its customers. Ex: Panera Bread's "Bakes before sunrise; donated after sunset" campaign.

Purveyor
A company or person who supplies provisions, especially food.

Push system
In production, a system in which the demand for goods is predicted by the company, so more goods are made to keep up with pre-set levels rather than customer demand.

Push/Pull strategies
Customers "pull" products towards themselves (creating channels that until now did not exist), while a producer "pushes" a product toward customers by promoting (advertising, sales promotion and discounts/ allowances) through an existing channel, one channel member at a time.

Put option
The right given a buyer to sell stock at a specified price within a specified period of time.

Put option
An option in a contract giving the holder the right to sell shares, materials, etc., at a specified price at, or up to, a fixed date.

Pyramid scheme
Illegal in several countries, a scheme in which people are paid for recruiting others who pay a fee, part of which goes to the person who recruited them as a commission. In order to get their payment the recruits then have to find new recruits to pay a fee. This goes on until there is no one left to recruit and the people who come into the scheme last end up losing their money. The difference between Pyramid Selling and a Pyramid Scheme is that is that the latter has no product.

Pyramid selling
A system in which people buy the rights (often a franchise) to sell a company's products to other distributors who have been recruited, who then sell the products on to other recruits. This type of selling often ends up with no final buyer for the products. The few people at the top of the pyramid commonly make a lot more money than the many people at the bottom.

Q

QR codes (Quick Response)

Digital graphic links found in magazine ads, webpages, billboards, and practically anywhere a marketer wishes to advertise his business. Read by cell phones and other digital devices with cameras to display additional information or promotional offers to potential customers.

Qualified opinion

A statement written by an independent auditor which accompanies a business's financial statements, saying that the audit has been limited, e.g., because the auditor may not have been able to collect all the information required to carry out a full audit.

Qualifying period

The length of time an employee must serve in a job before being entitled to various benefits, or being able to make a claim against unfair dismissal.

Qualitative

Associated with a thing's quality which cannot be measured, such as feel, image, taste, etc. Describes peoples qualities which cannot be measured, such as knowledge, behaviour, attitude, etc.

Quality

An attribute or level of excellence. The standard of a product, service, etc., as measured against similar products, services, etc. A distinctive characteristic or attribute possessed by someone or something.

Quality assurance

QA. A system in which the delivery of a service or the quality of a product is maintained to a high standard, especially by means of attention to every stage of the process.

Quality audit

An independent investigation and assessment of quality activities and results to determine whether or not the quality plan is effective and appropriate.

Quality circle

Originating in Japan, a group of workers in a company who meet regularly to discuss ways in which to improve working conditions for employees and productivity for the company.

Quality circles

1. Quality improvement teams or groups.
2. In Japan, groups of employees formed for the study of and sharing information regarding quality control issues and theory.

Quality control

The use of techniques and activities that compare actual quality performance with goals and define appropriate action in response to a shortfall.

Quality function deployment

A technique used to translate customer requirements into appropriate goals for each stage of product or service development and output. The two approaches to quality function deployment are known as the House of Quality and the Matrix of Matrices.

Quality improvement

A systematic approach to the processes of work that looks to remove waste, loss, rework, frustration, etc. in order to make the processes of work more effective, efficient, and appropriate.

Quality improvement team

A group of employees that take on a project to improve a given process or design a new process within an organization.

Quality loss function

An algebraic function that illustrates the loss of quality that occurs when a characteristic deviates from its target value. It is expressed often in monetary terms. Dr. Genichi Taguchi coined this term; his work suggests that quality losses vary as the square of the deviation from target.

Quality management

A system to make sure that a product or service meets standards of excellence, and that the process by which the product or service is created is efficient and effective as well. The three key components of this system are quality control, quality assurance and quality improvement.

Quantitive/quantitative

Related to or measured in numbers. Comparison based on quantity rather than quality.

Questionnaire

A form containing a list of research or survey questions for people to answer, so that information can be gathered for analysis

Quick ratio

Same as the Acid Test. The relationship between current assets readily convertible into cash (usually current assets less stock) and current liabilities. A sterner test of liquidity.

Quota

A specific imported amount imposed by one country on another, when once filled cannot be exceeded within a given time. When a quota is in force the price mechanism is not allowed to operate.

Quoted company

A company whose shares are listed on the Stock Exchange.

R

R&d
Research and Development. Investigative work carried out by a business to improve and develop products and processes.

Race relations act
A British government Act, introduced in 1976, making it unlawful to discriminate against someone because of their colour, race, nationality or ethnic origin.

Race to the bottom
A phrase said to be coined by US Supreme Court Justice Louis Brandeis. A situation in which competition between nations could result in lower standards, cheaper wages, poorer working conditions, etc.

Rack rate
The full price of something before discounts have been offered, especially hotel rooms.

Racketeer
A person who makes money through illegal business or crime, such as extortion, bribery, fraud, etc.

Raid
On the Stock Exchange, a situation where an individual or company makes a hostile bid to take over another company by buying a controlling interest in the company's shares.

Rainmaker
An employee, often an executive, who brings a lot of business and income to a company.

Ram
Random Access Memory. In computing, the place where current data is stored while a computer is being used. The data is removed when the computer is switched off.

Random sample
Often used in research, a method of sampling members of a large group, such as a population, in which everyone has an equal chance of being selected.

Random testing
Employer-administered drug and alcohol tests conducted at random intervals.

Range chart
Control chart in which the range of the subgroup is used to track the instantaneous variation within a process, i.e. the variation in the process at any one time, when many input factors would not have time to vary enough to make a detectable difference. Range charts are usually paired with average charts for complete analysis.

Rank and file
The ordinary members of a group, such as enlisted troops in an army, or

members of a union, who have no power.

Rat
Slang term for an informer, or to inform, typically for personal gain. Rat is also a verb, meaning to inform or betray.

Rat race
The exhausting, competitive struggle and routine of working and living in a large town or city.

Rate card
A printed list of charges and details regarding advertising costs on television, radio, websites, newspapers, etc.

Rate of return
The amount of profit or loss generated by an investment, expressed as a percentage of the total sum invested.

Ratify
To sanction formally. Validate an agreement with a vote or signature.

Rating
Broadcast size of an actual listening or viewing audience for a particular Programme or commercial as compared to the size of the potential audience (all households in a geographic area that have broadcast receivers—whether or not these broadcast receivers are turned on). One rating point represents 1% of the households making up the potential audience. Outdoor advertising estimates the number of persons exposed to an outdoor sign. Each outdoor structure is rated in terms of the number of persons who pass by on a daily basis as compared to the entire population in the area where the structure is located.

Rating agency
A company which assesses and rates businesses on their credit-worthiness and/or their ability to repay debts.

Ratings point
The measure of a size of an audience, i.e., one point equals one per cent of all households watching a television Programme or listening to a radio station at a particular time.

Ratio analysis
A study of a company's financial statements which show the relationships between items listed on a balance sheet and gives an indication as to whether the company can meet its current obligations.

Reach
Size of the audience who listen to, read, view or otherwise are exposed to a particular ad message over a defined time period. Reach may be stated either as an absolute number, or as a fraction of a given population (for instance TV households, men, or those aged 25-34).

Reactive marketing
Describes when companies or businesses wait for customers to contact them in order to buy their products or services.

Ready-to-wear
Describes clothing that is produced in standard sizes and designs and sold as finished products in retail outlets.

Real estate
Also called Realty. Property consisting of land with permanent structures on it, such as buildings, walls, fences, etc.

Real rate of return
The percentage of return on an investment over one year after adjustments for inflation or deflation.

Real time
In computing, systems which receive information and update it at the same time.

Ream
500 sheets of paper. A large quantity of written material.

Rebadge
To change the name , brand or logo of an existing product or business, especially cars.

Reboot
To switch a computer off and restart it again immediately.

Rebrand
Change the name, packaging, etc., of an existing product or business and advertise it as new and improved.

Recall
To ask customers to return a product which they have bought because it has been found to be faulty or dangerous.

Recall (Aided and Unaided)
Ascertaining whether potential customers saw/heard a specific product or service advertisement, often conducted via telephone after showing/playing the ad in test markets. Unaided question: "What ads do you recall from your TV viewing last night?" Aided question (often after negative unaided response): "Do you remember any ads for shampoos?"

Recapitalise
To put more money into a business, often one which is facing bankruptcy. To reorganise a company's capital structure by exchanging preferred stock for bonds, usually to reduce taxes.

Receivables
Shown as assets on a balance sheet, money which is owed to a company by customers who have purchased goods or services on credit.

Receiver
An independent person appointed by a court to manage and control the finances, property, etc., of a bankrupt company, who usually sells the company's assets in order to pay the creditors.

Recession
The decline of the economy of a country (or other region) over a period of time, resulting in increased unemployment, reduced productivity, reduced GDP (Gross Domestic Product), falling household income and livings standards, etc. Different nations and financial institutions, bodies, etc., have different definitions of a recession. Many economists and business commentators use the term very loosely without regard to a particular definition, other than it being a period of economic contraction with related factors. A common official definition at national/governmental level is broadly that a recession is: "Two consecutive quarters (i.e., total 6mths) of 'negative growth' (or contraction or reduction) in GDP (Gross Domestic Product)". Aside from the euphemistically unhelpful term 'negative growth' (used by UK governments notably) this definition of recession is open to debate because it is calculated over such a short period and is therefore very finely balanced. This definition tends to increase instances of 'double-dip'

or 'triple-dip' recessions (i.e., two or three recessions in very close succession, according to this particular definition of 'recession') when in fact many such 'ups and downs' may be due to seasonal effects and adjustments rather than being actually different recessions. By more general (and some would say sensible and realistic) definitions of a recession, a 'double-dip' or 'triple dip' recession may instead be plainly and simply one long recession, and is historically seen as such.

Recession shape

A common way to describe a recession, in terms of how the recession appears in a graph of GDP movement over time. 'Shapes' are mostly letter-shapes (V, W, U, etc). Here are the most common recession shapes: V-shaped recession - The simplest shape and basic form of recession, namely a broadly straight-lined angled decline to a trough or lowest point, followed by a relatively quick 'bounce' upwards again in a straight-lined angled rise back to the pre-recession level. U-shaped recession - Like the V-shaped recession but with a longer period at the lowest point. Alternatively called a 'Bathtub Curve'. W-shaped recession - Also called a double-dip recession, essentially characterized by a recession whose recovery is interrupted by a further decline into recession, before final recovery. L-shaped recession - A recession which fails to recover for a very long period, typically ten years or longer, or indefinitely, i.e., pre-recession levels of GDP and GDP growth are not seen again for many decades. Also, where extremely severe an L-shaped recession might more traditionally be called a depression. The Japanese recession of the 1990s is gererally regarded as an example of an L-shaped recession. The recessions in the US and large parts of Europe following the 2007/8 global financial crisis might easily be interpreted as similarly long-term and ominously L-shaped recessions. WW-shaped recession - A recession which lurches from recovery back into recession several times, which given the implication of the need for such a term, contains more ups and downs than a triple-dip recession. As with many of the terms referring to types of recessions, the need for the terminology is produced more by finely balanced definitions of a recession, rather than the ups and downs of economic performance, which are generally happening anyway whether in growth or recession. It's all a matter of degree; i.e., where recessions are defined by very tiny degrees of contraction (as happens in modern times), then 'multiple dip' and convoluted letter-shaped terminology tend to be used more frequently. J-shaped recession - This shape unusually and optimistically refers to a recession which recovers into a boom or period of high growth, i.e., the level of GDP immediately beyond recovery continues to increase strongly and substantially above pre-recesssion levels for a period exceeding the duration of the recession. This sort of recessionary recovery might be fuelled by technology innovation, or discovery and exploitation of new natural resources, etc. Inverted Square Root Sign-shaped recession - Otherwise technically the 'inverted radical symbol-shaped' recession, this term, apparently coined by financier George Soros, is very rarely used, and is included here mainly for curiosity. It refers to an L-shaped recession containing a small bounce (partial initial recovery) before a prolonged or indefinite period of depressed/ recessionary-level economic conditions. Confusingly an inverted radical sign, with or without the long horizontal overline, seems not to fit the effect Soros described. A reverse tick or check sign is more apt.

Reciprocal
Loosley meaning 'in return', based on the stricter mathematical sense of the word, found in financial and scientific theories, where reciprocal refers to the number or fraction which when multiplied by a specified other number or fraction will produce the number one. For example a half is the reciprocal of the number two; and a fifth is the reciprocal of the number five. The word derives from Latin 're' (back) and 'pro' (forward).

Reciprocal trade/trading
Exchange of product or services. A simple example might be an accountant providing book-keeping services to a telemarketing company which in return performs telemarketing services on behalf of the accountant.

Reciprocity
Based on the notion of mutuality or return in the term 'reciprocal', reciprocity means give-and-take, such as to achieve a mutually agreeable balance.

Recognition test
Also known as Readership Test. A test carried out after people have read a newspaper, magazine, etc., to see if they have remembered or read a particular advertisement.

Record date
A date set by a company by which an investor must be recorded as owning shares in order to qualify to receive dividends and be able to vote at a shareholders meeting.

Recorded delivery
A postal system for which an extra fee is charged in addition to postage. The sender is given a receipt at the time of posting and the recipient signs a form to confirm delivery.

Recorder
The team member that takes minutes during team meetings to capture team's progress. Once the team is well underway, this role can be rotated through out the group.

Recruit
To seek employees for a business or organisation. To enlist military personnel.

Recruitment
The process of finding and hiring the best-qualified candidate for a position.

Recruitment process outsourcing (RPO)
The outsourcing of the recruiting process to a third party.

Red ink
Term used when referring to a company's financial loss.

Red-circling
The practice of protecting the salary of employees whose jobs have been downgraded because of the restructuring, etc., of the company.

Redundancy
A situation in which an employer intends to cease business, so therefore the workforce lose their jobs, or an employee is made redundant because their job no longer exists in the company they work for. Employees in these situations often qualify for redundancy pay.

Refer to drawer
In the UK, a phrase used by banks when someone's account does not have sufficient funds to clear a cheque which they have written, or the cheque has been written incorrectly.

Reference
A letter/statement written about a person by someone who knows them, detailing their abilities, character, qualifications, etc., which is sent to a prospective employer.

Referral premium
Reward offered to customers that introduce new customers, or to employees that bring in suitable recruits. For example, customers at a Miami car wash can earn $ 3.00 off their next wash for each new customer referred. At the end of the month, the customer with the most referrals gets a $50.00 gift card.

Regiocentrism
A regional market orientation with world market strategies.

Registered capital
Also called Authorised Capital. The maximum value of shares which a company can legally issue.

Registered company
In the US, a company which has filed an SEC (Securities and Exchange Commission) registration, and may issue new shares. In the UK, a company which is listed on the Companies Register as a limited private company, a public limited company, or an unlimited company.

Registered trademark
A distinctive symbol, name, etc., on a product or company, which is registered and protected by law so it cannot legally be used by anyone else.

Registrar
A person in a company or organisation who is in charge of official records.

Registration statement
In the US, a legal document containing details about a company's activities, financial status, etc., which must be submitted to the SEC (Securities and Exchange Commission) before the company can issue shares.

Regression analysis
A statistical technique used to determine the best mathematical expression to describe the relationship between a response and independent variables.

Reinsurance
The practice of sharing insurance risk among several insurance companies, in case of major disasters such as floods, hurricanes, etc.

Relationship marketing
Emphasizing customer retention and satisfaction rather than a point-of-sale transactions by recognizing the long term value of keeping customers.

Reliability
Research study can be replicated and get some basic results (free of errors).

Remunerate
To pay a person for services rendered, goods, losses incurred, etc.

Renewal notice
An advanced notice of payment required to renew insurance cover, subscription, etc., by a certain date.

Rental fleet
Cars, vans, etc., which a business leases from a vehicle leasing

company for its workers to use, usually sales teams, executives, service engineers, etc.

Replacement charts
A tool in succession planning in which current and future job vacancies, as well as the number of employees in currently filled jobs, are visually summarized.

Reporting line
In a business or organisation, employees, managers, etc., who report to the next person higher up, usually their boss.

Repositioning
Changing a brand's status in comparison to competing brands, usually through changing the marketing mix in response to changes in the marketplace, or due to a failure to reach the brand's marketing objectives.

Repossess
To take back property, goods, etc., usually from an individual or organisation who has failed to repay a loan or has defaulted on a repayment plan.

Repudiate
Refusal to perform a contractual duty or repay a debt.

Request for proposal (RFP)
A request sent by a company to a vendor to submit a bid for a product or service. The bid includes a timeline, a description of the good or service, the type of contract, cost and other specifics.

Requisition
An official written request or demand for something.

Rescind
To make void or cancel, for example a law or contract.

Research
The gathering of information, facts, data, etc., about a particular subject.

Reserve currency
A reserve currency (or anchor currency) is a currency that is held in significant quantities by governments and institutions as part of their foreign exchange reserves, and that is commonly used in international transactions. Persons who live in a country that issues a reserve currency can purchase imports and borrow across borders more cheaply than persons in other nations because they need not exchange their currency to do so.

Reserve price
The lowest fixed price at which a seller will sell an item at auction. If the bidding does not reach the reserve price then the item is not sold unless the highest bidder comes to an arrangement with the seller.

Reserves
The accumulated and retained difference between profits and losses year on year since the company's formation.

Residual income
Part of a person's income which is left over after taxes and living expenses, for example mortgage, bills, etc., have been deducted.

Residual value
Also Called Salvage Value. The market value of an asset which is no longer in use or has reached the end of its useful life.

Resource
Economic or productive factors required to accomplish an activity, such as materials, components, land,

and capital. Others include energy, entrepreneurship, information, human skills/management expertise.

Resource allocation
The process of assigning available finances, materials, labour, etc., to a project.

Restitution
Money paid by an offender in compensation for loss, damages or injury. To give something back to its rightful owner.

Restricted funds
These are funds used by an organisation that are restricted or earmarked by a donor for a specific purpose, which can be extremely specific or quite broad, eg., endowment or pensions investment; research (in the case of donations to a charity or research organisation); or a particular project with agreed terms of reference and outputs such as to meet the criteria or terms of the donation or award or grant. The source of restricted funds can be from government, foundations and trusts, grant-awarding bodies, philanthropic organisations, private donations, bequests from wills, etc. The practical implication is that restricted funds are ring-fenced and must not be used for any other than their designated purpose, which may also entail specific reporting and timescales, with which the organisation using the funds must comply.

Restrictive covenant
Also known as a negative covenant; a provision in a contract excluding key employees from working for competitors in a certain geographic area and for a certain length of time.

Restrictive practice
A trading agreement between businesses or industries which prevents free competition. The practice of workers, often trade unions, of protecting their jobs in a manner which limits the freedom of other workers.

Resume
A written summary of a person's education, employment record, qualifications, etc., which is often submitted with a job application.

Retail
Channel members in a distribution network or commercialization schedule that sell directly to the end user. In the U.S., that's where sales tax is collected. If a producer sells direct to consumers, it is a retailer (it charges and collects sales tax.) It's where possession utility takes place.

Retail banking
Also called Consumer Banking. Banking services provided directly to the public, such as savings accounts, credit/debit cards, mortgages, etc.

Retail investor
Also called Small Investor. An individual who buys and sells shares, etc., for themselves, usually in small quantities.

Retail park
Usually situated on the outskirts of a large town, a large retail development consisting of shops, stores, car parking, and often cinemas and restaurants.

Retail price index
RPI. An inflation indicator, usually calculated on a monthly basis, reflected in the retail price of everyday goods, such as food, fuel, fares, etc.

Retail therapy
Shopping which is done for enjoyment and to relieve stress.

Retailer
A channel institution which acts as an intermediary between other channel institutions and the end user and who usually breaks bulk, charging a margin for its services.

Retained earnings
The earnings of a business or company which is used for reinvestment, rather than being distributed to shareholders as dividends.

Retained profits
A business profit, after tax and dividend payments to shareholders, which is retained by the business and often used for reinvestment.

Retainer
A fee paid in advance to someone, such as a lawyer, to engage their services as and when they are required.

Re-targeting
Tracking website visitors, often with small embedded coding on the visitor's computer called "cookies." Then displaying relevant banner ads relating to products and services on websites previously visiting as surfers visit other websites.

Retention ratio
The percent of a firm's earnings kept for investment purposes.

Retention strategy
In order to retain employees and reduce turnover managers must meet the goals of employees without losing sight of the organization's goals, utilizing valence and expectancy theories.

Retrench
To cut down on spending, economise, for example to reduce a workforce.

Return
The sum of the income plus capital gains.

Return on assets
Net income divided by total cost or value of assets. The more expensive a company's assets, the less profit the assets will generate.

Return on capital employed
A fundamental financial performance measure. A percentage figure representing profit before interest against the money that is invested in the business. (profit before interest and tax, divided by capital employed, x 100 to produce percentage figure.)

Return on equity (ROE)
The value found by dividing the company's net income by its net assets (ROE measures the amount a company earns on investments).

Return on investment
Another fundamental financial and business performance measure. This term means different things to different people (often depending on perspective and what is actually being judged) so it's important to clarify understanding if interpretation has serious implications. Many business managers and owners use the term in a general sense as a means of assessing the merit of an investment or business decision. 'Return' generally means profit before tax, but clarify this with the person using the term - profit depends on various circumstances, not least the accounting conventions used in the business. In this sense most CEO's

and business owners regard ROI as the ultimate measure of any business or any business proposition, after all it's what most business is aimed at producing - maximum return on investment, otherise you might as well put your money in a bank savings account. Strictly speaking Return On Investment is defined as: Profits derived as a proportion of and directly attributable to cost or 'book value' of an asset, liability or activity, net of depreciation. In simple terms this the profit made from an investment. The 'investment' could be the value of a whole business (in which case the value is generally regarded as the company's total assets minus intangible assets, such as goodwill, trademarks, etc and liabilities, such as debt. N.B. A company's book value might be higher or lower than its market value); or the investment could relate to a part of a business, a new product, a new factory, a new piece of plant, or any activity or asset with a cost attached to it. The main point is that the term seeks to define the profit made from a business investment or business decision. Bear in mind that costs and profits can be ongoing and accumulating for several years, which needs to be taken into account when arriving at the correct figures.

Revaluation
The increase in the value of one currency vis a vis other currencies.

Revenue
Amounts generated from sale of goods or services, or any other use of capital or assetsbefore any costs or expenses are deducted. Also called sales.

Revenue bond
A municipal bond (muni) backed by the revenue gained from a specific project such as the building of a stadium.

Revenue stamp
A stamp or sticker which is put on an item, for example a packet of cigarettes, as proof that a government tax has been paid.

Reverse auction
A type of auction in which there are several sellers and only one buyer. The buyer usually purchases the goods or service from the seller who offers the lowest price.

Reverse billing
A payment method used for messaging on mobile phones in which the recipient pays for the text message.

Reverse merger
When a private company acquires the majority of a public company's shares, therefore enabling the private company to get a public listing on the stock exchange.

Revolving credit
A type of credit agreement, e.g., a credit card, in which a person is given a specified credit limit which can be paid in full or in part, usually on a monthly basis. If the amount owing is paid in full in the first month then usually no interest is charged. When the full credit limit has been reached a payment must be made before the credit card can be used again.

Rider
An attachment which makes amendments or provisions to an original contract or official document. In the entertainment industry, a rider is a list of demands made by a performer, usually before a show, sometimes including particular foods and drinks, hotels and transport, free

tickets for friends and family, etc.

Right to manage

The "right" of management to conduct business without having to answer to internal or external forces for their decisions.

Rights issue

The issuing of new shares which are offered to a company's existing shareholders at a fixed price, usually lower than the market price.

Risk

Uncertainty of falling short of goals in a marketing plan. It's also all the unknowns that are uncontrollable by the marketer. That's why researching the needs of the target market is imperative towards reducing risk.

Risk management

The use of insurance and other strategies to minimize an organizations exposure to liability in the event a loss or injury occurs.

Risk/return trade-off

The compromise made between high- and low-risk investments (High-risk investments generally generate more earnings, while low-risk ones generate a lower rate of return.).

Roaming

Roaming is a general term referring to the extension of connectivity service in a location that is different from the home location where the service was registered. Roaming ensures that the wireless device is kept connected to the network, without losing the connection.

Robust

The ability of a product or service to function appropriately regardless of external conditions and other uncontrollable factors.

Robust design

An approach to the planning of new products and services that harnesses Taguchi methods.

Rogue trader

A stockbroker who makes unauthorised, usually high risk, trades on behalf of their employer, often resulting in huge losses.

Rolling contract

A contract which runs for a specific period of time and continues to be renewed for further periods, subject to review.

Roll-on roll-off

Ro-Ro. In the UK, describes ferries which vehicles can be driven onto at one end and driven off at the other end on reaching their destination.

Rotational training

A training method where employees are rotated among a variety of different jobs, departments or company functions for a certain period of time.

Round lot

Also called Normal Trading Unit. A block of shares, usually 100, which is traded on the Stock Market.

Route 128

Also known as Yankee Division Highway. A highway encircling Boston , Massachusetts, which is associated with the technology industry.

Router

A device which connects at least two computer networks and sends data from one to the other.

Royalty

A fee paid for the use of another person's property, for example a copyrighted work, a patent, a franchise, etc. A payment made to a writer, composer or singer when a book, CD or performance of their work is sold. A share of the profit paid to the owner of the land which an oil or mining company is leasing.

RSI
Repetitive Strain/Stress Injury. Damage caused to hands, arms and neck due to continual computer use, or by repetitive movements while performing a task.

RSS (Real simple syndication)
A commonly used protocol for delivering web-based content such as blogs. RSS is an XML-based format that allows webmasters to provide fresh web content in a succinct manner. It is fast becoming an easy and affordable way to spread content.

Rubber cheque
A cheque which bounces, due to insufficient funds in the account of the person who wrote the cheque for it to be cleared by the bank.

Run chart
Also known as a line chart, or line graph. A chart that plots data over time, allowing you to identify trends and anomalies.

Run Chart Showing Upward Trend

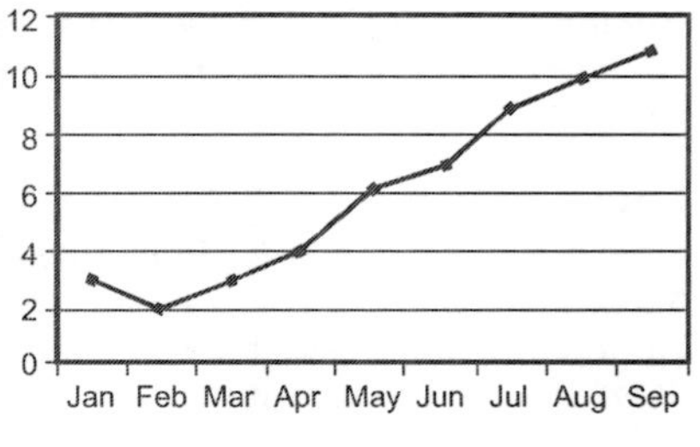

Run of network
RON. Describes when an advertisement is placed on any page on one or more websites and the advertisers have no say where their advert is placed, usually because the advertising rates are cheaper.

Running cost
The day to day running costs of a business, for example wages, rent, utilities, etc.

Rush hour
A rush hour or peak hour is a part of the day during which traffic congestion on roads and crowding on public transport is at its highest. Normally, this happens twice a day—once in the morning and once in the evening, the times during when the most people commute. The term is very broad but often refers to specifically private automobile transportation traffic, even when there is a large volume of cars on a road but not a large number of people, or if the volume is normal but there is some disruption of speed.

Rust belt
Also called The Manufacturing Belt. In the US, an area which contains many old, unmodernised factories, such as steel works, many of which are now closed or not very profitable.

R-value/u-value
Refers to insulation effectiveness in buildings, and to materials used in construction. Either term may be used. U-Value is the reciprocal of R-Value. The higher the R-Value the better the insulation. The lower the U-Value, the better the insulation.

S

Sabbatical
A period of leave which is granted to an employee, sometimes up to a year, in order for them to study, travel, rest, etc.

Sabotage
To deliberately destroy or damage property, tools, or machinery in order to hinder production. To cause an obstruction to something in order to make it unsuccessful.

Safe harbor regulations
Guidelines regulated by the Department of Labour, which, when fully complied with, may reduce or limit the liability of a plan fiduciary, on the condition that the party performed its actions in good faith or in compliance with defined standards.

Safety
Value Line Index's measure of stock volatility (magnitude of beta), measured from 1 to 5, 5 being most volatile.

Safety stock
Also called Buffer Stock. Extra stock kept by a company or business in case of extra demand or late deliveries of new stock.

Salami slicing
The process of carrying out small actions or removing something in very small amounts so that it goes unnoticed, i.e., stealing money.

Salary
An employees wages which are paid on a regular basis for performing their job.

Sale and leaseback
An arrangement in which property, machinery, etc., is sold to a business or individual, who then immediately leases it back to the seller.

Sale or return
An agreement in which unsold goods can be returned to the supplier without the goods having to be paid for.

Sales and marketing
The business of promoting and selling a company's products or services. The department of a business which carries our these activities.

Sales conference
A meeting at which members of a company's sales team(s) are brought together to discuss or review ways of marketing the company's products or services.

Sales ledger
Also known as Accounts Receivable. A company's record of transactions for goods and/or services which have been provided to a customer, and for which money is still owed.

Sales pitch
A salespersons attempts to persuade a potential customer to buy something,

often using demonstration and argument.

Sales resistance
The refusal of a potential customer to buy a product or service, often as a result of aggressive selling practices.

Sales tax
A tax based on the cost of a product or service which must be paid by the buyer. This tax does not apply to all goods or services.

Salvage value
Also known as Residual Value. The estimated value of an asset, for example a piece of machinery, which is to be scrapped or removed.

Sample
A subset of a population used to represent the population in statistical analysis. Samples are almost always random, which means that all individuals in the population are equally likely to be chosen for the sample.

Sample standard deviation chart (s chart)
Control chart in which the standard deviation of the subgroup is tracked to determine the variation within a process over time. Sample standard deviation charts are usually paired with average charts for complete analysis.

Sandbagging
In a court of law, the practice by a lawyer of not mentioning a possible error which has occurred during a trial in the hope that it goes unnoticed and the lawyer can then use it as a basis for appeal.

Sandwich course
An educational course, sometimes lasting three or four years, which involves alternate periods of study, e.g. at university, and periods of work experience in business or industry.

Sca
Sustainable Competitive Advantage – A position that a firm occupies in its competitive landscape. A firm possesses an SCA when it has value-creating processes and positions that cannot be duplicated or imitated by other firms over a long term. It takes time and sustained promotional expenditure to establish an SCA. Without both of these criteria, it's probably a USP (unique selling proposition).

Scab
A derogatory term for an employee who refuses to join a trade union, or who continues to work during a strike at their workplace. Also describes someone who accepts work or replaces a union worker during a strike.

Scalability
The degrees to which the system, network, or process of a computer's hardware or software can be expanded in size, volume, or number of users served and continue to function properly. An analogous business model of economic growth refers to a businesses ability to expand to a greater capacity.

Scam
Means of making money by deceit or fraud.

Scarcity value
A situation where the more scarce an item is, the more its worth.

Scatterplot
A tool that studies the possible relationship between two variables expressed on the x-axis and y-axis of a graph. The direction and density of

the points plotted will indicate various relationships or a lack of any relationship between the variables.

Schadenfreude

German word derived from Schaden (damage, harm) and Freude (joy). Malicious pleasure derived from the misfortune and suffering of others. Typically felt by individuals with low self-esteem.

Scheme of arrangement

In the UK, a legal agreement between a company and its shareholders and/ or creditors in which the company will pay what debts it can as an alternative to bankruptcy.

Schism

A split or division in a group into opposing factions, caused by differences of opinion.

Scorched-earth policy

A situation in which a company tries to prevent a hostile take-over by selling off its most valuable assets, thereby making the company unattractive to a potential buyer. Derives from a military strategy of 'leaving nothing for the enemy' by burning crops, buildings, etc.

Screen-based activity

A task which is carried out using a computer.

Screening interview

A brief, first interview, sometimes over the phone, with a company looking for potential job applicants. This process weeds out unsuitable applicants, and successful ones go on to the next stage of interviews.

Screensaver

A moving image on a computer screen which appears when there has been no screen activity for a specific time. Screensaver Programmes were originally used to prevent damage to the screen.

Scrip

A certificate which entitles someone to a parcel of shares. An issue of additional shares given to existing shareholders instead of dividends.

SD card

Secure Digital Card. A small memory card used in portable devices such as mobile phones, cameras, etc.

Sealed bid

A bid to buy an item, or a cost estimate for a contract, which is kept secret in a sealed envelope until all the bids have been received and are opened together.

Seaq

Stock Exchange Automated Quotation system. In the UK, a system used on the London Stock Exchange which continuously updates share prices and shows the information on computer screens around the world.

Search

The collection of relevant information by deliberate searching either formally or informally.

Search engine

Google, Bing, Yahoo, etc., are examples of Search Engines which locate, list and rank (according to various crietria and unknown algorithms) relevant websites and website content on the Internet when the user types in key words or phrases.

Second generation

Term which describes an improved product, service, etc.

Secondary action
A sympathy strike. Action which is taken by workers in one industry in support of striking workers in a separate but related industry.

Secondary boycott
An organised protest to prevent or persuade a company from doing business with another company which is involved in a dispute.

Secondary data
Facts and figures already recorded prior to a project. There may be a higher degree of risk due to the length of time that has passed when the data were collected.

Secondary market
On the Stock Exchange, the purchasing of shares from another investor rather than from the issuing company.

Secondary research
Also called Desk Research. The collating and analysis of existing data which has already been collected for another purpose often by an outside source.

Secretary
A person who works for another person , usually in an office, dealing with correspondence, filing, phone calls and other clerical duties.

Securities
A financial that indicated the holder owns a share or shares of a company (stock) or has loaned money to a company or government organization (bond).

Securities and Exchange Commission (SEC)
In the US, a government agency which is responsible for protecting investors against fraudulent and dishonest practices in the securities market.

Securities and futures Authority
Now part of the Financial Services Authority. In the UK, an organisation which regulates the trading in stocks and shares, bonds, etc., and protects investors against dishonest practices.

Securities market(s)
Exchange(s) where investments such a stocks and shares, etc., are traded. Traditionally and originally these exchanges were buildings containing traders and brokers, etc., whereas nowadays such trading is conducted virtually using modern communications and IT systems, usually online, so that markets and exchanges are virtual, i.e., existing mostly through connections between people and organizations and systems, rather than necessarily requiring a physical grouping in a building.

Security
The strict financial meaning of a security is a document that proves ownership of stocks, shares, bonds, etc., or other investments. More loosely securities refer to investments generally, for example in the term securities market.

Security analyst
A person who specializes in evaluating information regarding stocks and bonds.

Security deposit
A sum a buyer pays, which is not usually refundable, to protect the seller if the buyer does not complete a transaction or if a rented item gets damaged.

Seedcorn

Money or assets set aside by a business in order to generate more profit or benefit in the future.

Segmentation

Clusters of people with similar needs that share other geographic, demographic, and psychographic characteristics, such as veterans, senior citizens, or teens.

Seigniorage

Profit made by a government from printing and minting banknotes and coins. The profit being the difference between the cost of issuing the money and the face value of the money.

Selective attention

Term which applies to consumers who only notice, or are aware of, certain pieces of information in advertisements, etc., because that is the only part in which the consumer is interested.

Selective distribution

Contracting with several, but not all available channel members to move the product through the commercialization schedule. Attention is given to those channel members willing to give special attention to the product or service, such as employing a sales force to help sell/move the product to the next channel. (Not to be confused with Selective exposure: Providing several different choices where the customer can obtain possession utility. Often marketers select selective channel members based on their ability to push the product to the next channel member through its own sales force.)

Self reference criterion

Perceptual distortion brought about by an individual's own cultural experience.

Self-employed

A person who earns their income by operating their own business, rather than working for an employer and receiving a salary.

Self-funded (self-insured) plan

A health care insurance Programme in which employers (usually larger companies) pay the specified health care costs of their employees rather than insuring them. Self-funded plans may be self-administered, or the employer may contract a third party administrator (TPA) for administrative services only (ASO).

Self-supporting

Financially independent. Being able to operate without the help of others.

Sell limit order

An order to a stock broker to sell a specific number of shares at or above a specified price.

Seller's market

A situation in which there are more buyers than sellers, often resulting in high prices.

Selling cost

Costs which are incurred for the advertising and distribution of a product.

Selling orientation

A company-centered approach designed to motivate potential customers to buy products and services through various promotional offers, such as quantity discounts, free trial, money-back guarantees, and rebates. This orientation tends to ignore what the customer really needs. (All those extra rolls of toilet paper in your bathroom linen closet probably got there through a selling-oriented coupon or quantity price discount.)

Seminar

A business meeting for training purposes or for discussing ideas.

Semi-skilled

Having or requiring some skills or special training to perform a job, such as operating machinery.

Semi-structured interview

An informal method of research in which set questions are asked which allow other questions to be brought up as a result of the interviewees response.

Sensitivity analysis

Looks at the effects of the performance of a system, project, etc., by changing the variables, such as costs, sales, production, etc.

Sensitivity training

A form of individual or group counseling geared toward increasing self-awareness of one's own prejudices and sensitivity to others.

SEO (Search engine optimization)

The process of optimizing a web site (e.g., identifying and placing targeted keywords on web pages) to ensure the site places well when queried on search engines. It is important for corporate web sites to optimize their visibility on search engines.

Sequential sampling

A sampling method in which an unfixed number of samples are tested and enough data is collected before a decision can be made.

Sequester

Keeping a jury in isolation, under close supervision and away from the public and media, during a trial.

Sequestrate

To legally confiscate someone's property until a debt has been paid.

Serial bonds

Also called Instalment Bonds. Bonds which are issued on the same date but mature over a period of time, usually at regular intervals, so the issuer can spread the repayment to the investor.

Server

A computer which provides services, such as e-mail, file transfers, etc., to other computers connected to the network.

Service

An intangible economic activity (buying and selling transaction) that is not stored, and does not result in ownership—such as a check-up at the doctor, or being privileged to attend an EMBA marketing class in Houston at Texas Woman's University.

Service economy

Part of a country's economy which provides services, such as banking, tourism, education, retail, etc., rather than manufacturing or production.

Service level agreement

A contract, which can be legally binding, between a service supplier and a user, in which the terms of service are specified.

SET

Secure Electronic Transfer. A safe and confidential way of paying for goods which have been purchased over the Internet.

Set-aside scheme

Introduced in 1988 in the UK to reduce the overproduction of arable crops. Farmers are paid to keep land fallow rather than use it to grow produce.

Settlement date
Term used to describe the date by which shares, bonds, etc., must be paid for by the buyer, or a sold asset must be delivered by the seller.

Seven tools of quality
Quality improvement tools that include the histogram, Pareto chart, check sheet, control chart, cause-and-effect diagram, flowchart, and scatter diagram.

Shadow
To be with someone in the workplace as they perform their job so that you can learn all about it.

Shadow economy
Also called Black Economy. Business activities, including illegal activities, which are carried out without government approval or regulations.

Share
Percentage of a media audience reached with an advertisement among those watching at the time. This is often a misleading term. For example, a 50 share (half of all viewers) means only that half of those watching at that time had the potential to see the ad. But if only half of 2 million TV households in a given market had their TV sets tuned to that Programme, that would equate to 500,000 households (only half of 1 million TV households).

Share
Any of the equal units into which a company's capital stock is divided and sold to investors.

Share buyback
Also known as Stock Repurchase. A situation in which a listed company buys back its own shares from shareholders.

Share capital
The balance sheet nominal value paid into the company by shareholders at the time(s) shares were issued.

Share incentive plan
SIP. A way for employees to invest in the company for which they work. The company gives the employees shares or offers shares for them to buy, enabling the employees to receive some of the company's profit, i.e. in dividends.

Share index
A list of certain companies share prices, which can be compared on a day to day basis, i.e. showing whether prices have risen or fallen.

Shareholder
Also called Stockholder. An individual, business or group who legally owns one or more share in a company.

Shareholders' equity
The sum of preferred and common stock equity held by shareholders.

Shareholders' funds
A measure of the shareholders' total interest in the company represented by the total share capital plus reserves.

Shareware
Copyrighted computer software which is available for a free trial, after which a fee is usually charged if the user requires continued use and support.

Shark
A dishonest business person who cheats and swindles others.

Shark repellent
Measures taken by a company, such as creating different voting rights concerning shares, or requiring certain shareholders to waive rights to capital

gains resulting in a takeover, etc., in an attempt to keep a hostile bid from succeeding.

Shark watcher
An individual or company who monitors the stock market for another company and warns them of a potential takeover, e.g., if a lot of their shares are being bought by one person or one company.

Shelf talker
Also known as Shelf Screamer. A sign hung on the edge of a shelf in a shop to attract peoples attention to a product.

Sheriff's sale
In the US, a forced sale of property ordered by a law court, the proceeds of which settle unpaid debts.

Shewhart cycle
Another name for the Plan-Do-Check-Act cycle. It is also sometimes called the Deming cycle.

Shoestring
A very tight, barely adequate budget.

Shop floor
Workers, usually in a factory, as opposed to managers. The area in a factory where production of goods takes place.

Shop steward
A member of a Trade Union, usually in a factory, who is elected to represent other members in meetings with management and personnel officers.

Shopping bot
Also called Price Engine. Computer software which searches the Internet and compares prices from retailers for specific products.

Short covering
The purchase of the same number of shares, bonds, etc. which have been sold short.

Short selling
The sale of shares, etc., which are not owned by the seller but borrowed from a broker, on the understanding that they must be bought back, hopefully at a lower than what they were sold for in order to make a profit, and returned to the broker.

Short-change
Give too little change in a cash transaction, and metaphorically meaning to treat someone unfairly or dishonestly, deprive someone of something, or cheat, usually from a position of control or dominance.

Short-term disability
Disability income insurance designed to replace employee income for a temporary, specified time frame while they are unable to perform their duties due to illness or injury, before they return to work.

Shoulder season
In the travel industry, the time between high and low season.

Shovelware
A derogatory term for content which is put directly on to a web page, e.g. from a magazine, etc., without changing its appearance to make it suitable for the Internet. Also refers to pre-installed Programmes on some computers, which have little value to the user.

SHRM
Their self-definition : “The Society for Human Resource Management (SHRM) is the world's largest

association devoted to human resource management. Representing more than 250,000 members in over 140 countries, the Society serves the needs of HR professionals and advances the interests of the HR profession."

SIC
Standard Industrial Codes for the United States (up to four digits) used from 1930 to 1997. Replaced by the NAICS (National American Industrial Code) in 1997 for North America, 6-digit code.

Sick building syndrome
SBS. Ailments, such as headaches, fatigue, nose and throat irritations, etc., experienced by workers or residents in certain buildings, often believed to be caused by poor ventilation, air conditioning, heating, cleaning chemicals, or the materials from which the building has been made.

Sickout
A type of organised strike in which the employees refuse to work by staying away from the workplace and claiming they are ill.

SIG
Special Interest Group. On the Internet, a place where people can discuss and exchange information about a particular subject. A group or organisation whose aim is to influence political decisions by trying to persuade government officials to act or vote in the group's interest.

Sight unseen
To buy something which has not been available for inspection before the purchase.

Signature loan
Also called Unsecured Loan or Character Loan. A loan which is not backed by any security, and which only requires the borrowers signature.

Silicon alley
An area in Manhattan, New York, which is known for its Internet and multi-media companies.

Silicon valley
An area south of San Francisco, California, which is noted for its computer and high-technology industries.

Silver bullet
A simple extremely effective solution to a very challenging and serious problem. A metaphor alluding to the mythical method of killing a werewolf or similar monster.

Silver surfer
An older person who uses the Internet.

Sim card
From the full meaning, Subscriber Identification/Identity Module. A small removable card which stores personal information on a mobile phone or other small personal computerized device. There are other less serious interpretations of the SIM acronym.

Simple interest
Interest which is calculated on the original amount of money deposited or borrowed, and not on any interest which may have accrued.

Sin tax
A tax on certain goods or services which are considered bad for people, such as cigarettes, alcohol, etc.

Sinecure
A sinecure means an office that requires or involves little or no responsibility, labour, or active service. The term originated in the medieval church, where it signified a post without any responsibility for the

"care of souls", the regular liturgical and pastoral functions of a cleric, but came to be applied to any post, secular or ecclesiastical, that involved little or no actual work. Sinecures have historically provided a potent tool for governments or monarchs to distribute patronage, while recipients are able to store up titles and easy salaries.

Single-entry bookkeeping

A simple system of recording a company's finances in which transactions are recorded only once in one account.

Sinking fund

Money set aside on a regular basis by a company, that is used for paying debts, taxes, etc., which are due at a later date.

Situational leadership

A management theory stating that effective leadership varies, but is task-relevant, and the most successful leaders are those that adapt their leadership style to the maturity of their audience.

Six sigma

Six Sigma is a disciplined, data-driven methodology used to improve the quality of process outputs by identifying and removing the causes of defects and minimizing variability in manufacturing and business processes. It also cuts costs from manufacturing by creating a special infrastructure of people that are experts in these methods.

Skimming

Pricing strategy often used in the introductory and growth stages of the product life cycle to target innovators and early adopters that are willing to pay a relatively high price for the product. Over time, the price may be reduced to take advantage of production economies of scale achieved by selling higher volumes. A skimming strategy can attract competitors to the market if the product or technology can be easily duplicated. Luxury perfumes use a skimming strategy that takes advantage of the high perceived value, enabling them to sell perfume at hundreds of dollars per ounce. The term is derived from the concept of “skimming the cream” off unprocessed milk. In this case, the marketer is skimming the cream, or those consumers willing to pay the most, off the market.

Skimming price

The charging of a high price in order to gain maximum revenue conducted under conditions of product uniqueness and inelastic demand patterns.

SKU

Stock Keeping Unit. A unique number which identifies the price, size, manufacturer, etc., which is assigned to a product by a retail store.

Skunkworks

A production development Programme in a company which has the freedom to work outside the usual rules, without the restrictions of company procedures and policies.

Sleeper

Something, such as a film, book, share, etc., in which there is little interest but suddenly becomes a success.

Sleeping partner

Also called Silent Partner. A person who has invested capital in a company but does not take an active part in managing or running it.

Slogan

A catch-phrase used in advertising which is easy to remember so it is associated with a product or company when people hear or see it.

Slotting fees

Fees charged by retailers to obtain exposure (shelf space) for a product. This may take the form of promotional, advertising and stocking fees. Supermarkets often earn more profit from agreeing to carry a marketer's product than from actually selling the product to customers.

Slush fund

Also called Slush Money. Funds which are raised and set aside for dishonest or illegal purposes, e.g., for bribing government officials.

Small claims court

A UK court in which hearings are generally informal, without jury, for the judgment of civil claims for small amounts of money, and where parties commonly represent themselves instead of hiring a solicitor or lawyer, although legal assistance or representation is permitted.

Smoke and mirrors

Term based on a magician's illusions. To cover something up by drawing attention away from it.

SMS

Short Message Service. Allows a text message to be sent from one mobile phone to another.

Snail mail

Mail which is delivered in the traditional way by postal service, rather than e-mail.

Sneakernet

Humorous term describing the transfer of electronic information, such as computer files, by physically taking the disk, cd, etc., from one computer to another.

Social collabouration

Processes that help multiple people within an organization interact, share information to achieve common goals. Globalization and the rise of contingent workforces and telecommuting have given increased importance to social collabouration and social collabouration software.

Social culturism

Uncontrollable variables that relate to values, religion, tradition, age, and ethnicity that impact the effectiveness of marketing strategies and tactics. Ex: Sales of matzah balls increase dramatically during annual Jewish Passover; then level off for the remainder of the year.

Social currency (online)

A measure of a person's power, or influence, within a defined social group. Factors contributing to one's social currency are their visibility, activity and following on social networks like Twitter, LinkedIn, Facebook, Blogs.

Social enterprise

A business chiefly having positive social and/or environmental aims, in which community and staff tend to feature strongly in priorities, and where profit is a means towards social, environmental or community purposes rather being an aim itself for the enrichment of owners or shareholders.

Social HR

The extent to which human resource departments leverage social media tools (Facebook, LinkedIn, Twitter, etc.) to conduct human resource activities (recruiting, employment branding, etc.) aimed at aligning HR goals to the company's business goals.

Social marketing

Seeking to increase the acceptability of a social idea, cause, or practice in a target group or vested public. Ex: Oklahoma State University used social marketing to broaden its image as a conscious global solutions-oriented university. Both enrollment and alumni donations increased. Beyond shortening the distance between friends, Facebook is also an advertising site: Click "like" and you advertise to everyone in your network. Social marketing (social networking) Seeking to increase the acceptability of a social idea, cause, or practice in a target group or vested public. Ex: Oklahoma State University used social marketing to broaden its image as a conscious global solutions-oriented university. Both enrollment and alumni donations increased. Beyond shortening the distance between friends, Facebook is also an advertising site: Click "like" and you advertise to everyone in your network

Social media

Forms of electronic communication (as Web sites for social networking and microblogging) through which users create online communities to share information, ideas, personal messages, and other content (as videos).

Social media background screening

Using publicly available social media profiles of job candidates in the hiring decision process. Typically done after a company has extended or is about to extend and offer to a candidate. Recruiters and employers need to be aware of governing bodies like the Equal Employment Opportunity Commission (EEOC) and the Office of Federal Contract Compliance Programmes (OFCCP) when conducting social media screening to avoid discrimination.

Social media marketing

Various methods of obtaining online traffic and brand exposure through socially-based or driven websites. Blogs, videos, social book marketing sites and other social online communities often go viral (rapid attention and exposure).. Those who work to effectively leverage these efforts are often referred to as social mediologists.

Social networking

The building of online communities of people who have common interests. LinkedIn, Facebook and MySpace facilitate these interconnected systems. HR departments have begun to incorporate social networking into the recruiting process as a means to attract and evaluate candidates.

Social recruitment

The process of recruiting potential job candidates through the use of social networking platforms and/or websites such as Twitter, Facebook and LinkedIn. Social recruitment software is used to search social networks for passive candidate information, manage active social recruiting efforts, as well as distribute job postings and information related to open positions to job posting websites.

Socialism

A belief that a country's wealth should be distributed equally among its population, and to varying extent also that its industries should be under government ownership and control.

Socio-economic grouping
The process if identifying and dividing people into groups according to their social, economic and/or educational status.

Soft loan
Also known as Soft Financing. A loan which has attractive terms for the borrower, such as low or no interest rates and/or a long repayment period, often made by banks to developing countries.

Soft sell
A subtle, persuasive way of selling a product or service, as opposed to Hard Selling.

Software
A general term for Programmes, etc., used to operate computers.

Soldier of fortune
A mercenary. A person, sometimes ex-military, who is hired to work for another person or country. A freelance fighter.

Sole trader
Also called Sole Proprietor. A business which is owned and managed by one person who is responsible for any debts which are incurred, keeping their own accounts, etc.

Solomo
Blend of social, local, and mobile targeting trends to target customers with content designed to be shared via social networks, based on their location (via smartphones, tablets, or other mobile devices).

Solvency margin
The money a business requires in the form of cash or saleable assets, which must exceed the amount needed to pay bills, debts, etc.

Solvent
Having enough funds to pay all your debts.

Sort code
A number which is assigned to a branch of a bank, found on cheques, bank statements, etc., which enables that particular bank's address to be identified.

Sourcing
The developing of lists of potential candidates. Also relates to the task of requisitioning, or creating job descriptions, approval workflows and actual job postings. Most e-recruitment software providers include modules for requisitioning.

Spam
Unsolicited e-mail which is sent to numerous recipients.

Special causes
Causes of variation in a process that are not inherent in the process itself but originate from circumstances that are out of the ordinary. Special causes are indicated by points that fall outside the limits of a control chart.

Special commissioners
In the UK, special commissioners are present at appeals concerning disputes between the Inland Revenue and tax payers.

Special resolution
In business, a resolution which must be passed by a high majority of a company's shareholders, often 75%, as opposed to an ordinary resolution, which only requires more than 50% of the the vote.

Specialised
To be highly skilled in a particular branch of a profession, occupation,

activity, etc. Developed or adapted for a particular job or task.

Specification limit

An engineering or design requirement that must be met in order to produce a satisfactory product.

Specimen signature

An example of a person's signature required by a bank, etc., so that it can be compared with the same person's signature on cheques and documents.

Speculate

To risk investment in property, shares, etc., in the hope of making a profit when selling them.

SPHR (Senior Professional in Human Resources)

Senior Professional in Human Resources (PHR) is an industry certification for people working in the human resource management profession, awarded by the Human Resource Certification Institute. It is the senior-most human resources certification for those who have also demonstrated a strategic mastery of the HR body of knowledge.

Spider food

Key words or phrases which are placed, usually invisibly, on a web page in order to attract search engines.

Spiff

Money paid to sales people as an incentive to push/sell certain merchandise or services. It can include such items such as extended warranties, or in the case of auto salesmen, paint protection or window tinting for new car buyers.

Spin

Often a heavily-biased portrayal of an event or situation. Often used in PR campaigns to create and support favorable impressions among vested groups, such as customers, investors, or a specific community. It can also imply disingenuous, deceptive and manipulative tactics.

Spin doctor

A public relations official or press/ media spokesperson, in government or corporate work.

Splash page

Branding/introductory page or screen before you enter the main homepage on a website. Usually designed to prompt attention and make the viewer feel that the website has what's needed. It sets the tone and mood of the browsing experience.

Sponsor

A company or individual who helps to support, usually financially, a team, an event, such as a sports meeting or concert, etc., in return for publicity or to advertise their own company or product.

Spot check

A random inspection or examination, often with no warning, of a sample of goods or work performance to check for quality.

Spreadsheet

On a computer, a Programme used for entering, calculating and storing financial or numerical data.

Square mile

A term used for an area of London in which many financial institutions are based.

Staffing

A method of finding, evaluating, and establishing a working relationship with future employees. They may be current employees or future employees.

Stagflation
A situation in which there is a slow economic growth along with high inflation and high unemployment.

Stakeholder
A person or group, such as shareholders, customers, employees, suppliers, etc., with a vested interest in, and can affect the success of, a company or organisation, or successful completion of a project.

Stamp duty
Called Stamp Tax in the US. A stamp which must be put onto certain documents, contracts, etc., to show that he tax has been paid when property, land, etc., has been sold.

Standard & poor's 500 index (S&P 500)
A well-known, value-rated index of 500 major US companies: 400 industrial firms, 20 transportation firms, 40 utilities firms, and 40 financial firms.

Standardisation
Same goods or services marketed in either product, distribution or advertising form, unchanged in any country.

Standardised plans
A uniform planning system applied globally, based on economics of scale and consumer uniformity.

Standing order
In the UK. an instruction given to a bank to debit a fixed amount of money from an account, usually every month on the same date, to pay a bill, mortgage, etc.

Standing room only
A sales technique in which a company or individual selling a product gives the impression that many people wish to buy the product, encouraging people to purchase it immediately in case it sells out and they don't get another chance.

State benefit
In the UK, money given by the government to people who don't have enough funds to live on and need financial assistance, often because they are unemployed or too ill to work.

State of the art
The highest level of development and/or technology applied to a product or service which is currently available.

Statistical process control
Analysis and control of a process through the use of statistical techniques, particularly control charts.

Statistical quality control
Analysis and control of quality through the use of statistical techniques, essentially the same as SPC.

Statistician
A person who specialises in or works with statistics.

Status enquiry
In the UK, a request made to a bank asking for a report on a person's financial status, i.e., whether they can repay a loan, mortgage, etc.

Stay interviews
Unlike exit interviews, stay interviews are conducted during employment to help employers understand why good employees stay and what might make them leave.

Staycation
US term for spending one's vacation at home or near to one's home.

Stealth marketing
Also known as Buzz Marketing. A method of advertising a product where customers don't realise they are being persuaded to buy something, e.g., people recommending a product on Internet Chat Forums, without others realising that the person actually works for the company or manufacturer selling the product.

Steering committee
Also called Steering Group. A group of people who are responsible for monitoring a company's operations or project progress, by ensuring it complies with company policies, resources and costs are approved, etc.

Stenographer
A shorthand typist. From Greek: Stenos (narrow) and Graphie (writing)

Sterling
The basic monetary unit of the UK, e.g. the pound.

Stet
Latin for 'let it stand', a term from printing, which extends to proof-reading and copy-checking, editing, etc., to indicate that a word or section marked for deletion (crossed through) within a document or other media is to be retained.

Stevedore
Also called Longshoreman. A person who works on the docks, loading and unloading cargo.

Sticker shock
A US term for the feeling of surprise or shock experienced by some customers when they see that the price of an item they were thinking of purchasing is much higher than they expected.

Stipend
A fixed, often modest, payment, usually made on a regular basis, to someone, e.g. an apprentice, for living expenses during a training period.

Stock
An investor's share of ownership in a company which entitles them to equity in the company, dividends, voting rights, etc.

Stock dividend
A dividend paid in shares of stock as a substitute for cash (Stock dividends allow dividends to make money on themselves.).

Stock exchange
An organised market place where shares in companies are traded by professional stockbrokers.

Stock split
The splitting or dividing of shares to reduce the price needed for the formation of a round lot (To illustrate, in a 2-for-1 split, when 1 shares splits into 2, an investor would receive one additional share for each he formerly owned.).

Stock ticker
A display which automatically updates and shows the current prices and volumes of traded shares on the Stock Market.

Stockbroker
A broker who buys and sells stocks and other securities for his customers, charging commission.

Stockholder
A holder or owner of shares of stock.

Stocktaking
The process of listing all the items, materials or goods which a shop, company, etc., has in stock. An inventory of merchandise.

Stop list/stoplist
Excluded people, organizations, or other items, typically for reasons of disqualification for failing to meet standards or terms stipulated by the organization responsible for the exclusion. This might be customers excluded from a supply by a provider, or people prevented from membership or involvement with an organisation. Often a stoplist refers to customers 'on stop' because of poor credit rating or payment history, and notably payment default. More technically a stoplist may refer the words excluded ('stopwords') in computerized generation of a concordance, which in publishing refers to a detailed cross-referenced index of key words from a text or book or report, etc. Another example might be a schedule of banned substances or ingredients. Basically a stoplist may refer to a roster or schedule of potentially acceptable items/entities/people excluded or barred for reasons of not meeting qualifying standards.

Stop word/stopword
A word or term excluded from a word listing or index, notably from a computer-generated concordance in publishing where the exclusion of common words enables time-consuming cross-referencing processes to move faster.

Stop-limit order
An order placed with a stockbroker to buy or sell at a certain price or better during a limited period of time.

Stop-loss order
An order placed with a stockbroker to buy or sell a designated stock once a designated price has been reached (This order limits the amount an investor can lose on that investment.).

Storyboard
Used in films, TV Programmes, etc., drawings or photographs which are illustrations of the scenes which are to be shot.

Straight rebuy
When a business or individual orders the same goods, in the same quantity from the same supplier.

Strapline
A subheading in a newspaper or magazine. A slogan attached to a well known brand.

Strategic business unit
A self contained grouping of organisations, products or technologies which serve an identified market and competes with identified competitors.

Strategic HRM
Aligning human resource management (HRM) with the strategic goals of an organization.

Strategic industry
An industry which is considered essential to the economy of a region or country.

Strategic management
The process of predicting and assessing a company's opportunities and difficulties, and making decisions so the company can achieve its objectives and gain a competitive advantage.

Strategic planning
The process of considering an organization's future, usually three to five years ahead, and then working backward to create strategic plans and allot resources to realize this desired future state. This includes a hiring strategy.

Stress puppy
A person who seems to thrive on stress, but is always complaining about it.

Stress/stress management
Area of study and corporate/employer responsibility relating to workers' health, well-being, productivity.

Strike
A work stoppage caused by a disagreement between employees and management over working conditions, pay etc.

Strike-breaker
A person who continues to work, or is employed to work, during a strike.

Structural engineer
A professional who researches, plans and designs structures, such as buildings, bridges, etc.

Structural variation
Variation caused by recurring system-wide changes such as seasonal changes or long-term trends.

Sub judice
Term used when a legal case is currently under trial or is being considered by a judge, and any information about the case must not be disclosed to the public.

Subcontract
To hire someone to carry out some of the work that you have been contracted to do.

Subliminal advertising
An illegal form of advertising. An image which is flashed onto a screen, usually for about one second, or a message played at low volume, that can influence the person watching or listening but they are not aware of what they have seen and/or heard.

Subordinate
Someone who is lower in rank than another person, and is subject to the authority of a manager, etc. Less important.

Subpoena
An official summons which requires a witness to attend a court case and testify at a specific time and place. Failure to do so may result in them being punished for contempt of court.

Subrogation
The right of an insurer, who has paid out a claim to an injured party, to sue the person, company, etc., who caused the injury.

Succession planning
The process of identifying long-range needs and cultivating a supply of internal talent to meet those future needs. Used to anticipate the future needs of the organization and assist in finding, assessing and developing the human capital necessary to the strategy of the organization.

Succession planning
The process of identifying suitable employees who can be trained and prepared to replace senior staff when their positions become vacant.

Summary dismissal
The immediate firing of an employee, usually due to an act of gross misconduct.

Summary material modifications

A summary of modifications or changes made to an employee benefit plan that is not included in the summary plan description.

Summary plan description

A document that explains the fundamental features of an employer's defined benefit or defined contribution plan, including eligibility requirements, contribution formulas, vesting schedules, benefit calculations, distribution options, participation, coverage and employee rights for any ERISA-covered benefit plan. ERISA requires that the SPD be easy to understand and that each participant receive a copy within 90 days of joining the plan.

Summons

An official document which orders a person to appear in court to answer a complaint against them.

Sunk cost

A company's past expenditures which cannot be recovered, and should not be taken into account when planning future projects.

Sunset provision

Also called Sunset Clause. A provision which states that a particular law or regulation will expire on a certain date unless further action is taken to extend it.

Superannuation

A pension, for which regular sums are deducted from a person's salary while they are working, which is paid by an employer when the person retires from their job.

Superstitial

A web-based advertisement format that combines flash and other animation technology with Java Programmeming to deliver video-like commercials.

Superstitial

a web-based advertisement format that combines flash and other animation technology with Java Programmeming to deliver video-like commercials.

Supertax

Also called Surtax. An additional tax on something already taxed, e.g. an income above a certain level.

Supplemental unemployment benefits (SUB)

Pay benefits which are taxable payments that form a fund, which can be combined with state unemployment insurance benefits. Typically found in collective bargaining agreements, they provide a higher level of unemployment benefits during periods of temporary layoff.

Supplier

Anyone whose output (materials, information, service, etc.) becomes an input to another person or group in a process of work. A supplier can be external or internal to the organization.

Supply and demand

Supply is the amount of a product or service which is available, and demand is the amount which people wish to buy. When demand is higher than supply prices usually rise, when demand is less than supply prices usually fall.

Supply chain

A chain through which a product passes from raw materials to manufacturing, distribution, retailing, etc., until it reaches the end consumer.

Supply chain management

Management activities to maximize customer value by ensuring the most effective and efficient commercialization schedule.

Supply Chain Management – Main Component

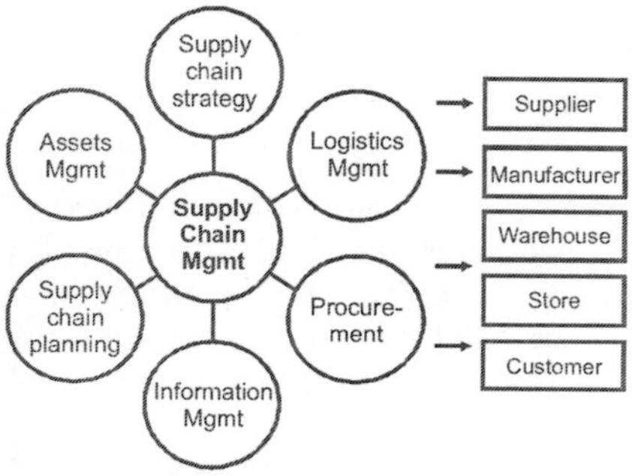

Surface mail

Mail which is transported over land or sea, not by air.

Surveillance

The collection of relevant information which crosses an individual's scanning attention field.

Suspension

An employee is sent home for a period of time, usually without pay, as a disciplinary measure.

Swag ("stuff we all get")

Useful items given to specific groups of people that are designed to reinforce a brand, experience, or theme. Also know as branded logo merchandise, promotional ad specialties — "freebies" used to stimulate thoughts about a product or service.

Sweat equity

Term used to describe a person's investment in a project, etc., by the contribution of their time and effort, rather than their money.

Sweatshop

A place, often a clothing factory, where people work long hours in poor conditions for low wages.

SWOT analysis (Strengths, Weaknesses, Opportunities, and Threat)

Internal and external factors identified in a situation analysis that can be both advantageous and disadvantageous to the organization in its efforts to satisfy the needs of its target market.

Sychophant

A servile person or follower, not necessarily of low rank, who tries to please a (more) powerful or influential person by using flattery, and often by informing on others, from which the word is derived in its original Greek meaning.

Symposium

A meeting or conference at which experts discuss a particular topic, often with audience participation.

Synergy

The working together of two or more individuals, groups, companies, etc., to produce a greater effect than working individually.

Systemic discrimination

A pattern of discrimination that permeates workplace practices, and is not apparent at first glance, but is actually systematic in its application of policies and practices.

T

T/t (telegraphic transfer)

Interntional banking payment method: a telegraphic transfer payment, commonly used/required for import/export trade, between a bank and an overseas party enabling transfer of local or foreign currency by telegraph, cable or telex. Also called a cable transfer. The terminology dates from times when such communications were literally 'wired' before wireless communications technology.

Table d'hote

Technically 'table d'hôte'-a food menu which offers a full meal with set courses and limited choices at a fixed price, from French 'host's table'.

Tachograph

A device which is fitted to vehicles, especially commercial vehicles, which records the speed, distance and time travelled.

Tag

A word or words assigned to or associated with electronic data, usually on a website, to aid searching, finding, analysis, display, organization, etc., of the data. Used as a verb also, for example, to tag or tagging articles, content, etc., when posted onto a website.

Tag line

Slogan or phrase that conveys important attribute or benefits of the product or service. Often, a theme to a campaign that's defined by the product's unique selling proposition or sustainable competitive advantage. Ex: Nike Just do it; Las Vegas What happens here, stays here; M&M Candies Melts in your mouth, not in your hands.

Taguchi, genichi

Developed a set of practices known as Taguchi Methods, as they are known in the U.S., for improving quality while reducing costs. Taguchi Methods focus on the design of efficient experiments, and the increasing of signal to noise ratios. Dr. Taguchi also articulated the developed the quality loss function. Currently, he is executive director of the American Supplier Institute and director of the Japan Industrial Technology Institute.

Tailor-made

Adapted or made for a particular purpose or individual.

Take-home pay

The amount of money received by an employee after deductions, such as tax, insurance, etc.

Takeover

The purchase of one company by another.

Takeover bid
A bid made by an organisation or individual to acquire a company, usually by offering to purchase the shares of the company's shareholders.

Takeover panel
A panel set up in certain countries to ensure that all company takeovers comply with laws and regulations, and that all shareholders are treated equally and fairly.

Talent management
Also called Human Capital Management, the process of recruiting, managing, assessing, developing and maintaining employees.

Tampering
Dr. Deming cautions against tampering with systems that are "in control." It is very common for management to react to variation which is in fact normal, thereby starting wild goose chases after sources of problems which don't exist. Tampering with stable processes actually increases variation.

Tangible asset
Physical assets, such as machinery, buildings, vehicles, cash, etc., which are owned by a company or individual.

Tangible rewards
Gifts in the form of merchandise, gift certificates, etc. that can be physically held or touched.

Tare
The weight of packaging used in wrapping and protecting goods which is deducted from the total weight of a product in order to ascertain the actual weight of the goods. The deduction in weight of a vehicle used to transport goods in order to determine the actual weight of the goods.

Target audience
TA – Group of persons to which the firm generates advertising or other e-marketing efforts towards gaining exposure of their product.

Target company
A company that another company or organisation wants to acquire.

Target market
Group of persons for which a firm creates and maintains a product mix that specifically fits the needs and preferences of that group. For example, the furniture market can be divided into segments described as Early American, contemporary, or traditional.

Tariff
An instrument of terms of access normally the imposition of a single or multiple excise rate on a imported good.

Task force
A group of people formed to work on a particular project or assignment.

Tax
A fee imposed by a government on personal or corporate income, products, services, etc., in order to raise revenue to pay for public services.

Tax abatement
Also known as a Tax Holiday. An exemption or reduction of taxes by a government for certain companies for a specific period of time, often as an incentive for industrial development.

Tax allowance
The amount of income that can be earned or received in one year before tax has to be paid.

Tax avoidance
Legal ways of paying the minimum amount of tax possible by making use of allowances and exemptions.

Tax bracket
Based on income levels, the higher the income the higher the tax bracket, therefore people earning more money have to pay a higher rate of tax on the part of their income which is below the lower tax bracket allowance.

Tax evasion
Illegally avoidng paying tax, usually by making a false declaration of income.

Tax exile
A person or business who chooses to leave a country to reside or operate in another country, usually called a Tax Haven, where taxes are much lower or there aren't any.

Tax lien
The right of a tax authority to claim assets belonging to a company or individual who default on tax payments.

T-commerce
Television Commerce. The purchasing and selling of products and services using interactive television.

Team building
A philosophy of job design which fosters teamwork to create a work culture that values collabouration. It is a training Programme designed to encourage employees to view themselves as members of interdependent teams instead of as individual workers, in which people understand and believe that thinking, planning, decisions and actions are better when done cooperatively.

Team player
A person in any type of profession who works well as a member of a team.

Teaser ad
A brief advertisement which reveals only a little bit of information about a product, usually not yet available, in order to arouse widespread interest.

Teaser rate
A low rate of interest, for example on a mortgage, loan, credit card, etc., which is below the going market rate and available for only a short period of time in order to attract borrowers.

Techie
A person who is very knowledgable, or an expert, in technology, especially computing.

Technical analysis
The analysis of historical trends of price, volume, and other related market indicators to aid in predicting future trends; commonly includes tables and graphs.

Technical analyst
A stock market analyst who uses charts and computer Programmes to study investments in order to predict the future of share prices, etc.

Technical support
A service provided by the vendor of technology products, such as computers, mobile phones, televisions, etc., which the purchaser can use if they need help using the product.

Telecommunications
Known informally as Telecoms. Communicating over long distances by telephone, e-mail, etc.

Teleconference
A conference involving two or more people at different locations, using telecommunications equipment, such as computers, video, telephone, etc.

Telemarketing
Also known as Telesales. The selling of goods or services by contacting potential customers by telephone.

Teleworking
An arrangement in which the employee works at home and contacts their office or workplace by telephone or computer.

Tenant
An individual or business who pays a fee for the use of land, property, etc., to the owner. An occupant.

Tenant at will
A tenant who continues to rent land, property, etc., past the expiration of the lease. Also a tenant who rents property without a written lease, therefore they can be forced to leave without notice from the owner.

Tender offer
An offer, usually above the market price, made to the shareholders of a company by another company or individual as part of a takeover bid.

Term assurance
A form of life insurance which pays out a lump sum if the policyholder dies within a fixed period of time.

Terminal anchor
TA or (Primary Optical Area / POA) – We learn to read by first scanning the page top left to bottom right. Primary Optical (POA) point is the top left corner, with the Terminal Anchor Point being the last thing we scan at the bottom right (TA).

Terms of access
The conditions imposed by one country which apply to the importation of goods from another country.

Terms of reference
A document which describes the objectives, scope and purpose of a project, committee, meeting, etc.

Terrestrial
Term used to describe broadcasting systems, such as television, which operate on land, rather than from a satellite.

Tertiary industry
Third sector of a country's economy which covers the provision of services, such as transport, schools, financial services, etc., rather than manufacturing or production.

Test case
Term used to describe a court case which establishes legal rights and serves as a precedent for future similar cases.

Test market
Research technique to test consumer behaviour under actual buying conditions before executing distribution on a mass scale to the target market. Involves selecting a metropolitan area with demographic and psychographic characteristics that mirror the target market.

Text message
A written message sent from one mobile phone to another.

Text-to-speech
Describes the converting of text into audible speech on a computer by using speech synthesis techniques.

The big three
The three largest credit ratings agencies: Standard and Poor's; Moody's, and Fitch. There are hundreds of smaller credit rating agencies, but historically 95% of the market is served/controlled by these three companies. As at 2013 their ownership is all American, except 50% of Fitch in French ownership. These companies have an enormous and controversial influence over corporate and international debt and the workings of credit and debt markets, banking, investments, etc., and consequently also on economies and societies around the world. 'The Big Three' are particularly controversial because of their considerable market dominance, considered by most commentators to be monopolistic (or at least a duopoly, given S&P/Moody's 80% market share), together with potential for conflict of interest in the way that the credit ratings industry operates: Credit rating agencies provide extensive high-value advisory services to the same markets/clients that are subject to the ratings issued by the agencies. Despite the heavy reliance on their assessments and pronouncements, the Big Three agencies failed to identify the toxic nature of the mortgage and related derivative debt 'products' prior to and regarded central to the 2008 global financial collapse, and in some cases awarded very positive ratings for these debts which subequently proved largely valueless and irrecoverable.

The daily official list
The daily record setting out the prices of shares that are traded on a stock exchange. The father of statistical process control or statistical quality control. He pioneered statistical quality control and improvement methods when he worked for Western Electric and Bell Telephone in the early decades of the 20th century.

The world bank
Known also as the International Bank for Reconstruction and Development (IBRD). A bank, with world wide country membership, (United nations) which provides long term capital to and economic development.

The big board
An informal name for the New York Stock Exchange on Wall Street.

Theory of constraints
Theory originally developed by Dr Eliyahu Goldratt, which states that every organisation must have at least one constraint that should be overcome by recognising and dealing with the cause of the 'bottleneck', thus enabling the company to achieve its goals.

Theory X
Developed by Douglas McGregor in the 1960s, a theory which states that most people in the workplace do not enjoy work and will take every opportunity to avoid doing their job because they are lazy and need to be closely supervised, threatened and disciplined by management.

Theory Y
Developed by Douglas McGregor. The opposite to Theory X, a method of managing people in the workplace

based on the idea that most workers enjoy their job, are self-motivated and want responsibility, and the managers role is to help the workers realise their full potential by giving them more responsibility, including them in decision-making, etc.

Theory Z
A Japanese management style based on the theory, developed by William Ouchi, that workers like to build relationships with other workers and management, to feel secure in their jobs, develop skills through training, and have their family life and traditions valued.

Think tank
A group or organisation which researches and advises on issues relating to technology, economy, politics and social strategy.

Third line forcing
A situation which occurs when a supplier will only sell a product or service to a customer on condition that it is purchased from a third party nominated by the supplier.

Third party
A person or organisation not principally involved with the other two parties but who has an interest in an agreement or contract. In an insurance policy, the third party is the person whose car, etc is damaged by you in an accident.

Third sector
Part of a country's economy which is non-profitmaking, such as voluntary work, charities, etc.

Third world
Refers to poor, underdeveloped nations in South Africa, Asia and South America.

Third-generation
3G. Describes wireless technology which has been developed to send messages and data over networks using mobile phones, computers, etc.

Third-party administrator (TPA)
An organization that is responsible for the administration of insurance for a self-insured group. It does not have any responsibility for paying claims. The self-insured group is financially responsible.

Thrift
In the US, a savings or loan association. The practice of not spending too much money or using up too many resources.

Through-the-line
(first helps to understand above-the-line: media advertising; below-the-line:traditional mix of promotional events, discounts, coupons and catalogs) Through-the-line is a combination of above- and below-activities for the purpose of building brand image and repeat sales among specific groups of customers.

Ticker symbol
In the US, a set of characters, usually letters, used to identify a particular share on the Stock Exchange.

Tied agent
A sales agent or business who represents or sells and/or offers advice only on one company's products, such as insurance.

Tier pricing
a promotional price-setting tool that generally affords customers unit price savings for purchasing in higher quantities. This is an effective way to

move more merchandise. For example: customers that purchase 3 boxes of printer paper save money. The retailer sign might read: — Buy 2 and save 6% — Buy 3 and save 15% — Buy 5 and save 42%

Time and a Half

Rate of pay which is 50% more than the regular rate, usually for overtime work.

Time and Motion Study

The study and analysis of a specific job within an organisation, the results of which are used to improve efficiency and production.

Time to market

Range or amount of time that precedes the commercialization of an enterprise (time it takes to realize an idea and deliver a product to the marketplace). Often this period of time is used to research, refine, and adapt a product to meet customer needs; in addition, promotion can also be used to introduce and educate customers about what it to come.

Timekeeper

Team member who keeps track of time spent on each agenda item during team meetings. This job can easily be rotated among team members.

Timeliness

Value Line Index's measure of a stock's price performance for the upcoming year.

Timeshare

A lease on a (usually holiday) property jointly owned by several people who have the right to use it during agreed times of the year, usually for one or two weeks. The industry is often associated with high-pressure or unethical selling methods.

Title deed

A legal document which proves a person's rights of ownership of property or land.

Tokenism

The practice of doing the minimum required, especially by law, by making small token gestures, such as employing or including a single person who represents a minority or ethnic group.

Toolbar

On a computer screen, a set of icons or symbols, usually under the menu bar, which allow you to perform different tasks on your computer, such as print documents, change font size, use a paintbrush , etc.

Top brass

The most important people in a company or organisation.

Top dog

The person who has the highest authority and is in charge of a whole operation, business, etc.

Top dollar

The very highest price paid for a product, service, worker, etc.

Top-heavy

Describes a company or business which has too many managers and/or administrators in comparison to the number of workers.

Top-level domain

TLD. The last part of a domain address on the Internet, for example .com (commerce), .gov (government), etc.

Tort

A wrongful act, other than a breach of contract, which is not criminal but harmful to another person, against which legal action for damages may be taken.

Total assets
The sum found by adding property, plant, and equipment asset values to current asset values.

Total costs
In business, the costs of manufacturing, overheads, administration, etc. i.e., the sum of fixed costs and variable costs. In investments, the price paid for a share, security, etc., plus brokerage fees, taxes, interest due to the seller, etc.

Total debt to total assets
The ratio found by dividing short- and long-term debts by the total assets of the firm (This ratio measures a company's financial risk, showing how much of the firm's property has been financed by debt.).

Total liabilities
The liabilities found by adding current liabilities to long-term debts.

Total quality management
An integrative philosophy of management for continuously improving the quality of products and processes. Practices and systems include: cross-functional product design, process management, supplier quality management, customer involvement, information and feedback, committed leadership, strategic planning, cross-functional training, and employee involvement.

Total remuneration
An employee's complete annual pay package, including benefit and pension plans, bonuses, incentives, and paychecks.

Touch base
To make contact, usually managers who want to communicate with their staff.

Trade
The buying and selling or exchange of goods and services. The buying and selling of shares on the Stock Market. A skilled occupation such as builder, carpenter, plumber, electrician, etc.

Trade agreement
An agreement, usually between countries, to limit or change their policies when trading with one another.

Trade descriptions act
In the UK, a 1968 Act of Parliament which prevents misrepresentation of goods and services to customers by manufacturers, retailers or service providers.

Trade name/trading name
These are vague terms and care needs to be taken if deciding serious matters based on interpretation. Precise interpretation may depend local state/national company law definitions. Generally business names and trade/trading names may be registered and licensed. A lot depends on the interpretation of the term 'Business name' which could refer to a legal/parent/holding company, or merely to a branded product or division. A trade name could be a brand or a division or branded operation/service within/of a (legally titled) business. Avoid applying a strict definition to these terms, and if there are serious implications then seek expert local clarification, or a ruling from your legal department/advisor.

Trade secret
A secret device or formula used by a company in the manufacturing of a product which gives it an advantage over the competition.

Trade war
A conflict between countries in which each country puts up trade barriers in order to restrict or damage the others trade.

Trademark
A symbol, logo, word or phrase which is used exclusively by a company, individual, etc., so their products or services can be easily identified, A Trademark cannot legally be used by anyone else.

Trading floor
An area of a Stock Exchange where dealers trade in stocks, shares, etc.

Trading range
The range of prices within which a stock is normally traded.

Trailblazer
An innovator or pioneer. An individual or company who is the first to do or discover something, and leads where others follow.

Training and development
Providing information and instruction that equips employees to better perform specific tasks or attain a higher level of knowledge.

Training needs analysis
An assessment to determine the training needs of a group of employees, taking into account the employees' prior education and skills and the desired outcome once training is completed.

Tranche
Describes part of a loan, investment, etc., which is a portion of the whole amount.

Transaction costs
The costs that are brought about by the buying or selling of securities, including broker commissions and the difference between dealer buying and selling price (called a dealers' spread).

Transactions
An exchange. What one gives up for something else without any change in form to the object, as in buying a pack of gum at the drugstore vs. having a roll of film developed. The latter involves both a transformation (developing the film and printing photo) and a transaction (paying for processing and printing).

Transfer deed
Also called Deed Of Transfer. A legal document which shows that the ownership of property, land, etc., has been changed from its legal owner to another party who now legally owns it.

Transfer pricing
The price at which goods or services are transferred between one country and another within the same organisation.

Transformational leadership
A systematic form of leadership that enhances the motivation, morale and performance of followers through change, innovation, and group dynamics.

Transformations
Change in form, function, condition or outward appearance of a good or service. For example, a plastics

company buys polymer pellets (transaction) which are then melted and poured into molds to make a child's toy (transformation).

Transitional employment

The arrangement of lessened or altered duties for an employee who has been absent from the workplace because of illness or injury, but has been given leave by their medical provider to return.

Transnational

Multinational. Refers to businesses, organisations, etc., which operate in or between several countries.

Transvection

Series of transformations and transactions that take place throughout the commercialization schedule (from producer to consumer). The transvection is a measure of efficiency in turning raw materials into finished goods. Used by marketers to evaluate and optimize efficiency of their channels.

Treasurer

A person in a company, organisation, club, etc., who is responsible for the management of funds and accounts.

Treasury bill (T-bill)

A certificate representing a short-term loan to the federal government for periods not exceeding one year.

Treasury bond

A certificate representing a long-term loan to the federal government for periods exceeding ten years.

Treasury note (T-note)

A certificate representing a median-term loan to the federal government for a duration of between two and ten years.

Tree diagram

A chart used to break any task, goal, or category into increasingly detailed levels of information. Family trees are the classic example of a tree diagram. In PathMaker, the structure of the tree diagram is identical to that of the cause & effect diagram.

Trial offer

A temporary offer by a company usually aimed at first-time buyers in which a customer can try a product or service free or at discounted rates for a short period of time.

Triple-dip Recession

A recession during which there is are two brief periods of economic growth, each followed by a slide back into recession, before final recovery.

Troubleshoot

To identify and solve problems which arise in the workplace.

Trust fund

Property or funds which are legally held in control of a trustee on behalf of an individual or organisation.

Trustafarian

An informal term for a wealthy young person, who gives the appearance of being unemployed and living a Bohemian lifestyle in less than comfortable circumstances, but who is living off a trust fund.

Trustbuster

A government agent whose job is to break up monopolies or corporate trusts under the anti-trust laws.

Trustee

An individual or organisation who is legally responsible for managing the financial affairs or another person or company.

Turd polishing
Australian equivalent of not being able to make a silk purse out of a pigs ear. An engineering term for fixing the defects in a product, process, system, etc., then repeating as new defects appear, rather than re-engineering it with fewer defects.

Turnover
The number of employees lost and gained over a given time period.

Turntablist
A person who uses vinyl records, a turntable of a record player and a DJ mixer all together as an instrument to create sounds.

Tycoon
A wealthy, prominent, successful business person, also referred to as a mogul, magnate, baron ,etc.

Type I error
Rejecting something that is acceptable. Also known as an alpha error.

Type II error
Accepting something that should have been rejected. Also known as β error.

Tyre kicker
A person who appears to be interested in purchasing an item, especially a secondhand car, but has no intention of buying it.

U

U chart
A control chart showing the count of defects per unit in a series of random samples.

Ultra vires
Latin for 'Beyond The Powers'. Legal term which refers to actions or deeds, especially performed by a corporation, that exceed official powers.

Unanimous
A complete agreement on a decision or opinion by everyone in a group.

Unauthorised
Without official endorsement or permission.

Unbundling
Dividing a company into separate companies, usually after a takeover, in order to sell some or all of the subsidiaries. Supplying a product, service or equipment in separate components.

Uncalled capital
The value of shares which have been issued by a company but which have not yet been paid for by the shareholders.

Unconsolidated
Describes subsidiary companies whose financial statements, shares, etc., are not included in the parent company's finances.

Uncontested
Without opposition or competition. A lawsuit which is not disputed by the person against whom it has been filed.

Undercut
To sell a product, service, etc., cheaper than the competition.

Undermanned
Describes a company, business, etc., which does not have enough workers to function properly. Understaffed.

Undershoot
To fall short of reaching a goal or target.

Undersubscribed
When a product, service, etc., is not being bought by enough people.

Underwriter
A person who assesses the risk and eligibility of an insurance company's potential client. On the Stock Market, an organisation, such as a bank, that agrees to purchase any unsold shares which are offered for sale by a company.

Undischarged bankrupt
A person who has officially been declared bankrupt but has not yet been given permission to start another business, and must not stop paying debts which are still owed.

Unearned income
Personal income which has not come from employment but from investments, dividends, interest, etc.

Unemployment
An economic situation in which jobless people, often those who have been made redundant from their jobs, are actively seeking employment.

Unfair dismissal
Term used when a person's employment is terminated by their employer without a good reason.

Unfair labour practice (ULP)
An action carried out by an employer or union that violates the Federal Service Labour-Management Relations Statute, part of the National Labour Relations Act (NLRA), and would be investigated by the National Labour Relations Board (NLRB).

Unfavourable trade balance
Describes when a country's value of its imports exceeds the value of its exports.

Unhappy camper
Someone who has complaints about their employers. An unsatisfied customer.

Unilateral
Performed by one person, group, side, party, etc-basically 'going alone'. For example a unilateral decision is one made without dependence or condition upon others who might have interests in the matter in question.

Unilateral contract
A one-sided agreement in which one party promises to do something (or refrain from doing something) in return for an action, not a promise, from a second party.

Union
Workers who organize a united group, usually related to the kind of work they do, to collectively bargain for better work conditions, pay or benefit increases, etc.

Unique visitor
Describes a person who visits a website, as one unit, even if they have made several visits to the same site in a particular period of time, usually 24 hours.

Unit trust
A fund which raises money from a number of investors, usually investing only a small amount each, which is then invested on their behalf by a fund manager in a range of shares, securities, bonds, etc.

Universal product code
Assigned 12-digit number used to identify a product. Translated into barcodes consisting of a series of vertical parallel bars, it can be used for scan entry, by an electronic cash register, or information for product sales and inventory tracking. The first set of digits are the same for all of the manufacturer's products and represent the name of the manufacturer. The next set refers to the product itself and are assigned by the manufacturer to the product of his choice.

Unjustifiable dismissal
Firing an employee in a way that the courts do not find justifiable (i.e. unfairly or in violation of the employment contract).

Unlimited company
In the UK, a company whose owners have unlimited liability, e.g. if the company goes into liquidation the owners are required to raise the funds to pay the company's debts.

Unlimited liability
The obligation of a company's owners or partners to pay all the company's debts, even if personal assets have to be used.

Unlisted
Refers to company whose shares are not traded on the Stock Exchange.

Unofficial strike
Also known as a Wildcat Strike. A form of industrial action which does not have the approval or permission of a trade union.

Unsolicited
Not requested or invited, for example junk mail.

Unsystematic risk
Also called Residual Risk. The risk that can affect a company's share prices, production, etc., such as a sudden strike by employees.

Unzip
On a computer, to return files to their original size after they have been compressed.

UPC
Universal Product Code. A bar code, using thick and thin vertical lines, which is printed on labels, packets, etc., to identify a specific product, and is used for stock control.

Upload
To transfer data or Programmes from a smaller computer, camera, etc., or a computer at a remote location, to a larger computer system.

Upselling
A sales technique in which the salesperson tries to persuade the customer to purchase more expensive and/or more goods than they originally intended.

Uptick
Also called Plus Tick. On the Stock Market, a transaction or quote at a price above the preceding transaction for the same security.

Uptime
The period of time which a computer, piece of machinery, etc., is operational and available for use.

Upwardly mobile
Describes someone who is moving towards a higher social and/or economic position.

Urban regeneration
Also called Urban Renewal, the redevelopment of run-down parts of a towns or cities, to include business and housing projects, typically funding by governments or agencies.

Url (uniform resource locator)
Internet service provider address of a document or website, usually a protocol consisting of a name(s). Also expressed as a series of numbers: Example: *stevetoms.net* is the base URL for this glossary, which references its IP (Internet Protocol) address of 75.53.135.140.

Usance
In international trade, the period of time allowed, which varies between countries, for the payment of a bill of exchange.

USB - universal serial bus
A device on a computer which is used for connecting other devices, such as telephones, scanners, printers, etc. Bus is derived from busbar, a metal conductor strip within a switchboard.

User friendly
Easy to learn or use by people who are not experts.

Username
In computing, refers to the name that uniquely identifies the person using a computer system or Programme and is usually used with a password.

Usp
Unique Selling Proposition – Differentiates and positions it in the mind of the consumer. Unlike an SCA (sustainable competitive advantage), a USP can be adapted, modified, and even changed depending on fluctuations in the market.

Utility
Ability of the product to satisfy customers needs and wants. The 4 major marketing utilities include form utility, time utility, place utility, and possession utility. More recent studies include psychological utility.

Utopia/utopian
An imaginery society or world or situation which is ideal and everyone has everything they want, from the highly revered English statesman, scholar, lawyer and writer, Sir Thomas More's 1516 century book Utopia, whose full Latin title loosely translates to mean 'On the Best State of a Republic and on the New Island of Utopia'. The opposite term Dystopia, was devised two centuries later.

U-value
Buildings and construction industry term referring to insulation effectiveness of materials.

V

Vacancy
A job opening which is offered by a company that wants to hire an employee. An available room in a hotel.

Vacancy rate
The percentage of unoccupied rental space or units, e.g hotel rooms, compared to total available rental area at a given time.

Valid
Legally or formally acceptable or binding. Unexpired, e.g. a passport.

Validity
In research studies, it means the data collected reflects what it was designed to measure. Often, invalid data also contains bias.

Valuation
The process of determining the current value of stock or other assets.

Value added
Each time work is done to inputs to transform them into something of greater usefulness as an end product.

Value engineering
In manufacturing, a method of producing a product at the lowest price but without sacrificing quality, safety, etc., and at the same time meeting the customers needs.

Value investor
An investor who buys shares, etc., which they believe to be underpriced, in order to make a profit by selling them when they price rises.

Value line index
An index representing 1700 equally-weighted companies from the NYSE, AMEX, and the over-the-counter markets.

Value proposition
Giving customers what they pay for — unique value that competitors don't offer or emphasize. In Houston, Rice Epicurean Supermarkets host gourmet cooking demonstrations, grocery delivery, unique gourmet products, and catering services.

Value share
A share, etc., which is considered to be underpriced and is therefore a good investment prospect.

Value-added reseller
VAR. A company which purchases a product and modifies or enhances it before reselling it to the consumer. This practice is common in the computer industry.

Valued policy
An insurance policy in which the insurer agrees to pay a claim for a specified amount in the event of loss, damage, etc., for items insured, such as works of art.

Vampiring
Star-power overshadowing an advertiser's promotional message. When Chrysler contracted Celine Dion to appear in an ad for its Pacifica model, it generated more sales for her music than sales of the auto.

Vanilla
Plain and ordinary without any extras. Basic.

Vapourware
Term used to describe computer software which is advertised before it has been, and may never be, developed, often to damage sales of a competitor's product which has already been launched.

Variable cost
In business, costs which vary according to the changes in activity, production, etc. of the company, such as overheads, labour and material costs.

Variables data
Data that is measured on a continuous and infinite scale such as temperature, distance, and pressure rather than in discreet units or yes/no options. Variables data is used to create histograms, some control charts, and sometimes run charts.

Variance
A measure of deviation from the mean in a sample or population.

Variation
Change in the output or result of a process. Variation can be caused by common causes, special causes, tampering, or structural variation.

VAT
Value Added Tax. A tax paid by consumers which is added to the price of certain goods and services.

VDU
Visual/Video Display Unit. A computer screen or monitor which displays text and/or pictures.

Vendee
A person or business who buys goods, property, etc.,

Vendor
Manufacturer, producer, or seller (can also include wholesalers and retailers and their affiliated sales agents).

Venture capital
Money invested in a new business which is expected to make a lot of profit but which also involves considerable risk.

Vertical disintegration
A situation in which a company that previously produced parts and materials is now buying them from other suppliers.

Vertical equity
A concept of economic fairness, for example people who are better off should contribute more taxes than those who are less well off.

Vertical integration
Strategy for growth in which a company adds new facilities to existing manufacturing or distribution facilities, reducing risk by extending control through its commercialization schedule (distribution channels). It primary purpose is to enable the firm to become more effective and efficient. Ex: By owning the mines, ships, and railroads tracks, Carnegie Steel became vertically integrated as a means to expand/grow.

Vertical integration
A situation in which a company acquires one or more of the companies which are involved in the

production or distribution processes of its goods/services, for example a brewer which buys a pub chain, or a clothing retailer which buys a knitwear factory.

Vertical market/vertical sector

Vertical market sector-Often shortened to 'vertical' - this refers to an industrial activity or trade comprising producers, manufacturers, makers, providers and users, etc - basically the supply chain or all the linked purchasers - of the same products/services, for example media, coal production, healthcare, automotive, education, retail, etc. Imagine a bar chart in which each vertical bar is an industry; or imagine a series of vertical lines, each one connecting suppliers and customers in a supply chain for a single industry. A sub-section of a vertical market sector, such as car magazines (within the media vertical), or private schools (within education), or shoe-shops (within retail) is typically called a niche or a niche market.

Vested interest

When an individual, business or group has a special interest in something, such as property, an activity, etc., from which there is a personal or financial gain.

Veto

Latin for 'I Forbid'. To vote against. The right to block a law, etc.

Vexatious litigant

A person or party who regularly brings unsustainable lawsuits against another party in order to harass or annoy them.

Viable

Capable of being done or working successfully.

Vicarious liability

Having legal responsibility for the actions of another, e.g. the liabilty of an organisation for the actions of its employees.

Video game marketing

Activities that generate product sales via gaming consoles. This includes digital advertising while playing games, attending trade shows, watching movie trailers, TV commercials, and online or printed materials. Online gaming characters include Mario, Pac Man, and "Soap" MacTavish of Grand Theft Auto.

Vigorish

A slang term, also abbreviated to vig, for the commission or fee charged by a bookmaker or casino on a wager. Also the interest on a loan from a loan shark or unregulated loan provider. The term is Yiddish (Jewish) deriving from the Russian word vyigrysh, meaning winnings.

Viral marketing

Any marketing technique that induces people (or web sites) to pass on a marketing message to other people or sites, creating a growth in the message's visibility and effect. A classic example of this concept was Hotmail whereby each email sent via Hotmail included Hotmail's own advertisement in the footer (Get your Free Email....").

Virtual HR

The use of various types of technology to provide employees with self-serve options. Voice response systems, employee kiosks are common methods.

Virtual memory

On a computer, a technique of simulating additional memory by moving data between the computers memory and a hard disk.

Virtual reality

An artificial three-dimentional (3-D) image or experience, created by a computer, and which seems real to the person looking at it.

Virus

A computer Programme with a hidden code, designed to infect a computer without the owners knowledge, and which causes harm to the computer or destroys data, etc.

Vision

Often incorporated into an organizational mission (or vision) statement to clarify what the organization hopes to be doing at some point in the future. The vision should act as a guide in choosing courses of action for the organization.

Vocation

An occupation for which a person is strongly suited and/or to which they are dedicated.

Vocational

Relating to an occupation for which a person has undergone special training or has special skills.

Voice recognition

Technology which allows computers, mobile phones, etc., to be operated by being spoken to.

Voice-over

A presenter or actor in a TV commercial or Programme who is heard but who is not seen on the screen.

Void

A contract, agreement, document, etc., which is no longer valid or legal.

Voluntary bankruptcy

A situation in which a debtor voluntary files for bankruptcy because they cannot pay their creditors.

Voluntary benefits

Benefits that are paid for by the employee through payroll deductions. The employer pays for administration. Examples of these benefits include life insurance, dental, vision, disability income, auto insurance, long-term care coverage, medical supplement plans and homeowners insurance.

Voluntary liquidation

A situation where the owners/directors of a solvent company decide to cease business, sell the company's assets and pay all the creditors.

Volunteerism

How a company supports an employee who wishes to volunteer or otherwise offer unpaid services to a community organization, often by providing paid leave of sponsorship.

Vote of no confidence

A vote which shows that the majority of those voting have lost confidence in something, usually a government.

Voting shares

Called Voting Stock in the US. A company share which gives the shareholder the right to vote on matters regarding company policy, etc.

W

Wage differential
The difference in wage rates between different types of worker, often those with similar jobs but who work in different regions of a country, have different skills, hours of work, etc.

Wage drift
A situation when basic rates of pay are not as high as levels of wages actually paid. This is often because of increases in overtime, bonuses, profit share, etc.

Wage slave
Someone whose is totally dependent on the wages they earn.

Waiver
A formal statement in which someone gives up a right or privilege.

Walk back the cat
A metaphor for troubleshooting. When something goes wrong, the situation is analysed in chronological order to find out when the problem happened and why, and correct mistakes so they don't happen again. Like when a cat unravels a ball of string and you have to rewind the twisted yarn to find the flaw.

Walking papers
Also called Walking Ticket. A notification of dismissal from a job.

Wall street
A street in Lower Manhattan where the New York Stock Exchange and financial centre is situated.

WAN
Wide Area Network. A communications network which covers a wide area of a region or country, connecting computers, phones, etc.

Wants
To feel the need for, craving, desire, or wish to have or possess. It is often said that "wants are manifestations of unmet needs."

WAP
Wireless Application Protocol. An open network communications system which enables information to be sent between hand-held devices such as mobile phones, pagers, etc.

Warrant
A certificate which entitles the holder to buy a specific number of shares at a fixed price within a specified period of time. A legal document issued by a court of law authorising the police to make an arrest, search premises, etc.

Watch list
A list of investments being monitored because they are showing signs of unusual activity, often because the companies who own the shares may be takeover targets.

Watchdog

A person or organisation that monitors the practices of companies to ensure they are nor acting illegally.

WATS

Wide Area Telecommunications Service. In the US and Canada, a long distance telephone service which provides discounted calls for companies that place large volumes of long distance telephone calls.

Wayzgoose

A traditional August outing or party for printers, typically around St Bartholomwe's Day, 24th August, marking the end of summer, when work by candlelight began each year. The term persisted in the print industry in more general use referring to a company party, although its use is now rare since large-scale automation and workforce reduction.

Web traffic

Number of hits or unique visitors that a website receives. This traffic results from marketers' efforts to drive more people (potential customers) to their sites.

Webinar

Web-based seminar. A meeting, conference, etc., which is transmitted over the Internet, with each participant using their own computer to connect to the other participants.

Webmaster

A person who is responsible for maintaining a website.

Webzine

An electronic magazine which is published on the Internet.

Weighbridge

Known as a Weigh Station in the US. A vehicle weighing system which consists of a metal plate set into a road which vehicles, usually trucks with loads, are driven onto to be weighed to check if they are overladen.

Weighting

An allowance paid to workers who live in certain areas of the country, such as London, to compensate for higher living costs.

Well-being/wellbeing/well being

Significant term and consideration concerning personal health and happiness in the workplace, with implications for performance, quality, organizational effectiveness and profitability. Well-being, and specifically the promotion and strategic improvement of personal well-being in the workplace, is a major extension of earlier principles and issues of stress and stress management.

Wet lease

An arrangement in which an airline leases an aircraft, complete with crew, insurance, etc., to another company, usually for a short period of time.

Wheeling and dealing

Making a profit, sometimes dishonestly, buy buying and selling things, or acting as a go-between for two parties.

Whistleblower/Whistle-blower

A person who informs the public (usually via websites or news media) and/or relevant authorities (watchdogs, government, ombudsman, standards body, etc) about wrong-doings, failings, corruption, or other illegal activities within an organization. The wrong actions might be of a colleague, superior, workgroup, or any number of individuals working in the organization, or otherwise working with the organization. Typically, but not essentially, the whistleblower is or was employed by the organization concerned, or becomes quickly unemployed or at least suspended.

White collar

Refers to employees who work in offices or business rather than manual workers.

White collar crime

An illegal act such as fraud, embezzlement, bribery, etc., committed by a worker in business or administrative function.

White goods

Large domestic electrical appliances, such as cookers, washing machines, fridges, etc.

White knight

A company, individual, etc., who offers favourable terms in a takeover, usually saving the acquired company from a hostile takeover.

White van man

A derogatory term for drivers of white commercial vans, who have a reputation for driving recklessly and intimidating car drivers by driving about three inches from their rear bumper.

Wholesale

Channel members in a distribution network (commercialization schedule) that sell to other wholesalers and retailers. Generally, it involves sales to other organizations that are not the intended end user (customer) for the product. Marketers enroll channel members to perform functions which they cannot perform as effectively or efficiently, such as transporting, grading, sorting, assorting, financing, or researching other channel members/customers. In the U.S., no sales taxes are collected at the wholesale level. Thus, a Sam's Club or Costco can operate as both wholesaler and retailer. For example, a Little League organization may have a tax I.D. number (to avoid paying sales tax) when purchasing hot dogs, buns, mustard, and ketchup at Sam's Club, because it will then transform these items into finished hot dogs for sale at the ballpark—where tax will be collected from the fan.

Wholesale

The sale of goods in large quantities, usually to retailers who then sell them for a profit.

Wholesale bank

A bank which provides services to large organisations, financial institutions, etc., rather than individual customers.

Wholesaler

A channel institution which purchases and sells in bulk from either original suppliers and/or other channel intermediaries, charging a margin for its services.

Widget

A small Programme which is run by certain computers. A small device, switch, gadget, etc., whose name is not known.

Wi-fi

Wireless Fidelity. A wireless technology which enables computers, mobile phones, video games, etc., to be operated by using radio frequency.

Wilshire 5000 equity index

A stock market index composed of approximately 7000 securities, including most issues from NYSE, AMEX, and the over-the-counter markets.

Wind farm

A large area of land, which has strong winds, on which a group of wind turbines are placed in order to produce electricity by driving generators.

Windfall

A sudden, unexpected sum of money or piece of good fortune received by someone.

Win-win

Describes a situation or arrangement in which all parties benefit or profit.

With profits

Describes an insurance policy which pays the sum assured plus any bonuses which may have accumulated over the term of the policy.

Without prejudice

Written on a document in legal proceedings, negotiations, etc., meaning that any information contained in the document does not affect the legal rights of a party involved in a dispute.

Without recourse

A legal term written on a bill of exchange which signifies that the buyer accepts the risk of non-payment from a third party, rather than the seller.

Word-of-mouth (referral marketing)

WOM marketing is an alternative marketing strategy supported by research and technology that encourages consumers to dialogue about products and services through various online and offline tactics, often facilitated by brand ambassadors.

Work in progress

Also called Work In Process. Work on a product, contract, etc., that a company has invested in but is not yet completed. A piece of music, art, etc., which is unfinished but may be available for viewing or listening.

Work permit

A legal document which gives a person a right to employment in certain foreign countries.

Work/life employee benefits

Work/Life benefits are "non-traditional" employee benefits that assist employees in managing their lives. Employers purchase these services from vendors and they are offered to employees as benefits. These services can make the difference in attracting and retaining employees. Common life management benefits include : child and elder care referral services, employee assistance Programme (EAP), concierge, legal assistance, and emergency back-up childcare.

Workaholic

A person who is addicted to work.

Workers compensation

A form of insurance to reimburse employees who are injured or contract an illness in the course of preforming their job, in exchange for mandatory relinquishment of the employee's right to sue his or her employer for the sort of negligence. Laws vary by state, but employers are required to carry appropriate workers' compensation insurance, to ensure sufficient funding to cover the types of injures that are likely to occur in their workplace. Such insurance types include disability insurance, health insurance, life insurance, or a wage replacement provision.

Workforce planning
The assessment of the current workforce in order to predict future needs. This can consist of both demand planning and supply planning. Many e-recruitment software providers include modules for workforce planning.

Working capital
Current assets less current liabilities, representing the required investment, continually circulating, to finance stock, debtors, and work in progress.

Working time directive
Rules set by the European Union which limits the maximum number of hours in a working week, the minimum amount of annual leave and the minimum amount of rest period in a working day to which an employee is entitled.

Work-life Balance
The attempt to balance work and personal life in order to have a better quality of life. A person with a balanced life is an asset to his or her business, as he or she experiences greater fulfillment at work and at home.

World economic forum
WEF. Based in Geneva, Switzerland, an non-profit, international organisation which brings together politicians, business and education leaders from all over the world to discuss ways to improve economic and social growth, health and environment issues, etc.

World trade organisation
WTO. An international organisation, established in 1995, with more than 150 member nations, based in Geneva, Switzerland. The WTO monitors international trade, helping importers and exporters conduct their business, and provides assistance to developing countries.

World wide web
WWW. Also known as The Web, a computer network system in which documents are inter-linked using hypertext computer code, and allows information to be accessed using the Internet.

Wow factor
The instant appeal of a product, property, etc., which impresses and surprises people the first time they see it.

Wrap
The end of a film shoot when everything is finished, the set can be taken down and everyone can go.

Writ
A written order issued by a court of law which orders someone to do, or not do, something.

Writ of execution
A court order which ensures that a judgement is enforced.

Write-off
In accounting, to reduce the book value of an asset, sometimes to zero, or cancel a debt which has not been, or is unlikely to be, paid.

X

X-efficiency
A concept introduced by economist Harvey Liebenstein. A company's ability to use its workers, machines, technology, etc., to produce maximum output at lowest cost and as quickly as possible.

Xenology
The scientific study and/or research of alien cultures and biology.

Xerox machine
A piece of equipment which makes paper copies of documents, etc.

X-inefficiency
When a company is not using its employees, machinery, resources, etc., effectively, often because of lack of competition.

XML and HR-XML
Extensible Markup Language. A common system used for defining data. Unlike HTML, XML is not a fixed set of elements. XML allows information creators to apply descriptive markup (or "tags") around each discrete element of data. The HR-XML Consortium strives to spare employers and vendors the risk and expense of having to negotiate and agree upon data interchange mechanisms on an ad-hoc basis. By using XML, the Consortium provides the means for any company to transact with other companies without having to establish, engineer, and implement many separate interchange mechanisms.

Y

Yarnstorming
Also called yarnbombing, an intriguingly specialised type of peaceful demonstration and activism in which objects such as works of art, sculpture, railings, phone boxes, considered unattractive by the activists, are covered by knitting or crochet, usually at night, and mainly by young women.

Yellow pages
A telephone directory, usually printed on yellow paper, which lists businesses, organisations, retailers, etc., in alphabetical order in categories according to the service they provide.

Yellow sheets
Published every day in the US by the National Quotation Bureau, a list which shows information and prices of corporate bonds.

Yeoman
A servant or attendant in a royal or noble household.

Yield
The value found by dividing the amount of interest paid on a bond by the price, thus measuring the income from a bond (The term also refers to the dividend from stock divided by its price. Yield, however, is not a measure of total return since it does not include capital gains or losses.).

Yield to maturity
The return expected on a bond held until the maturity date.

Youth court
A court of law, which members of the public are not allowed to attend, that deals with juvenile (under 18 years of age) offenders.

Yuppie
Derives from Young Urban Professional. Term used since the 1980s to describe a young person who has a well-paid job and an affluent lifestyle.

Z

Zero defects

Philip Crosby's recommended performance standard that leaves no doubt regarding the goal of total quality. Crosby's theory holds that people can continually move closer to this goal by committing themselves70 to their work and the improvement process.

Zero-based budgeting

ZBB. A system in which a yearly budget for a department in a company starts at zero with no pre-authorised funds, and the department has to justify its budget requests.

Zero-rated

Describes goods or services on which the buyer pays no value-added-tax.

Zero-sum game

A situation in which what is lost by one person, company, etc., is matched by a gain by another/others. Used in economics and Game Theory to describe the relatively simple 'strictly competitive' situation whereby all the losses and gains balance each other to zero. Potential gains are finite; what is gained by one must be lost by another, and vice-versa.

Zip

In computing, compressing data to make a file smaller in order for it to be stored or sent to another computer. Also, slang for nothing.

Zone pricing

A pricing strategy by which all customers within a specific geographic zone or region are charged the same price; those more distant pay more due to higher shipping costs. Price zones are set by marketers, not by law.

Z-score

Developed by Dr Edward Altman of New York University in the 1960s, a measurement of the financial health of a company which predicts the probability of the company going bankrupt.